ECONOMIC ISSUES, PROBLEMS AND PERSPECTIVES

STRATEGIES OF ECONOMIC GROWTH AND CATCH-UP

INDUSTRIAL POLICIES AND MANAGEMENT

ECONOMIC ISSUES, PROBLEMS AND PERSPECTIVES

Additional books in this series can be found on Nova's website under the Series tab.

Additional E-books in this series can be found on Nova's website under the E-books tab.

ECONOMIC ISSUES, PROBLEMS AND PERSPECTIVES

STRATEGIES OF ECONOMIC GROWTH AND CATCH-UP

INDUSTRIAL POLICIES AND MANAGEMENT

HANS W. GOTTINGER
AND
MATTHEUS F.A. GOOSEN
EDITORS

Nova Science Publishers, Inc.
New York

Copyright ©2012 by Nova Science Publishers, Inc.

All rights reserved. No part of this book may be reproduced, stored in a retrieval system or transmitted in any form or by any means: electronic, electrostatic, magnetic, tape, mechanical photocopying, recording or otherwise without the written permission of the Publisher.

For permission to use material from this book please contact us:
Telephone 631-231-7269; Fax 631-231-8175
Web Site: http://www.novapublishers.com

NOTICE TO THE READER

The Publisher has taken reasonable care in the preparation of this book, but makes no expressed or implied warranty of any kind and assumes no responsibility for any errors or omissions. No liability is assumed for incidental or consequential damages in connection with or arising out of information contained in this book. The Publisher shall not be liable for any special, consequential, or exemplary damages resulting, in whole or in part, from the readers' use of, or reliance upon, this material. Any parts of this book based on government reports are so indicated and copyright is claimed for those parts to the extent applicable to compilations of such works.

Independent verification should be sought for any data, advice or recommendations contained in this book. In addition, no responsibility is assumed by the publisher for any injury and/or damage to persons or property arising from any methods, products, instructions, ideas or otherwise contained in this publication.

This publication is designed to provide accurate and authoritative information with regard to the subject matter covered herein. It is sold with the clear understanding that the Publisher is not engaged in rendering legal or any other professional services. If legal or any other expert assistance is required, the services of a competent person should be sought. FROM A DECLARATION OF PARTICIPANTS JOINTLY ADOPTED BY A COMMITTEE OF THE AMERICAN BAR ASSOCIATION AND A COMMITTEE OF PUBLISHERS.

Additional color graphics may be available in the e-book version of this book.

LIBRARY OF CONGRESS CATALOGING-IN-PUBLICATION DATA

Strategies of economic growth and catch-up industrial policies and
management / editors, Hans W. Gottinger and Mattheus F.A. Goosen.
    p. cm.
  Includes index.
  ISBN 978-1-61122-422-1 (hardcover)
 1. Industrial policy. 2. Economic policy. 3. Economic development. I.
Gottinger, Hans-Werner. II. Goosen, Mattheus F. A.
  HD3611.S775 2010
  338.9--dc22
                        2010041605

Published by Nova Science Publishers, Inc. † New York

CONTENTS

Preface		vii
Introduction and Overview		xi
	Hans W. Gottinger and Mattheus F. A. Goosen	
Part I: Catch-Up for Economic Growth		1
	Hans W. Gottinger and Mattheus F. A. Goosen	
Chapter 1	Industrial and Macro Competition	3
	Hans W. Gottinger	
Chapter 2	Technology and Industrial Races	21
	Hans W. Gottinger	
Chapter 3	Overview of Economic Growth and Development	41
	Hans W. Gottinger	
Chapter 4	Modelling Aggregate Technological Racing: Catching Up, Falling Behind and Getting Ahead	61
	Hans W. Gottinger	
Chapter 5	Urban Economic Growth and Development	87
	Hans W. Gottinger	
Chapter 6	Increasing Returns Mechanism and Economic Growth	103
	Hans W. Gottinger	
Chapter 7	Growth and Institutions	127
	Mattheus F. A. Goosen	
Part II: Japanese Economic Growth and Industrial Policy		157
	Makoto Takashima	
Chapter 8	Asian Economies to Take off	159
	Makoto Takashima	
Chapter 9	Dynamic Cooperative Industrial Policy	181
	Makoto Takashima	

Chapter 10	Innovation Systems and Japanese R&D Policies *Makoto Takashima*	**203**
Epilogue		**223**
	Hans W. Gottinger and Mattheus F. A. Goosen	
About the Editors		**231**
Index		**233**

PREFACE

Economic growth is a major source of wealth creation at the national and international level. It elevates a nation's standard of living as well as being able to lift it out of poverty. With suitable guidance on population growth, fiscal soundness, environmentally sustainable development and resource use, an acceptable distribution of income and a constant rate of technical progress, economic growth will always have a quantitative (i.e. real income per capita) as well as a qualitative dimension (i.e. real income equivalent), both of which improve general living conditions and individual growth. Calls for zero growth or sustaining wealth without growth are misguided. Policies in this direction are bound to fail, indeed, they do not solve social problems but actually create new ones.

A major vehicle to sustain economic expansion among nations lies in the industrial catch-up processes among leaders and laggards that are born out of rivalry for enhanced market performance. How the interactive patterns of growth and development emerge in an evolutionary context is the foremost subject of this book. It establishes a link between progress and expansion of economies and assesses the mechanisms of growth facilitating factors that support technology-based growth processes over time, with technology as a leading source and institutional inefficiencies as binding constraints. Furthermore, understanding how industries, supported by effective industrial policies, make optimal investments in the face of dynamic competition will help to reveal the nature of inter-country competition and industrial advantage. Another source of racing behaviour in the Schumpeterian tradition can be linked to innovation through entrepreneurship. In competitive analysis involving R&D decisions the focus is on breakthrough innovations which could create entirely new markets; for example, as occurs in studies featuring patent racing between competing firms.

Though a broad range of industrial and developing economies are covered in this volume over the past fifty years the authors make a special reference to East Asia which for that period appears to be the most dynamic growth propagating region of the world, and as such a special showcase of growth diagnostics. In particular, the economies of South-East Asia have taken different strategies to acquire knowledge. Moreover, China and India are now in the situation of looking on a sustained growth for advanced industrialization and the government has begun the effort to make itself an innovative state. The book discusses how the success of this effort will depend upon how the country can improve its political and social institutions in order to overcome obstacles to efficiency improvement.

A deeper explanation of expansion consists of a mixture of theoretical insights on growth economics, evidence and experience from economic history after the industrial revolution, econometric-statistical observations on a cross-country basis and a broad concern on institutional, cultural and governance factors the latter of which are primarily of a qualitative nature. If we were to try and weigh institutional factors, for example, in as far as they tend to affect economic growth, positive factors include consensual political systems that are flexible, a competitive environment with fiscal incentives that allows for continuous improvement in efficiency, industrial competition that allows for economic choices, and a well developed educational system to help provide competent human capital for formal institutions such as courts. There is now convincing evidence that countries that have an open, technologically competitive and creative environment tend to perform better economically.

The major message the authors want to deliver in the book is that strategic decisions and policies on designing mechanisms on future or long-term growth should rely strongly on the micro sources of economic development to be built into a macro framework rather than the macro mechanism itself. Considerable research has been reported on economic development over the past 50 years. The current book differs from these previous publications by emphasizing industrial policies and management as they relate to competition and catch-up.

Much of the work presented here has emerged from lectures given at various international conferences, workshops and summer schools in Europe, Japan and China with our appreciation of feedbacks given by the audience, Chap. 7 is a complementary survey on institutional factors to economic growth. The authors are especially grateful to Prof. Makoto Takashima, O-Hara Graduate School of Business, Tokyo, for contributing Chaps. 8 to 10, on Japan's and East Asian sources of growth, their experience and institutional framework as a 'benchmark model' to modern economic growth and 'late industrialization'.

The intended audience for this book includes economists, decision makers, policy analysts, and advanced undergraduate and graduate students. The book could serve as a supplementary text in development economics and industrial catch-up processes. It is hoped that the information provided in this book would help to promote a better understanding of how a key driver of economic growth among nations is an intrinsic, ongoing, perpetual and historically observable rivalry aimed at boosting their reputation, prestige, power and economic performance through getting ahead of or not falling too far behind their competitors.

Hans W. Gottinger
STRATEC, Munich, Germany
Mattheus F. A. Goosen
Alfaisal University, Riyadh, Saudi Arabia
15 August 2010

ACKNOWLEDGMENTS

This volume is a joint effort by three researchers in an international context. As it is common practice in working together on such a comprhensive theme some of the material is sourced from previous journal and book publications of the authors which are indicated in chapterwise order:

Part I Catch-up for Economic Growth ,
Chap. 1 Industrial and Macro Competition
H.W. Gottinger:, Technological races in global industries, Int. J. Technology , Policy and Management 3(1), 2003, pp. 22-37; Global technological races, Japan and the World Economy 18, 2006, pp. 181-193

Chap. 2 Technology of Industrial Races
H.W. Gottinger, Modeling stochastic innovation racess, Technological Forecasting and Social Change 69, 2002, 607-624 and High speed technology competition, Int.J. Business and Systems Research 10, 2007,pp.1-18 ; Stochastic racing as competition in network markets, Int.J. Technology, Policy and Management 4(3), 2004, pp. 240-256

Chap. 3 Overview of Economic Growth and Development
Session Paper Presentation, H.W. Gottinger, Economic Growth and Industrial Policy, 3rd Intern. Conference on Business, Management and Economics, Izmir, Turkey, June 13-17, 2006 and H.W. Gottinger, Economic growth, catching-up, falling behind and getting ahead, World Review of Science, Technology and Sustainable Development. 10, 2007, pp. 1-20

Chap. 4 Modelling Aggregate Technolological Racing
H.W. Gottinger, Economic growth, catching-up, falling behind and getting ahead, World Review of Science, Technology and Sustainable Development. 10, 2007, pp. 1-20

Chap. 5 Urban Economic Growth and Development
H.W. Gottinger, Sustainable urban growth and policies, Journal of Policy Studies (Japan), 14, 2003, pp. 1-10
Conference Paper,H.W. Gottinger, Sustainable Urban Growth for East Asian Cities, Beijing Univ. of Public Finance, Beijing, Nov. 2010

Chap. 6 Increasing Returns Mechanism and Economic Growth
H.W. Gotttinger. Competition in increasing returns of network industries, World Review of Entrepreneurship, Management and Sustainable Development, 2007, pp 1-21, also World Sustainable Development Outlook 2006, pp 1-8. With regard to the micro foundations of technological development and growth in network economies precursors have been the books by H.W. Gottinger, Innovation, Technology and Hypercompetition (Routledge, London, 2006) and Strategic Economics of Network Industries (NovaScience 2009)

Chap. 7 Growth and Institutions (M. Goosen)
Comprehensive novel survey and synthesis of the political-economy aspects of institutions for growth and development

Part II Japanese Economic Growth and Industrial Policy (M. Takashima)
Chaps. 8 - 10
Development and applications of classical growth models linked to industrial policy in Japan

INTRODUCTION AND OVERVIEW

Hans W. Gottinger and Mattheus F. A. Goosen

In this book the authors argue that a key driver of economic growth among nations or regional economic entities is an intrinsic, ongoing, perpetual and historically observable rivalry to propel a state's standing, prestige, power and economic performance through getting ahead of or not to fall too much behind its rivals in a pecking order. As we observe in economic history through the age of industrialization from the mid 18th century, the cumulative process of industrial development in a dynamic time context can be correlated with some countries emerging as early leaders being challenged by others, later adopters that strived for new leadership positions. This is in contrast to those that were not part of the techno-economic race, falling behind in economic prosperity, and inevitably not being able to catch-up over decades or even centuries.

The design mechanism for strategies of economic growth essentially embodies a science and technology competition between nations and its industries as the creator of value added products and processes through competition as reflected in the level of gross domestic product (GDP). This is in the Schumpeterian tradition. It follows from exploring the varying implications of the notion, clearly advanced by Schumpeter (1942) that it is the expectation of supernormal profits from a temporary monopoly position following an innovation that is the chief driver of R&D investment.

The cumulative nature of science and technology development is at the heart of industrialization and economic expansion. Simon Kuznets (1966) characterized it as 'Modern Economic Growth'. More than anything else in industrial policy, a technology race today is guided by strategic considerations in identifying the most promising skill options, by launching technology entrepreneurship initiatives, and by inducing multiple value generating increasing returns industries with positive externalities (Baumol, 1993). In previous work on these issues (Reinganum, 1989) there have been attempts to categorize similarities and differences among various technological races due to a range of incentivized behavior rules. The very robust feature that appears to be common to some races is that there is a pronounced tendency for a firm to innovate more when it falls behind in the race. In less dynamic industries, the race seems most prone to catch-up rather than frontier-pushing behaviour. Furthermore, even the catch-up behaviour evidenced by firms in this race is less aggressive, in that it seldom tries to leapfrog the frontier. Rather, these firms tend to exhibit more frontier-sticking behaviour.

At the micro-level of our considerations on technological racing are stochastic models that view corporations as interactive moving objects that approach a stochastic destination. A major focus is the strategic orientation of corporations in participating in such a race, revealing empirically observable phenomena such as catch-up and leapfrogging, as reflected by statistical measurements. Next to the analysis of behavioral patterns, on the corporate or industry level, is their aggregation on a national scale that induces racing on economic growth among (groups of) countries. Beyond the micro-meso level of explaining changes in industry structures the model also addresses comparable issues on the macro level of global industry change.

Aggregation of racing behaviour may result in catch-up behavior among countries that are another subject level of our exploration. Simple catchup hypotheses as brought forward by Alexander Gerschenkron (1962) and Moses Abramovitz (1986) put emphasis on the great potential of adopting unexploited technology in the early stage and the increase in self-limiting power at the later stage. However, an actual growth path of technological trajectory of a specific economy may overwhelmingly be constrained by social capability. And the capability endogeneously changes as states of the economy and technology evolve.

The success of economic growth due to diffusion of advanced technology or the possibility of leapfrogging is mainly attributable to how social capability evolves, (i.e., which effects become more influential, growing responsiveness to competition or growing obstacles to it on account of vested interests and established positions). In a time of overcoming a major financial crisis with a slowing pace of deregulation, privatization, liberalization and lifting of trade barriers it remains an interesting question regarding an international competitive order whether industry racing patterns are sufficiently controlled by open world-wide markets or whether complementary international agreements (e.g. regulations, controls) are needed to eliminate or mitigate negative externalities without compromising the positive externalities that come with industry racing.

The authors investigate multiple kinds of races, frontier races among leaders and would be' leaders on a global, regional and local scale corresponding to different leagues like in major sports events, as there are in each category catchup races among laggards and imitators. Technological frontiers at the firm and industry race levels offer a powerful tool through which to view evolving technologies within an industry. By providing benchmarking roadmaps that show where an individual firm is relative to other firms in the industry, they highlight the importance of strategic interactions in the firm's technology decisions.

Let TF(C) be each racing company's technological knowledge frontier (its firm technology frontier or FTF) while TF(I) would be the respective industry's frontier (the industry technology frontier or ITF) represented by the most advanced companies as a benchmark. All firms engage in pushing their frontier forward which determines the extent to which movements in the individual TF(C) of the racing firms translate into movements of the TF(I). While a variety of situations may emerge, the extremal cases involve: either one firm may push the frontier at all times, with the others following closely behind or all firms share more or less equally in the task of advancing the TF(I). The first situation corresponds to the existence of a unique technological leader for a particular race, and a number of quick followers. The other situation corresponds to the existence of multiple technological leaders. In some industries firms share the task for pushing the frontier forward more equally than in other industries. This is usually the case the more highly paced and dynamic the race is in an industry.

In any race, 'closeness' is an important but relative attribute. The races are more or less close by construction; however, some might be closer than others. As a closeness measure (metric) of a race at any particular time we may define:

$$C(t) = \sum_0^N [TF(C_i) - TF(I)]^2 / N(t) \qquad (1)$$

where $N(t)$ is the number of active firms in that industry at time t. The measure thus constructed has a lowest value of 0 which corresponds to a "perfectly close" race. Higher positive values in the unit interval correspond to races that are less close.

Unlike other characteristics such as the domination period length during a race, innovation when ahead versus when behind, and leapfrogging versus frontier-sticking which describe the behaviour of a particular feature of the race and of a particular firm in relation to the frontier, the closeness measure is more of an aggregate statistic of how close the various racing parties are at a point in time. The closeness measure is simply an indication of the distance to approach a benchmark; it does not say anything about the evolution of the technological frontier. To see this, note that if none of the frontiers were evolving, the closeness measure would be 0, as it would be if all the frontiers were advancing in perfect lock-step with one another.

From the point of view of technology or innovation races between countries we look at clusters of advanced and developing economies with diverse value generating industries who's ITFs remain close enough through a given lengthy period. We could then identify at least two different kinds of races for a given time duration. One comprises the world frontier race in each of these industries, the other a subfrontier race (say, North America, Europe, South/East Asia) which technically would constitute a subfrontier to the world, also allowing in extreme cases for the subfrontier to be very close or identical to the frontier.

The technology frontiers of the firms in any race (that is generating the ITF) is constucted in a manner similar to the individual FTFs. Essentially, the maximal envelope of the FTFs in a particular race form the ITF for that race. So the ITF indicates, as a function of calendar time, the best achievable performance by any firm in that race. This begs the question how to assign industry value to multi-national companies in particular industries. They would be assigned to any national/regional industry where they have their headquarters and where most of their major R&D activities take place.

In an economic history perspective getting ahead, catching up and falling behind processes are taking place toward leaders and followers, trailers and laggards within a group of industrialized, industrializing and developing countries in pursuit of higher levels of power, welfare and productivity. Moses Abramovitz (1986) explains the central idea of the catch-up hypothesis as the trailing countries adopting behaviour of a backlog of unexploited technology. Supposing that the level of labor productivity were governed entirely by the level of technology embodied in capital stock, one may consider that the differentials in productivities among countries are caused by the 'technological age' of the stock used by a country relative to its 'chronological age'.

The technological age of capital is an age of technology at the time of investment plus years elapsing from that time. Since a leading country may be supposed to be furnished with the capital stock embodying, in each vintage, technology which was at the very frontier at the time of investment, the technological age of the stock is, so to speak, the same as its chronological age. While a leader is restricted in increasing its productivity by the advance of new technology, trailing countries, along Abramovitz' line, have the potential to make a larger leap as they are provided with the privilege of exploiting the backlog in addition to the newly developed technology. Hence, followers being behind with a larger gap in technology will have a stronger potential for growth in productivity. The potential, however, will be reduced as the catchup process goes on because the unexploited stock of technology becomes smaller and smaller.

This hypothesis explains the diffusion process of best practice technology and gives the same sort of S-curve change in productivity rise of catching-up countries among a group of industrialized countries as that of followers to the leader in an industry. Although this view can explain the tendency to convergence of productivity levels of follower countries, it fails to answer the historical puzzles why a country, such as the United States, has preserved the standing of the technological leader (taking exceptions for two world wars) for a long time since taking over leadership from Britain and Germany before the First World War and why the shifts have taken place in the ranks of follower countries in their relative levels of productivity, i.e., technological gaps between them and the leader.

Abramovitz poses some extensions and qualificatios on this simple catchup hypothesis in an attempt to explain these facts. Among other factors than technological backwardness he lays stress on a country's social capability, i.e., years of education as a proxy of technical competence in its political, commercial, industrial, and financial institutions. The social capability of a country may become stronger or weaker as technological gaps close and thus, he states, the actual catch-up process does not lend itself to simple formulation. This view has a common understanding to what Mancur Olson (1982) expresses to be 'public policies and institutions' as his explanation of the great differences in per capita income across countries, stating that "any poorer countries that adopt relatively good economic policies and institutions enjoy rapid catchup growth." This view should be taken seriously when we wish to understand the technological catching up to American leadership in some key industries by Japan, in particular, during the post-war period and explore the possibility of a shift in standing between these two countries. This consideration will directly bear on the future trend of the state of the art which exerts a crucial influence on the development of the world economy.

In a micro racing environment of industrial economics between leader and follower, or incumbent and entrant, we observe two contradistinctional behavioural rules. The incumbent's behaviour is influenced by what the literature identifies as the 'replacement effect' (Tirole, 1988, Chap. 10). The conventional replacement effect says that in an effort to maximize the discounted value of its existing profit stream an incumbent monopolist invests less in R&D than an entrant, and thus expects to be replaced by the entrant (for example, when the innovation is drastic enough that the firm with the older technology would not find it profitable to compete with the newer technology). This replacement effect could cause the incumbent to be replaced only temporarily, subsequently he regains a dominant position in the market since he has a superior version of the new technology. The analog event may happen on the macro scale, eventually somewhat more slowly, when one country passes another in innovation induced growth performance. This would be a natural thing consistent with the convergence hypotheses in neoclassical growth models. On the other hand, in the micro industrial economics literature it has been shown that the monopoly term is increasingly important to a firm as it gets ahead of its rival, and that the duopoly term is increasingly important to a firm that falls behind.

One question of interest is whether chance leads to a greater likelihood of increasing the lead, or in more catch-up behavior. The existing literature (Grossman and Shapiro, 1987; Harris and Vickers, 1987) has suggested that a firm that surges ahead of its rival increases its investment in R&D and speeds up while a lagging firm reduces its investment and slows down. We call this the Grove paradigm, after Andy Grove (1996) for an Intel economy. On a macro scale an Intel economy would be the prototype of an R&D driven endogenous growth model when both industry leaders and follower firms invest in R&D in each industry (Segerstrom, 2005). This behavioural pattern would suggest that the lead continues to increase, and there will be divergence.

On a macro scale this racing paradigm would suggest that the U.S. would mobilize all its technology/science/entrepreneurial resources to increase or keep its distance to other large emerging economies (such as China or India). With science/ technology being an evolutionary cumulative enterprise, for a dominating country with a portfolio of major increasing returns industries, the odds of leapfrogging oneself are higher than being leapfrogged by close followers, thus this asymmetry could play a distinctive role. Abramovitz' advantage of backwardness may hold on up to a certain limit but with decreasing returns.

In an interesting paper, under some seemingly reasonable assumptions on linear technology investment and dynamic equilibrium path of capital accumulation in a neoclassical type model Lau and Wan (1993) obtain the following results which they argue are fully consistent with empirical growth economics: These are: "(a) Not all economies converge in growth with each other. (b) Economies with an initial technical capability will converge in growth with the advanced economies. The difference in per capita output grows exponentially, if the developing economy engages only in imitation (and not innovation). (c) With an initial technical capability there is a 'high growth' period, preceded (followed) by a phase of 'trend acceleration' ('trend deceleration'). (d) With an initial technical capability the the technology gap widens forever." The previous analysis indicates that the possibilities opened through competitive industrial racing are far richer and more surprising than they would emerge from the macro-scale models.

In Part I, chapters 1-7, we shape the mechanism design in setting up the essentials for technology racing and catch-up processes. The proper tools for single or multiple-type racing are forms of stochastic differential games which allow strategic actions and positions between different cooperative or non-cooperative partners. The multi-faceted concept of economic growth at its poles covers urban growth as positve externalities through new technology and innovation drives city growth with spillovers in surrounding areas. A similar transformation applies to the composition of industries changing from constant/ decreasing returns industries to increasing returns to accelerate growth processes along the way achieving more value added.

A dynamic competitive national economy with its underlying institutional factors is fed by a consistent industrial policy intrinsically supported by a strategic innovation system. Although this view can explain the tendency to convergence of productivity levels of follower countries, it fails to answer the historical puzzle why a country, the United States, has preserved the standing of the technological leader for a long time this century, and why it has intermittently been threatened by Germany, Japan and lately by emerging China and to a lesser degree by India. We show the empirical proliferation of comparative growth and development over the main period of industrialization. Why have the shifts taken place in the ranks of follower countries in their relative levels of productivity, i.e., technological gaps between them and the leader?

In Part II we concentrate on a leader of economic growth and catch-up, Japan, as a precursor for a follow-up and model of other fast growing East Asian economies. The final three chapters 8-10 adapt the growth model methodology to growth processes in the East Asian arena, as in Japan, that covers the spectrum of consistent sources of growth. In fact, Wan (2004, Chap.2) considered Japan as a 'benchmark model' for industriaization, and Rosovsky (1966) argues that Kuznets' (1966) term, modern economic growth applies to Japan as a national objective by the end of the nineteenth century against which late industrialization in terms of Amsden (1998) can be measured up. Chap. 8 deals with the problems of sustained economic growth of East Asian countries, concentrating on their conditions of growth.

After discussing some of the main issues about the so-called 'Asian Miracle', a simple mathematical and policy relevant model of their economic growth is designed with emphasis on accumulation of technological knowledge. A theoretical investigation is made into possible conditions for sustained economic growth in developing economies. Besides such theoretical considerations, in order to examine the actual growth trajectories of such developing economies, special attention must be paid to their policy efforts under the different situations of each country and to the possible changes in political institutions according to their economic growth stage. This problem may be a theme for future studies on their state of affairs.

As a central source for the sustained growth of East Asian NIEs, attention is paid to the problem of national policy for technological advancement. This is the theme of Chap. 9. It addresses a problem of innovative strategies planned and practiced by private public partnership in a scheme of national technological policy. Although both the parties have their own objectives, they appear to behave cooperatively due to the public nature of technology. The optimal behaviors of both parties are investigated during a certain planning period in a differential game framework. Such a dynamic study as this may play a role in analyzing the evolution of the optimal strategies to be taken by each of the participants in innovative activities and the associated dynamics of technological state of an economy.

Post-war Japan has implemented national strategies for strengthening its industrial technology by introducing a cooperative scheme called "research consortium". Its activities have been financed by commingled funds from the government and the private sector. Chap. 10 explores the behavior of both parties to make the optimal choices under their respective objectives in this R&D scheme. Analysis is made based on a static game-theoretic model representing the essential scheme of the actual consortia. After obtaining some theoretical results about this policy scheme, we examine statistically how they explain the actual R&D activities taken by Japan during its development stage after World War .

REFERENCES

Abramovitz, M. (1986),' Catching Up, Forging Ahead, and Falling Behind', *Journal of Economic History* 66, 385-406

Amsden, A. H. (1998), Asia's Next Giant–South Korea and Late Industrialization, New York, Oxford: Oxford University Press

Baumol,W,J.(1993), Entrepreneurship,Management and the Structure of Payoff, Cambridge,Ma., MIT Press

Gerschenkron,A. (1962), Economic Backwardness in Historical Perspective: A Book of Essays, Cambridge,Ma., Harvard Univ. Press

Grossman,G. and C. Shapiro (1987),'Dynamic R&D Competition', *Economic Journal* 97, 372-387

Grove, A. (1996), Only the Paranoid Survive, New York, Doubleday

Harris,C. and J. Vickers (1987)'Racing with Uncertainty', *Review of Economic Studies* 54, 305-321

Kuznets,S. (1966), Modern Economic Growth, New Haven, Yale Univ. Press

Lau,M-L and H. Wan (1993) ,On the Mechanism of Catching Up', *European Economic Review* 38, 952-963

Olson, M. (1982) The Rise and Decline of Nations, New Haven, Yale Univ. Press

Reinganum,J.(1989)'The Timing of Innovation', in Handbook of Industrial Organization, Vol. I, Schmalensee,R. and R. Willig eds., North Holland, Amsterdam, Chap. 14

Rosovsky, H (1966), 'Japan's Transition to Modern Economic Growth' in H. Rosovsky,ed., Industrialization in Two Systems, Essays in Honor of A. Gerschenkron, New York, Wiley, 91-139

Schumpeter,J. (1942), Capitalism, Socialism, and Democracy, New York, Harper and Row

Segerstrom, P.S. (2005), Intel Economics', mimeo, *Stockholm School of Economics,* Stockholm, August 22

Tirole,J.(1988) ,The Theory of Industrial Organization, Cambridge,Ma., MIT Press

Wan Jr., Henry Y. (2004), Economic Development in A Globalized Environment:East Asian Evidences, Kluwer Academic Publishers

PART I: CATCH-UP FOR ECONOMIC GROWTH

Hans W. Gottinger[1] and Mattheus F. A. Goosen[2]
[1]STRATEC, Munich, Germany
Email: info@stratec-con.com, http://stratec-con.com
[2]Alfaisal University, Riyadh, Saudi Arabia
Email: mgoosen@alfaisal.edu, www.afaisal.edu

Chapter 1

INDUSTRIAL AND MACRO COMPETITION

Hans W. Gottinger

1.1 INTRODUCTION

The striking pattern that emerges in the innovative activities of firms is their rivalries for a technological leadership position in situations are best described as races or competitions. A race is an interactive pattern characterized by firms or nations constantly trying to get ahead of their rivals, or trying not to fall too far behind. In high-technology industries, where customers are willing to pay a premium for advanced technology, leadership translates into increasing returns in the market through positive network externalities. Abramovitz (1986), the American economist, in explaining the catch-up hypothesis, lays stress on a country's social capability in terms years of education as a proxy of technical competence and its institutions. Competing behaviour is also a dynamic story of how technology unfolds in an industry. In contrast to any existing way of looking at the evolution of technology, racing behaviour recognizes the fundamental importance of strategic interactions between competing firms. Thus firms take their rivals' actions into account when formulating their own decisions. The importance of this characterization is at least twofold. At one level, racing behaviour has implications for appreciating technology strategy at the level of the individual firm; at the other level, for understanding the impact of policies that aim to spur technological innovation in an industry or country

On a national scale, simple catch-up hypotheses have put emphasis on the great potential of adopting unexploited technology in the early stage and the increase of self-limiting power in the later stage. However, the actual growth path of the technological trajectory of a specific economy may be overwhelmingly constrained by social capability. The capability endogenously changes as states of the economy and technology evolve. The success of economic growth due to diffusion of advanced technology or the possibility of leapfrogging is mainly attributable to how the social capability evolves. In other words, which effects become more influential: growing responsiveness to competition or growing obstacles to it on account of vested interests and established positions?

Observations on industrial patterns in Europe, the United States or Asia point to which type of racing behaviour is prevalent in global high- technology industries. The pattern evolving from such conduct could be benchmarked against the frontier pursuit type of the global technological leaders. Another observation relates to policy inferences on market structure, entrepreneurship, innovation activity, industrial policy and regulatory frameworks in promoting and hindering industry frontier races in a global industrial context. Does lagging behind one's closest technological rivals' cause a firm to increase its innovative effort? The term 'race' suggests that no single firm would want to fall too far behind, and that everyone would like to get ahead. If a company tries to innovate more when it is behind than when it is ahead, then 'catch-up' behaviour will be the dominant effect. Once a firm gets far enough ahead of its rivals, then the latter will step up their efforts to get closer. The leading company will slow down its innovative efforts until its competitors have drawn uncomfortably close or have surpassed it. This process repeats itself every time a firm gets far enough ahead of its rivals. An alternative behaviour pattern would correspond to a business increasing its innovative effort if it gets far enough ahead, thus making catch-up by the lagging companies increasingly difficult. For any of these businesses there appears to be a clear link to market and industry structure, as termed 'intensity of rivalry'.

We investigated two different kinds of races: one that is a frontier between itself and the technological leader at any point in time ('frontier- sticking' behaviour), or it might try to actually usurp the position of the leader by 'leapfrogging' it. When there are disproportionately large payoffs to being in the technical lead (relative to the payoffs that a firm can realize if it is simply close enough to the technical frontier), then one would expect that leapfrogging behaviour would occur more frequently than frontier-sticking behaviour. Alternatively, racing toward the frontier creates the reputation of being an innovation leader hoping to maintain and increase market share in the future. All attempts to leapfrog the current technological leader might not be successful since many lagging firms might be attempting to leapfrog the leader simultaneously and the leader might be trying to get further ahead simultaneously. Correspondingly, one could distinguish between attempted leapfrogging and realized leapfrogging.

Among the key issues to be addressed is the apparent inability of technology-oriented corporations to maintain leadership in fields that they pioneered. There is a presumption that firms fail to remain competitive because of agency problems or other suboptimal managerial behaviour within these organizations. An alternative explanation is that technologically trailing firms, in symmetric competitive situations, will devote greater effort to innovation, so that a failure of technological leaders to maintain their position is an appropriate response to the competitive environment. In asymmetric situations, with entrants challenging incumbents, research does demonstrate that startup firms show a stronger endeavor to close up to or leapfrog the competitors. Such issues highlight the dynamics of the race within the given market structure in any of the areas concerned.

We observe two different kinds of market asymmetries with bearing on racing behaviour: risk-driven and resource-based. When the incumbents' profits are large enough and do not vary much with the product characteristics, the entrant is likely to choose the faster option in each stage as long as he has not fallen behind in the contest. In view of resource-based asymmetries, as a firm's stage resource endowment increases, it could use the additional resources to either choose more aggressive targets or to attempt to finish the stage sooner, or both. Previous work has suggested that a firm that surges ahead of its rival increases its investment in R&D and speeds up, while a lagging firm reduces its investment and slows down. Consequently, preceding effort suggests that the lead continues to increase. However, based on related work for the US and Japanese telecommunications industry when duopolistic and monopolistic competition and product system complexity for new products are accounted for, the speeding up of a leading firm occurs only under rare circumstances. For example, a company getting far enough ahead such that the (temporary) monopoly term dominates its payoff expression, will always choose the fast strategy, while a company that gets far enough behind will always choose the aggressive approach. Under these conditions, the lead is likely to continue to increase. If, on the other hand, both monopoly and duopoly profits increase substantially with increased aggressiveness then even large leads can vanish with significant probability.

Overall, this characterization highlights two forces that influence a firm's choices in the various stages: proximity to the finish line and distance between the firms. This probability of reaping monopoly profits is higher the farther ahead a firm is of its rival and even more so the closer the firm is to the finish line. If the lead company is far from the finish line, even a sizeable lead may not translate into the dominance of the monopoly profit term, since there is plenty of time for the lead situation to be reversed, and failure to finish first remains a probable outcome. In contrast, the probability that the lagging company will get to be a monopolist becomes smaller as it falls behind the leader. This raises the following question: what kind of actions cause a firm to get ahead? Intuitively, one would expect that a firm that is ahead of its rival at any time t, in the sense of having completed more stages by time t, is likely to have chosen the faster strategy more often. We will construct numerical estimates of the probability that a leading firm is more likely to have chosen a strategy faster to verify this intuition.

Moving away from the firm-led race patterns revolving in a particular industry to a clustering of racing on an industry level is putting industry in different geo-economics zones against each other and becoming dominant in strategic product/process technologies. Here racing patterns among industries in a relatively free-trade environment could lead to competitive advantages and more wealth creating and accumulating dominance in key product/process technologies in one region at the expense of others. There appears to be a link that individual races on the firm level induce similar races on the industry level and will be a contributing factor to the globalization of network industries.

Thus similar catch-up processes are taking place between leaders and followers within a group of industrialized countries in pursuit of higher levels of productivity. Supposing that the level of labour productivity were governed entirely by the level of technology embodied in capital stock, one may consider that the differentials in productivities among countries are caused by the 'technological age' of the stock relative to its 'chronological age'. The technological age of capital is the age of expertise at the time of investment plus years elapsing from that time. Since a leading state may be supposed to be furnished with the capital stock embodying, in each vintage, technology which was 'at the very frontier' at the time of investment, the technological age of the stock is, so to speak, the same as its chronological age.

While a leader is restricted in increasing its productivity by the advance of new technology, trailing countries have the potential to make a larger leap as they are provided with the privilege of exploiting the backlog in addition of the newly developed technology. Hence, followers being behind with a larger gap in technology will have a stronger potential for growth in productivity. The potential, however, will be reduced as the catch-up process goes on because the unexploited stock of technology becomes smaller and smaller. However, as new technologies arise and are rapidly adopted in a Schumpeterian process of 'creative destruction', their network effects induce rapid accelerating and cumulative growth potentials which are catalyzed through industry competition. In the absence of such a process we can explain the tendency to convergence of productivity levels of follower countries. Historically, however, it fails to answer alleged puzzles as to why a country, such as the United States, has preserved the standing of the technological leader for a long time since taking over leadership from Britain in around the end of the nineteenth century and why the shifts have taken place in the ranks of follower states in their relative levels of productivity (i.e. technological gaps between them and the leader). The American economist Abramovitz (1986) poses some extensions and qualifications on this simple catch-up hypothesis in an attempt to explain these facts. Among other factors than technological backwardness, he lays stress on a country's social capability in terms of years of education as a proxy of technical competence and its political, commercial, industrial, and financial institutions. The social capacity of a state may become stronger or weaker as technological gaps close and thus he argues that the actual catch-up process does not provide itself to simple formulation. This view has a common understanding to what another economist, Olson (1996), expresses to be 'public policies and institutions' as his explanation of the great differences in per capita income across countries, stating that any poorer states that implement relatively good economic policies and institutions enjoy rapid catch-up growth.

The suggestion should be taken seriously when we wish to understand the technological catching-up to American leadership by Japan, in particular during the post-war period, and explore the possibility of a shift in standing between these two countries. This consideration will directly bear on the future trend of the state of the art which exerts a crucial influence on the development of the world economy (Juma and Clark, 2002; Fagerberg and Godinho, 2004). These explanations notwithstanding, we venture as a major factor for divergent growth processes the level of intensity of the racing process within the most prevalent value-added industries with cross-sectional spillovers. These are the communications and information industries which have been shaped and led by leading American firms and where the rewards benefited their industries and country. Although European and Japanese companies were part of the race they were left behind in core markets reaping lesser benefits. (Since ICT investment relative to GDP is only less than half in states such as Japan, Germany and France compared to the US, 2% vs. more than 4% in 1999, this does not bode well for a rapid catch-up in those countries and a fortiori, for the EU as a whole).

Steering or guiding the process of racing through the pursuit of industrial policies aiming to increase competitive advantage of respective industries, as having been practiced in Japan, would stimulate catch-up races but appears to be less effective in promoting frontier racing. Another profound reason lies in the phenomenon of network externalities affecting ICT industries. That is, racing ahead of rivals in respective industries may create external economies to the effect that such economies within dominant industries tend to improve their international market position and therefore pull ahead in competitiveness vis-à-vis their (trading) partners. As Krugman (1997) observed: 'It is probably true that external economies are a more important determinant of international trade in high technology sectors than elsewhere'. The point is that racing behaviour in leading high-growth network industries by generating frontier positions, create critical cluster and network externalities pipelining through other sectors of the economy and create competitive advantages elsewhere, as supported by the increasing returns debate (Arthur, 1996). In this sense we can speak of positive externalities endogenizing growth of these economies and contributing to competitive advantage. All these characteristics lay the foundations of the 'Network Economy'.

The Network Economy is formed through an ever-emerging and interacting set of increasing returns industries; it is about high-intensity, technology driven-racing, dynamic entrepreneurship, and focused risk-taking through (free) venture capital markets endogenized by societal and institutional support. With the exception of pockets of activity in some parts of Europe (the UK and Scandinavia), and in specific areas such as mobile communications, these ingredients for the Network Economy are only in the early stage of emerging in Continental Europe, and the political mindset in support of the Network Economy is anything but prevalent. As long as we do not see a significant shift toward movements in this direction, Europe will not see the full benefits of the Network Economy within a Global Economy.

Racing behaviour on technological positions among firms in high- technology industries, as exemplified by the globally operating telecommunications and computer industries, produce spillover benefits in terms of increasing returns and widespread productivity gains. Due to relentless competition among technological leaders the network effects result in significant advantages in the value added to this industry contributing to faster growth of GDP, and through a flexible labour market, also to employment growth. This constitutes a new paradigm in economic thinking through network economies and is a major gauge to compare the wealth-creating power of the US economy over the past decade against the European and advanced Asian economies. It is interesting to speculate on the implications of the way companies in major high-technology markets, such as telecommunications, split clearly into the two major technology races, with one group of firms clearly lagging the other.

The trajectories of technological evolution certainly seem to suggest that firms from one frontier cannot simply jump to another trajectory. Witness, in this regard, the gradual process necessary for a firm in the catch-up race to approach those in the frontier race. There appears to be a frontier 'lock-in', in that once a company is part of a race, the group of rivals within that same race are the ones whose actions influence that company's strategy the most. Advancing technological capability is a cumulative process. The ability to advance to a given level of technical capability appears to be a function of existing technical capability. Given this path dependence, the question remains: why do some firms apparently choose a path of technological evolution that is less rapid than others? Two sets of possible explanations could be derived from our case analysis, which need not be mutually exclusive. The first explanation lingers primarily on the expensive nature of Research and Development (R&D)in industries like telecommunications and computers which rely on novel discovery for their advancement. Firms choosing the catch-up race will gain access to a particular technical level later than those choosing the frontier, but will do so at a lower cost.

1.2 TECHNOLOGICAL FRONTIERS

The evolution of a cross section of high technology industries reflects repetitive strategic interactions between companies in a continuous quest to dominate the industry or at least to improve its competitive position through company level and industry level technological evolution. We can observe several racing patterns across industries, each of which is the result of a subset of firms jockeying for a position either as a race leader or for a position near the leader constituting a leadership club. The identification and interpretation of the races relies on the fact that different firms take very different technological paths to target a superior performance level with the reward of increasing market shares, maintaining higher productivity and profitability. In a Schumpeterian framework such races cannot be interpreted in a free-riding situation where one firm expands resources in advancing the state of technology and the others follow closely behind. Such spillover interpretations are suspect when products are in the domain of high complexity, of high risk in succeeding, and different firms typically adopt different procedural and architectural approaches.

The logic underlying this evolution holds in any industry in which two broad sets of conditions are satisfied. First, it pays for a firm to have a technological lead over its rival; it also boosts its market image and enhances its reputational capital. Second, for various levels of technological complexity among the products introduced by various firms, technological complexity can be represented by a multi-criteria performance measure, that is, by a vector-valued distance measure. The collection of performance indicators, parameters, being connected with each other for individual companies form an envelope that shapes a 'technological frontier'. The technological frontier is in fact a reasonable indicator of the evolving state of knowledge (technical expertise) in the industry. At any point in time the industry technology frontier (ITF) indicates the degree of technical sophistication of the most advanced products carried by companies in that industry in view of comparable performance standards. Firm level technology frontiers (FTF) are constructed analogously and indicate, at any point in time, the extent of technical sophistication achieved by the firm until that point in time. The evolution of company and industry level frontiers is highly interactive. Groups of company frontiers are seen to co-evolve in a manner that suggests that the respective firms are racing to catch up with, and get ahead of each other.

A data set could focus on a given set of products (systems) by major European, American and Asian enterprises in those industries for a sufficiently representative period of market evolution. In principle, we can identify at least two races in progress in the industries throughout a given period of duration. One comprises the world frontier race in each of those industries, the other, for example, the European frontier race which technically would constitute a subfrontier to the worldwide race. The aggregate technology frontier of the firms in a particular race (that is, ITF) is constructed in a manner similar to the individual FTFs. Essentially, the maximal envelope of the FTFs in a particular race constitutes the ITF for that race. The ITF indicates, as a function of calendar time, the best achievable performance by any firm in the race at a given date.

A statistical profiling of technological evolution and innovation relates to competitive racing among rival companies. Among the (non-exclusive) performance criteria to be assessed are (1) frequency of frontier pushing, (2) technological domination period, (3) innovations vs. imitations in the race, (4) innovation frequency when behind or ahead, (5) nature of jumps, leapfrogging or frontier-sticking, (6) inter-jump times and jump sizes, (7) race closeness measures, (8) inter-frontier distance, (9) market leading through 'market making' innovations and (10) leadership in 'innovation markets'.

A race may or may not have different firms in the leadership position at different times. It may be a tighter race at some times than at others, and in general, may exhibit a variety of forms of interesting behaviour. While analysis of racing behaviour is left to various interpretations, it is appropriate to ask why the firms are motivated to keep on racing at all. As access to superior technology expands the scope of opportunities available to the firms, the technology can be applied in a range of markets. However, leading edge technology is acquired at a cost. It seems unlikely that all the companies would find it profitable to compete to be at the leading edge all the time. Also not every firm has access to equal capabilities in leveraging a given level of technological resources. Firms may, for example, be expected to differ in their access to complementary assets that allows them to appropriately reap the benefits from their innovation. It is reasonable to assume that whatever the level of competence of a company in exploiting its resources it will be better off the more advanced the technology. Based on this procedure an analysis will show how dynamic competition evolved in the past.

Unlike other (statistical) indicators (such as patent statistics) referring to the degree of competitiveness among industries, regions and countries concerned, the proposed measures cover behavioral dynamic movements in respective industries, and therefore are able to lend intrinsic predictive value to crucial economic variables relating to economic growth and wealth creation. The results are likely to provide strategic support for industrial and technology policy in a regional or national context and will enable policy makers to identify strengths and weaknesses of relevant players and their environments in those markets. While this process looks like a micro representation of dynamic technological evolution driving companies and industries into leadership positions, we may construe an analogous process that drives a region or a nation into advancement on a macro scale in order to achieve a higher level pecking order among its peers. This may allow using the micro foundations of racing as a basis for identifying clubs of nations or regions among them to achieve higher levels and rates of growth.

1.3 CATCH-UP OR LEAPFROGGING

It was Schumpeter (1942) who observed that it is the expectation of supernormal profits from a temporary monopoly position following an innovation that is the chief driver of R and D investment. Along this line, the simplest technology race model can be explained as follows: A number of firms invest in R&D. Their investment results in an innovation with the time spent in R and D subject to some varying level of uncertainty. However, a greater investment reduces the expected time to completion of R&D. The model investigates how many firms will choose to enter such a contest, and how much they will invest. However, despite some extensive theoretical examination of technological races there have been very few empirical studies on this subject (Lerner, 1997) and virtually none in the context of major global industries, and on a comparative basis.

Technological frontiers at the firm and industry race levels offer a powerful tool through which to view evolving technologies within an industry. By providing a benchmarking roadmap that shows where an individual firm is relative to the other firms in the industry, they highlight the importance of strategic interactions in the firm's technology decisions. From the interactive process of racing could emerge various behavioral patterns. Does lagging behind one's closest technological rivals cause a firm to increase its innovative effort? The term 'race' suggests that no single company would want to fall too far behind, and that everyone would like to get ahead. If a firm tries to innovate more when it is behind than when it is ahead, then 'catch-up' behavior will be the dominant effect. Once a firm gets ahead of its rivals noticeably, then rivals will step up their efforts to catch up. The leader will slow down its innovative efforts until its rivals have drawn uncomfortably close or have surpassed it. This process repeats itself every time a company gets far enough ahead of its rivals. An alternative behavior pattern would correspond to a firm increasing its innovative effort if it gets far enough ahead, thus making catch-up by the lagging firms increasingly difficult. This looks like the 'Intel Model' where only the paranoid survives (Grove, 1992). For any of these forms there appears to be a clear link to market and industry structure, as termed 'intensity of rivalry' by Kamien and Schwarz (1982).

We group two different kinds of races: one that is a frontier race among leaders and would-be leaders (first league) and another that is a catch-up race among laggards and imitators (second league). Though both leagues may play their own game, in a free market contest, it would be possible that a member of the second league may penetrate into the first, as one in the first league may fall back into the second. Another aspect of innovation speed has been addressed by Kessler and Bierly (2002). As a general rule they found that the speed to racing ahead may be less significant the more 'radical' (drastic) the innovation appears to be and the more likely it leads to a dominant design. These two forms have been applied empirically to the development of the early Japanese computer industry (Gottinger,1998), that is, a frontier racing model regarding the struggle for technological leadership in the global industry between IBM and 'Japan Inc.' guided by MITI (now METI), and a catch-up racing model relating to competition among the leading Japanese mainframe manufacturers as laggards.

It is also interesting to distinguish between two sub-categories of catch-up behaviour. A lagging firm might simply try to close the gap between itself and the technological leader at any point in time ('frontier-sticking' behaviour), or it might try to actually usurp the position of the leader by 'leapfrogging' it. When there are disproportionately large payoffs to being in the technical lead (relative to the payoffs that a firm can realize if it is simply close enough to the technical frontier), then one would expect that leapfrogging behaviour would occur more frequently than frontier-sticking behaviour (Owen and Ulph, 1994). Alternatively, racing toward the frontier creates the 'reputation' of being an innovation leader facilitating to maintain and increase market share in the future (Albach, 1997). All attempts to leapfrog the current technological leader might not be successful since many lagging firms might be attempting to leapfrog the leader simultaneously and the leader might be trying to get further ahead simultaneously. Correspondingly, one should distinguish between attempted leapfrogging and realized leapfrogging. This phenomenon (though dependent on industry structure) appears as the predominant behaviour pattern in the US and Japan frontier races (Brezis et al., 1991). Albach (1993) cites studies for Germany that show otherwise.

Leapfrogging behavior influenced by the expected size of payoffs as suggested by Owen and Ulph (1994) might be revised in compliance with the characteristics of industrial structure of the local (regional) markets, the amount of R&D efforts for leapfrogging and the extent of globalization of the industry. Even in the case where the payoffs of being in the technological lead are expected to be disproportionately large, the lagging companies might be satisfied to remain close enough to the leader so as to gain or maintain a share in the local market. This could occur when the amount of R&D efforts (expenditures) required for leapfrogging would be too large for a lagging firm to be viable in the industry and when the local market has not been open enough for global competition: the local market might be protected for the lagging local companies under the auspices of measures of regulation by the government (e.g. government purchasing, controls on foreign capital) and the conditions preferable for these firms (e.g. language, marketing practices).

When the industrial structure is composed of multi-product companies, as for example it used to be in the Japanese computer industry, sub-frontier firms may derive spill over benefits in developing new products in other technologically related fields (e.g. communications equipment, consumer electronic products). These companies may prefer an R&D strategy just to keep up with the technological frontier level (catch-up) through realizing a greater profit stream over a whole range of products.

What are the implications of the way firms split cleanly into the two technology races, with one group clearly lagging the other technologically? The trajectories of technological evolution certainly seem to suggest that firms from one frontier cannot simply jump to another trajectory. Witness, in this regards the gradual process necessary for the companies in the Japanese frontier to catch up with those at the global frontier. There appears to be a front line 'lock-in' in that once a firm is part of a race, the group of rivals within that same race are the ones whose actions influence the firm's strategy the most.

Advancing technological capability is a cumulative process. The ability to advance to a given level of technical capability appears to be a function of existing technical potential. Given this 'path dependence', the question remains: why do some firms apparently choose a path of technological evolution that is less rapid than others? We propose two sets of possible explanations which need not to be mutually exclusive. The first explanation hinges primarily on the expensive nature of R&D in industries like the computer industry which rely on novel scientific discovery for their advancement. Firms choosing the subfrontier will gain access to a particular technical level later than those choosing the frontier, but will do so at a lower cost. Expending fewer resources on R&D ensures a slower rate of technical evolution. The second explanation relates mainly to technological spillovers. Following the success of the frontier firms in achieving a certain performance level, these become known to the subfrontier firms. In fact, leading edge research in the computer industry is usually reported in patent applications and scientific journals and is widely disseminated throughout the industry. The hypothesis is that partial spillover of knowledge occurs to the subfrontier firms, whose task is then simplified to some extent. Notice that the subfrontier firms still need to race to be technological leaders, as evidenced by the analysis above. This implies that the spillovers are nowhere near perfect. Company specific learning is still the norm. However, it is possible that knowing something about what research avenues have proved successful (for the frontier firms) could greatly ease the task for the firms that follow and try to match the technical level of the frontier company.

1.4 STATISTICAL METRICS OF INDUSTRIAL RACING PATTERNS

Statistically descriptive measures of racing behaviour can be established that reflect the richness of the dynamics of economic growth among competing nations. The point of departure for a statistical analysis of industrial racing patterns is the aggregate technological frontier represented by the national production function as a reasonable indicator of the evolving state of knowledge (technical expertise) in a nation or region which is the weighted aggregate of all industries or activities that themselves are represented by industry technology frontier (ITF). Firm level technology frontiers (FTF) are constructed analogously and indicate, at any point in time, the weighted contribution of that firm to the industry on standard industry classification.

In this context we define 'race' as a continual contest for technological superiority among nations or regions with key industries. Under this conceptualisation a race is characterised by a number of countries whose ITF's remain 'close' together over a period (T) of, say, 25 to 50 years. The distinctive element is that countries engaging in a competition have ITF's substantially closer together than those of any company not in the race. A statistical analysis should reflect that a race, as defined, may or may not have different countries in the leadership position at different times. It may be a tighter contest at some times than at others, and in general, may exhibit a variety of forms of industrial behavior. We look for clusters of firms who's ITFs remain close enough throughout the duration (formal measures of closeness are defined and measured). We identify races to take place at any level of industrial performance between the very top and the very bottom throughout 50 years duration that is racing from the bottom to racing to the top.

One comprises the world frontier race in each of those industries, the other a subfrontier race (say, North America, Europe, East Asia, China, India, Latin America, Africa) which technically would constitute a subfrontier to the world, allowing under the best of circumstances for the subfrontier to be the frontier. Since the level and breadth of industrial activity is reflected as an indicator for economic welfare, racing to the top would go parallel with economic growth and welfare enhancing, whereas racing from the bottom would correspond to poverty reduction and avoiding stationary (under)development traps.

1.5 CHARACTERIZATION OF STATISTICAL INDICATORS OF INDUSTRIAL RACING

While a variety of situations are possible, the extremes are the following: (a) one country may push the frontier at all times, with the others following closely behind, (b) some countries share more or less equally in the task of advancing the most value generating industry technology frontiers (ITFs). Depending on the situation the most value generating industries may be high technology based increasing returns or network industries that are able to induce complementary emerging industries with high potentials (see Chapt. 4). Extreme situation (a) corresponds to the existence of a unique technological leader for a particular race, and a number of quick followers. Situation (b), on the other hand, corresponds to the existence of multiple technological leaders.

Assessment of Frontier Pushing

The relevant statistics for the races relate to counting the times the ITFs are pushed forward by countries or regions at large within a global or regional frontier. Frontier pushing can be triggered through industrial policy by governments or well fostered entrepreneurship in an advanced capitalistic system

Domination Period Statistics

Accepting the view that a country/region has greater potential to earn income and build wealth from its technological position if it is ahead of its race suggests that it would be interesting to examine the duration of time for which a country can expect to remain ahead once it finds itself pushing its ITF. We statistically define the 'domination period' to be the duration of time for which a country leads its particular race. It is interesting to note that the mean domination period is virtually indistinguishable for the three races, and lies between three and four years. A difference of means test cannot reject the hypothesis that the mean years of domination tend to cluster but hardly converge. So countries in each of the races can expect to remain ahead approximately in proportion to their technological capability and more than the amount of time after they have propelled themselves to the front of their respective races. However, the domination period tends to be a more uncertain quantity in the world frontier race, to a lesser degree in the EU frontier race than in any smaller regional races (as evidenced by the lower domination period standard deviation).

Catch-up Statistics

If key industries of a country push to innovate more when they are behind than when they are ahead, then 'catch- up' behavior will be the dominant effect. For each country/region, these statistics compare the fraction of the total innovations carried out by industries in that country (i.e. the fraction of the total number of times that their ITFs advance) when it was engaging in its race when lagging, with the fraction of times that the country actually led its race. In the absence of catch-up behaviour, or behaviour leading to a country increasingly dominating its rivals, we would expect to see no difference in these fractions. Then the fraction of time that a country is ahead of its race could be an unbiased estimator of the fraction of innovations in its key industries that it engages in when it is ahead. As will be shown in Chapters 3 and 4, the data, however, suggest that this is usually not the case. They appear to show that the fraction of times a state leads its race at any development level in a group or club is larger than the fraction of innovations that occur when the country is ahead, i.e. more innovations occur when the country is lagging than would be expected in the absence of catch-up or increasing dominance behavior. A major exception would arise if the country would act like an 'Intel Economy', where unchallenged leadership in key industries creates incentives to increase the lead to its rivals. Catch-up behavior is supported by additional observations, as derivable from convergence and conditional convergence in the economic growth process that countries make larger jumps (i.e. the ITFs advance more) when they are behind than when they are leading the race

Leapfrogging Statistics

From this, the distinction emerges between two kinds of catch-up. A lagging country might simply try to close the gap between itself and the technological leader at any point in time (frontier-sticking behavior), or it might try to actually usurp the position of the leader by 'leapfrogging' it. When there are disproportional larger incomes per head when being in the technical lead (relative to a situation that a country can realize if it is simply close enough to the technological frontier), then one would expect that leapfrogging behaviour would make it a more attractive incentive than frontier-sticking behaviour.

All attempts to leapfrog the current technological leader might not be successful since many lagging firms/industries might be attempting to leapfrog the leader simultaneously. Correspondingly, we observe both the attempted leapfroggings and the realized leapfroggings. It appears likely that the leapfrogging phenomenon would be more predominant in the premier league than in following up leagues.

Interfrontier Distance

How long does 'knowledge' take to spillover from frontier to subfrontier industries? This requires investigating "interfrontier distance". One measure of how much subfrontier industries' technology lags the frontier industries' technology could be graphed as "subfrontier lag" in terms of calendar time. At each point in time, this is simply the absolute difference in the subfrontier performance and the frontier performance time. The graph would clearly indicate that this measure has been declining or increasing more or less monotonically over the past 50 years to the extent that the subfrontier industries have been able/unable to catch up with the frontier industries. A complementary measure would be to assess the difficulty of bridging the lag. That is, how much longer does it take the subfrontier to reach a certain level of technical achievement after the frontier has reached that level? Thus it might very well turn out that the interfrontier distance may be decreasing though the difficulty in bridging the gap is increasing.

Race Closeness Measure (RCM)

None of the previous analyses tell us how close any of the overall races are over a period of time. The races are all distant/close by construction, however, some might be closer than others, We define 'a measure of closeness' of a race (RCM) at a particular time as follows:

$$\text{RCM}(t) = \Sigma_0^N [F_i(t) - F_j(t)]^2 / N(t) \tag{1.1}$$

where $F_i(t)$ is country's i ITF at time t, $F_j(t)$ is country's j comparable ITF at time t = max [ITF(t)] for each i, j and N(t) is the number of active key value-generating industries at time t.

The measure (Equation 1) thus constructed has a lowest value of 0, which corresponds to a 'dead heat' race. Higher values of the measure correspond to races that are less close. Unlike the earlier characteristics (domination period length, innovation when ahead versus when behind, leapfrogging versus frontier-sticking) which investigate the behaviour of a particular feature of the race and of a particular industry in relation to the race frontier, the RCM is more of an aggregate statistic of how close the various racing parties are at a point in time. The closeness measure is simply an indication of parity, and not one that says anything per se about the evolution of the technological frontier. To see this, note that if none of the frontiers were evolving, the closeness measure would be 0, as it would be if all the frontiers were advancing in perfect lock-step with one another.

We talk about value-added increasing returns industries over a period of 30 years. The industries comprise ICT, Consumer Electronics, Chemicals and Materials, Automobiles, Pharma/Biotech, Machine Tools, Medical Instruments, Aerospace/Defense, Energy Technologies, and HT Transportation Systems. Industry sectors can be assigned to various countries/regions such as US, EU, China, Russia, India, Brazil, Japan. We benchmark the industry technology frontiers (ITFs) accordingly, that is, highest 'state of knowledge' at time t is 100 pc. The countries' rank to the max ITFs is assessed as the share of the max ITF. The assessment intervals are spaced in five year intervals starting in 1980 until 2010. After aggregating across industries for each observation point, altogether 7, we get trend graphs over the entire observed period (Table 1.1).

Table 1.1. ITF Trends across Industries in Different Industries.. The industries comprise ICT, Consumer Electronics, Chemicals and Materials, Automobiles, Pharma/Biotech, Machine Tools, Medical Instruments, Aerospace/Defence, Energy Technologies, HT Transportation Systems

ICT Industry 1980	ITF (max = 100)
US	80
EC	60
China	15
USSR	30
India	25
Brazil	20
Japan	70
All 10 Industries	GDP Share (pc)
US	70
EU	60
China	50
USSR	40
India	30
Brazil	25
Japan	65

1.6 FURTHER DISCUSSION

Observations on firm-led racing patterns emerging in oligopolistic market structures of particular high tech industries, and the clustering of racing on an industry level are putting companies in different geo-economic zones against each other, becoming dominant in strategic product/process technologies. Here racing patterns among industries in a relatively free trade environment could lead to competitive advantages and more wealth creating and accumulating dominance in key product / process technologies in one region at the expense of others. The question is whether individual contests on a firm level induce similar effects on an industry level and if so, what controlling effects may be rendered by regional or multilateral policies on regulatory, trade and investment matters? The point is that racing behaviour in leading high technology industries by generating frontier positions create cluster and network externalities pipelining through other sectors of the economy and creating competitive advantages elsewhere, as supported by the 'increasing returns' debate (Chapt.6). In this sense we can speak of positive externalities endogenizing growth of these economies and contributing to competitive advantage.

We are about to show in the upcoming chapters how technological racing, rivalry and competition instigates a process of innovation, industrial and market evolution and how it extends to larger entities than firms and industries to regions and national economies or economy networks. It will show what drives economic growth and globalization, which industries are most significantly affected and how technological racing results in value generation in increasing returns and network industries. Furthermore, we explore how the emergence of selective managerial strategies is most likely to carry success in the pursuit of corporate and industrial policies.

Welfare enhancing technology racing as a constituent element of the capitalist process reinforced by globalization provides social benefits far exceeding the costs. Even more important, any alternative path, other than the competitive, would likely be inferior given the costs in that it would generate a less valued and less welfare producing technology portfolio. That is, even if the competitive process is wasteful, (for example, in parallel or correlated technology development) its unique high value innovation outcome far exceeds the benefits of any alternative path. There is historical, observational and analytical evidence given in this book (see Chapters, 2, 4 and 7).

On a national scale simple catch-up hypotheses have put emphasis on the great potential of adopting unexploited technology in the early stage and the increase of self-limiting power in the later stage. However, an actual growth path of technological trajectory of a specific economy may overwhelmingly be constrained by social capability. The capability also endogenously changes as states of the economy and technology evolve. The success of economic growth due to diffusion of advanced technology or the possibility of leapfrogging is mainly attributable to how the social capability evolves (i.e., which effects become more influential: growing responsiveness to competition or growing obstacles to it on account of vested interests and established positions). Another observation relates to policy inferences on market structure, entrepreneurship, innovation activity, industrial policy and regulatory frameworks in promoting and hindering industry frontier races in a global industrial context. Does lagging behind one's closest technological rivals cause an industry to increase its innovative effort?

On an industry level, among the key issues to address is the apparent inability of technology oriented corporations to maintain leadership in fields that they pioneered. There is a presumption that firms fail to remain competitive because of agency problems or other suboptimal managerial behaviour within these organizations. An alternative explanation is that technologically trailing firms, in symmetric competitive situations, will devote greater effort to innovation, so that a failure of technological leaders to maintain their position is an appropriate response to the competitive environment. In asymmetric situations, with entrants challenging incumbents, research does demonstrate that start-up firms show a stronger endeavour to close up to or leapfrog the competitors. Such issues highlight the dynamics of the race within the given market structure in any of the areas concerned.

Catch-up processes are taking place between leaders and followers within a group of industrialized countries in pursuit of higher levels of productivity and economic growth. Supposing that the level of labour productivity were governed entirely by the level of technology embodied in capital stock, one may consider that the differentials in productivities among countries are caused by the 'technological age' of the stock used by a country relative to its 'chronological age'. The technological age of capital is a period of technology at the time of investment plus years elapsing from that time. Since a leading country may be supposed to be furnished with the capital stock embodying, in each vintage, technology which was 'at the very frontier' at the time of investment, 'the technological age of the stock is, so to speak, the same as its chronological age' (Abramovitz, 1986). While a leader is restricted in increasing its productivity by the advance of new technology, trailing countries 'have the potential to make a larger leap' as they are provided with the privilege of exploiting the backlog in addition of the newly developed technology. Hence, followers being behind with a larger gap in technology will have a stronger potential for growth in productivity. The potential, however, will be reduced as the catch-up process goes on because the unexploited stock of technology becomes smaller and smaller. However, as new technologies arise and are rapidly adopted in a Schumpeterian process of 'creative destruction', their network effects induce rapid accelerating and cumulative growth potentials being catalyzed through industry racing.

In the absence of such a process we can explain the tendency to convergence of productivity levels of follower countries. Historically, it fails to answer alleged puzzles of why a country, such as the United States, has preserved the standing of the technological leader for a long time since taking over leadership from Britain in around the end of the nineteenth century and why the shifts have taken place in the ranks of follower countries in their relative levels of productivity (i.e. technological gaps between them and the leader). The American economist Abramovitz (1986) poses some extensions and qualifications on this simple catch-up hypothesis in the attempt to explain these facts. Among other factors than technological backwardness, he lays stress on a country's 'social capability' (i.e. years of education as a proxy of technical competence and its political, commercial, industrial, and financial institutions). The social capability of a country may become stronger or weaker as technological gaps close and thus, he states, the actual catch-up process does not lend itself to simple formulation. This view has a common understanding to what another economist, Olson (1996), expresses to be public policies and institutions as his explanation of the great differences in per capita income across countries, stating that any poorer countries that adopt relatively good economic policies and institutions enjoy rapid catch-up growth. The suggestion should be taken seriously when we wish to understand the technological catching-up to American leadership by Japan, in particular, during the post-war period and explore the possibility of a shift in standing between these two countries. This consideration will directly bear on the future trend of the state of the art which exerts a crucial influence on the development of the world economy.

These explanations notwithstanding, we venture as a major factor for divergent growth processes the level of intensity of the racing process within the most prevalent value-added industries with cross sectional spillovers. These are the communications and information industries which have been shaped and led by leading American firms and where the rewards benefited their industries and country. Though European and Japanese companies were part of the race they were left behind in core markets reaping lesser benefits. The IT investment relative to GDP, for example, used to be only less than half in countries such as Japan, Germany and France compared to the US. This does not bode well for a rapid catch-up in those countries. Steering or guiding the process of racing through the pursuit of industrial policies aiming to increase competitive advantage of respective industries, as having been practised in Japan, would stimulate catch-up races but appears to be less effective in promoting frontier racing. Another profound reason lies in the phenomenon of network externalities affecting IT industries. That is, racing ahead of rivals in respective industries may create external economies to the effect that such economies within dominant industries tend to improve their international market position and therefore pull ahead in competitiveness vis-a-vis their (trading) partners.

As Krugman (1997) observed, 'It is probably true that external economies are a more important determinant of international trade in high technology sectors than elsewhere'. The point is that racing behaviour in leading high growth network industries by generating frontier positions create critical cluster and network externalities pipelining through other sectors of the economy and creating competitive advantages elsewhere, as supported by the increasing returns debate (Arthur, 1996). In this sense we can speak of positive externalities endogenizing growth of these economies and contributing to competitive advantage.

All these characteristics lay the foundations of the 'Network Economy'. The latter is formed through an ever emerging and interacting set of increasing returns industries, it is about high-intensity, technology driven racing, dynamic entrepreneurship, focussed risk-taking through (free) venture capital markets endogenized by societal and institutional support. With the exception of pockets of activity in some parts of Europe (the UK and Scandinavia), and in specific areas such as mobile communication, these ingredients for the Network Economy are only in the early stage of emerging in Continental Europe, and the political mindset in support of the Network Economy is anything but prevalent. As long as we do not see a significant shift toward movements in this direction Europe will not see the full benefits of the Network Economy within a Global Economy.

Racing behaviour on technological positions among firms in high technology industries, as exemplified by the globally operating telecommunications, and computer industries, produce spillover benefits in terms of increasing returns and widespread productivity gains. Due to relentless competition among technological leaders the network effects lead to significant advantages in the value added to this industry, contributing to faster growth of GDP, and through a flexible labor market, also to employment growth. This constitutes a new paradigm in economic thinking through network economies and is a major gauge to compare the wealth creating power of the US economy against the European and advanced Asian economies.

REFERENCES

Abramovitz, M. (1986) 'Catching up, forging ahead, and falling behind', *Journal of Economic History*, 66, 385–406.

Albach, H. (1994) Information, Zeit und Wettbewerb (Information, Time and Competition), J. H. von Thuenen Lecture, in Jahrestagung des Vereins fuer Sozialpolitik, Muenster 1993, Berlin: Duncker und Humblot, 113–154."

Albach, H. (1997) 'Global competition among the few', The Ehrenrooth Lectures, Swedish School of Economics and Business Administration, Res. Reports 40. Helsingfors.

Arthur, B. (1996) 'Increasing returns and the new world of business', Harvard Business Review, July–August, 100–109.

Brezis, E., Krugman, P. and Tsiddon, D. (1991) 'Leapfrogging: a theory of cycles in national technological leadership', National Bureau of Economic Research (NBER), Working Paper # 3886.

Fagerberg,J. and M.M. Godinho (2004),' Innovation and Catching-Up', Chapt. 20 on Handbook of Innovation, Oxford:Blackwell

Gottinger, H. W. (1989) 'Stochastics of innovation processes', *Journal of Economics*, 49, 123–138.

Gottinger, H. W. (1998) 'Technological races', *Annual Review of Economics* (Japan), 38, 1–9.

Grossman, G. and Shapiro, C. (1987) 'Dynamic R&D Competition', *Economic Journal,* 97, 372–387.

Group of Lisbon, The (1995) Limits to Competition, Cambridge, MA: MIT Press.

Harris, C. and Vickers, J. (1987) 'Racing with uncertainty', Review of Economic Studies, 54, 305–321.

Juma, C. and N. Clark (2002), 'Technology Catch-Up: Opportunities and Challenges for DevelopingCountries', Supra Occ.Papers, Research Centre for the Social Sciences, Univ. of Edinburg, UK

Kessler, E. H. and Bierly, P. E. (2002) 'Is faster really better? An empirical test of the implications of innovation speed', *IEEE Transactions on Engineering Management*, 49, 2–12.

Kamien, M. I. and Schwarz, N. L. (1982) Market Structure and Innovation, Cambridge: Cambridge University Press.`

Krugman,P. (1991) 'Myths and Realities of U.S. Competitiveness', Science Nov. 8, 811-815

Lerner, J (1997) 'An empirical exploration of a technology race', *The Rand Journal of Economics*, 28(2), 228–224.

Olsen, M. (1996) 'Big Bills left on the Sidewalk: Why some nations are rich and others poor', *Journal of Economic Perspectives* 10, 1996, 3-24

Owen, R. and Ulph, D. (1994) 'Racing in two dimensions', Journal of Evolutionary Economics, 4, 185–206.

Schumpeter, J. (1947), Capitalism, Socialism and Democracy, New York: Harper, Rev. edition

In: Strategies of Economic Growth and Catch-Up...
Editor: Hans W. Gottinger, Mattheus F. A. Goosen

ISBN: 978-1-61122-422-1
©2012 Nova Science Publishers, Inc.

Chapter 2

TECHNOLOGY AND INDUSTRIAL RACES

Hans W. Gottinger

2.1. INTRODUCTION

In highly competitive technological industries new challenges and opportunities arise in the new product development arena. Driven by global markets, global competition, the global dispersion of scientific/engineering talent, and the advent of new increasing returns industries based on core emerging technologies enhance the intensity of rivalry among countries or regions to dominate the regional or global marketplace. A central question to address is how should countries form investments in innovation and pursue innovation strategies and what are the implications of such investments for competitive advantage? Understanding why in aggregate a national economy benefits from investments in innovation and product quality illuminates issues of competitive strategy and industrial dominance. In the field of competitive strategy, much attention has been given to the concept of core capabilities (Teece et al., 1997). Understanding how industries possibly supported by effective industrial policy make optimal investments in the face of keen competition will help to reveal the nature of inter-country competition and industrial advantage. Another source of racing behaviour can be linked to 'animal spirits' and innovation through entrepreneurship (e.g. Schumpeter's creative destruction) inducing cyclical waves around a long-run growth path (Francois and Lloyd-Ellis, 2002).

In major parts of industrial competitive analysis involving R&D decisions the focus is on breakthrough innovations which could create entirely new markets, for example, in studies featuring patent racing between competing firms. In more common competitive situations we observe firms, however, competing by investing in incremental improvements of products. It is an important aspect when innovation is considered to be manifested in product quality, process improvements and in the overall quality culture of an organization (Moss Kanter, 2006). For example, after product launch, incremental improvement of different aspects of product quality, improvements in various business processes and an incremental adoption of a quality culture are quite real-world phenomena. Some firms operate in a simultaneous product launch situation while others compete sequentially by adopting the role of leader or follower.

The strategic implications in these diverse circumstances can be treated within a unified framework of dynamic stochastic differential games.

To represent the features of leader-follower type in a sequence of technological racing we consider a class of (non-cooperative) differential games in which some countries try to establish priority of moves over others depending on the level of industrial strength in relation to others. This situation is modelled initially as a War of Attrition and Attack which resemble long-term technological races among countries or regions (Isaacs, 1965; Friedman, 1971)

The country that takes the right to move first is called the leader and the other competing country is called the follower unless it itself becomes the leader. A well-known example of this type of sequential move game in an economic context is the Stackelberg model (of duopoly). In this type of interaction the open-loop Nash equilibrium conditions in a sequential move game can be derived. It would lead to a comparison of the strategies of leader and follower. In what follows, Section 2.2 presents the essence of leader-follower type interactions through the format of a differential game which is accommodated to a competitive economic rivalry of national economies in Section 2.3. The properties of their interactions are derived in Section 2.4. Section 2.5 handles various economy asymmetries in the leader follower type situation. Finally, Section 2.6 summarizes and draws up conclusions and directions for future research.

2.2. A Differential Game Formulation

For our modelling effort we follow the notations and symbols as explained below. N: number of countries (or countries of certain category), T: finite time horizon for the strategies, i,j: superscripts to denote competing economies, t: an instant of time in the dynamic game setup, $u(t)$: R&D investment(expenditure per unit time), $R(t)$: net social product at t, R_o :industry category net revenue rate for the existing industry, R_1 : industry category net revenue rate for the new Industry, x_o: quality (technology)level of the existing industry.

In the model we assume that enhancements of quality are achieved by climbing a performance ladder that may squarely embrace technology but could expand to other criteria uniquely identified with quality, say, transportation system and infrastructure. Let the quality of the social product at time t be $x(t)$. In the context of total quality management, as quality levels increase it becomes even more difficult to climb the performance ladder. The hypothesis behind the formulation is that an economy needs to make higher innovation investments targeted towards improvement of quality. To capture this dynamics a negative feedback effect of the present state quality on the rate of change of industry quality ($x^{\bullet}(t)$) is considered. The state dynamics is:

$$x^{\bullet}(t) = K[u(t)]^{\alpha} - Lx(t) \qquad (2.1)$$

where K is proportional to the level of capital investment in development technology and L is the proportionality constant for the influence of present quality on the speed of further quality improvements, α is the national innovation resource productivity parameter. Based on Equation 2.1 the quality of the product at time t is:

$$x(t) = x_o \int_0^t [K[u(s)]^\alpha - Lx(s)] ds \qquad (2.2)$$

The industry quality provides a means for evaluating the product's attractiveness in the market in the presence of other competing products. The economy's industrial market share is a function of both its own industry quality and the industry quality of rivals.(The initial industry quality x_o may reflect the reputational capital of the economy, either low or high, and may induce her to different innovation investment efforts) The difference lies in the planning horizon. In this competitive setup, the planning horizon extends beyond the date of industry launch and the competing economies continue investing in comprehensive innovation efforts until the end of the growth phase of the industry. Further:

$$R(t) = \begin{cases} R_0 \cdot \dfrac{x_0}{x_0^i + x_0^j}, & 0 \leq t < T_p, \\ R_1 \cdot \dfrac{x^i(T)}{x^i(T) + x^j(T)}, & T_p \leq t < T, \end{cases} \qquad (2.3)$$

The cumulative development cost of the new industry at time t is given as:

$$TC(t) = \int_0^T \{u(s)\} ds \qquad (2.4)$$

The industry's cumulative profit at time t is determined as follows:

$$T\Pi(t) = TR(t) - TC(t) \qquad (2.5)$$

where $TR(t)$ and $TC(T)$ are total revenues and costs at time t, respectively. The total revenue function is given by:

$$TR(t) = \int_0^T R(s) ds \qquad (2.6)$$

where $R(\cdot)$ is given in (2.3). The industry's decision set is $\Delta = \{u(t)\}$. Notice that the industry precommits on the date of product launch T_p. The cumulative profit function, $T\Pi(\delta)$, is defined as the total profit by end of the window of opportunity with decision $\delta \in \Delta$. The industry's decision problem can be stated as:

$$\max_{\delta \in \Delta} T\Pi(\delta) = TR(\delta^*) - TC(\delta^*) = T\Pi^*(\delta^*) \qquad (2.7)$$

The combination of equations (1) through (6) generates an explicit representation of industry's i's cumulative profit (or value added) by the end of time horizon. This substitution yields:

$$T\Pi^*(\delta^*) = \max_{\delta \in \Delta} [R_0 \cdot \frac{x_0}{x_0^i + x_0^j} \cdot T_p +$$

$$+ R_1 \cdot \frac{x_0 + \int_0^T K_1 [u(s)]^\alpha - L x(s) ds}{x_0 + \int_0^T K[u(s)]^\alpha - Lx(s)ds + x^j(T)} \cdot (T - T_p) - \quad (2.8)$$

$$- \int_0^T \{u(s)\} ds]$$

where x_0^j and $x^j(T)$ respectively are the quality of existing and new industries of the competitor.

Considering a high intense industry rivalry of i and j, the optimization problem written above can be reformulated as a differential game problem with the state variable for industry i (the competing industry is represented by superscript j) given as $x^i(t)$; the control variable $u^i(t)$. In the terminology used in optimal control and differential games, the salvage term for industry i, $\Phi^i(T, x(T))$ is defined as follows:

$$\Phi^i(T, x(T)) \triangleq R_0 \cdot \frac{x_0^i}{x_0^i + x_0^j} \cdot T_p^i +$$

$$+ R_1 \cdot \frac{\left\{ x_0^i + \int_0^T K_1 [u^i(s)]^{\alpha^i} - L_1 x^i(s) ds \right\} (T - T_p)}{x_0^i + \int_0^T K_1 [u^i(s)]^{\alpha^i} - L_1 x^i(s) ds + x^j(T)} \quad (2.9)$$

where

$$x^j(T) = x_0^j + \int_0^T \left[K_2 [u^j(s)]^{\alpha^i} - L_2 x^j(s) \right] ds \quad (2.10)$$

2.3. A Sequential Differential Game between Two Competing Countries

We extend the conceptualization of a hyper-competitive scenario by considering a sequential differential game as being representative for a leader-follower or incumbent-entrant competitive situation. The game is characterized by information asymmetry where the follower is aware of the innovation and quality levels of the leader's industries and social product. The motivation for considering this scenario is its close correspondence with many real life competitive cases in high technology markets. Knowing the investment strategy of the leader, the rival countries can formulate their own strategies. Therefore, the firm acting as a leader chooses a decision path that maximizes the objective for all conceivable responses that can be taken by the follower(s). In the case of sequential games a hierarchical play differential game approach is used to model the competitive situation and to obtain the open-loop Stackelberg Nash equilibrium. The issue of subgame perfectness and commitment is extremely important in these solutions. Adding to the previous notation we let T_p, date of product launch by the leader, $T_p + \tau$, date of product launch by the follower. The leader is represented by the superscript i and the follower is represented by the superscript j. Since it is a sequential game the time of product launch for the two players is such that the leader launches the product at time T_p. Later, the follower launches the product after time τ at $T_p + \tau$. A continuous improvement in the product is considered and therefore the entire time interval t $\in [0, T]$ for the leader, and t $\in [T_p, T]$ for the follower needs to be optimized. The state dynamics of the leader is:

$$x^{\bullet i}(t) = K_1 [u^i(t)]^\alpha - L_1 x^i(t) \qquad (2.11)$$

The rate of quality improvement $x^{\bullet i}(t)$ increases with investments $u^i(t)$. The factor $L_1 x^i(t)$ suggests a natural decay in quality in the absence of any investments. The differential game formulation for leader is:

$$max \; T\Pi \; (u^i(t), T_p) = - \int_0^T \{(u^i(s)\}ds + \Phi^i(T, x^i(T))\} \qquad (2.12)$$

with the first component under the integral identifying the investment costs and the second the returns on investment (ROI) where $\Phi^i(T, x^i(T))$ is defined as:

$$\Phi^i(T, x^i(T)) \cong R_0 \cdot x_0^i/(x_0^i + x_0^j) \cdot T_p^i + R_1 \cdot x^i(T)(\tau)/(x^i(T) + x_0^j) +$$
$$+ R_1 \cdot x^i(T)(T - T_p - \tau)/(x^i(T) + x^j(T)) \qquad (2.13)$$

subject to:

$$x^{\bullet}(t) = K_1 [u^i(t)]^\alpha - L_1 x^i(t) \; , \; x^i(0) = x_0^i, \; T \; fixed, \; x^i(T) \; free \qquad (2.14)$$

Next, the follower's problem formulation is discussed. Owing to the sequential nature of the game, the information concerning the leader's quality and investments is known to the follower. Specifically, it is assumed that the knowledge gained by the leader's investments "spills over" to the follower's quality improvement dynamics. It is plausible to assume that in the context of a leader-follower competition, the level of quality improvements of the follower indeed depends not only on its own innovation efforts but also on the knowledge pool available because of the leader's investments. The fact that the leader often cannot wholly conceal her efforts nor can she credibly announce the commitment she has made makes the situation quite complicated. To address these issues fully in this context would require a subtle and rich analysis of games with incomplete information (Robson, 1990).

A formal treatment of "spillover effects" would enrich this model. The spillover effect is modeled by considering a linear additive term $M_2 u^i(t)$. The follower's state dynamics is:

$$x^{\bullet j}(t) = K_2 [u^j(t)]^\alpha - L_2 x^j(t) + M_2 u^i(t) \qquad (2.15)$$

It is assumed that the spillover is a function of the investments made by the leader $u^i(t)$. In this term M_2 is some number which quantifies the amount of spillover from the leader to the follower. The term $M_2 u^i(t)$ would restrict the analysis to the case where the follower emulates the innovation and product quality of the leader, as opposed to setting his own technology and quality standards. Now with all considerations wrapped up, a leader-follower dynamics can be stated. The follower's differential game formulation is given as:

$$\max T\Pi^j(u^j(t), T_p) = -\int_{T_p}^{T} \{u^j(s)\} ds + \Phi^j(T, x^j(T)) =$$
$$= -\int_{0}^{T-T_p} \{u^j(s+T_p)\} ds + \Phi^j(T, x^j(T)) \qquad (2.16)$$

where $\Phi^j(T, x(T))$ is defined as:

$$\Phi^j(T, x(T)) \triangleq R_0 \cdot \frac{x_0^j}{x_0^i + x_0^j} \cdot T_p +$$
$$+ R_0 \cdot \frac{x_0^j}{x^i(T) + x_0^j} \cdot \tau + R_1 \cdot \frac{\{x^j(T)(T - T_p - \tau)\}}{x^i(T) + x^j(T)} \qquad (2.17)$$

subject to:

$$x^j(t) = K_2 \left[u^j(t) \right]^\alpha - L_2 x^j(t) + M_2 u^i(t) \qquad (2.18)$$

where $M_2 u^i(t)$ represent the spillover of knowledge, assumed to be a function of investments by the leader, M_2 is a small constant such that $0 < M_2 \ll 1$. Furthermore, $x^j(0) = x_0^j$, T is fixed, $x^j(T)$ is free, where:

$$x^i(T) = x_0^i + \int_0^t \left[K_1 \left[u^i(s) \right]^{\alpha^i} - L_1 x^i(s) \right] ds \qquad (2.19)$$

$$x^j(T) = x_0^j + \int_{T_p}^{t} \left[K_2 \left[u^j(s) \right]^{\alpha^j} - L_2 x^j(s) + M_2 u^i(s) \right] ds \qquad (2.20)$$

In this type of competitive game with a lagged response of the follower we would approach a catch-up equilibrium.

2.4. ANALYSIS OF THE MODEL AND DISCUSSION

A conventional tool for solving the problem is the application of Pontryagin's maximum principle for open-loop Stackelberg equilibrium conditions. Interested readers can refer to Dockner et al. (2000) for details regarding Pontryagin's approach to solving sequential differential game problems. The equilibrium results are adapted to the present racing situation and expressed in the form of properties as given below.

Equilibrium Results

Property 1: The maximized costate variables for the follower are function of time and are given by:

$$\lambda_1^* = \lambda_{01} e^{L_2 t} \qquad (2.21)$$

$$\lambda_2^* = \lambda_{02} e^{L_1 t} \qquad (2.22)$$

where λ_1^* and λ_2^* are the costate variables reflecting the marginal price for a unit increase in follower industry's own state and the state of the leader i, $\lambda_1(0) = \lambda_{01}$, $\lambda_2(0) = \lambda_{02}$ are known constants.

Property 2: The Stackelberg equilibrium investment by the follower in national product development is given as:

$$u^j(t)^* = \left[K_2 \alpha^j \lambda_{01} e^{L_2 t} \right]^{\frac{1}{1-\alpha^j}} \qquad (2.23)$$

Next the leader's problem is investigated. The leader knows the follower's best response to each control path $u^i(\cdot)$.

Property 3: The maximized costate variables for the leader are given by:

$$\psi_1^* = \psi_{01} e^{L_1 t} \qquad (2.24)$$

$$\psi_2^* = \psi_{02} e^{L_2 t} \qquad (2.25)$$

$$\psi_3^* = -\psi_{03} e^{-L_2 t} \qquad (2.26)$$

where ψ_1^*, ψ_2^* and ψ_3^* are the costate variables reflecting the marginal value for a unit increase in the leader's own state, the state of the follower and the costate of the follower. ψ_{01}, ψ_{02} and ψ_{03} are constants.

Property 4: The Stackelberg equilibrium investment by the leader in product development is given as:

$$u^i(t)^* = \left[\frac{K_1 \alpha^i \psi_{01} e^{L_1 t}}{1 - M_2 \psi_{02} e^{L_2 t}} \right]^{\frac{1}{1-\alpha^i}} \tag{2.27}$$

Property 5: The equilibrium state trajectory of performance improvement of the follower is given as:

$$x^j(t) = \frac{e^{-L_2 t}}{L_2} \left[L_2 x_0^j + (-1 + e^{L_2 t}) M_2 \left[\frac{K_1 \alpha^i \psi_{01} e^{L_1 t}}{1 - M_2 \psi_{02} e^{L_2 t}} \right]^{\frac{1}{1-\alpha^i}} + \right.$$
$$\left. + (-1 + e^{L_2 t}) K_2 (K_2 \alpha^j \lambda_{01} e^{L_2 t})^{\frac{\alpha^j}{(1-\alpha^j)^2}} \right] \tag{2.28}$$

Property 6: The equilibrium state trajectory of performance improvement of the leader is given as:

$$x^i(t) = \frac{e^{-L_1 t}}{L_1} \left[L_1 x_0^i + (-1 + e^{L_1 i}) K_1 \left[\frac{K_1 \alpha^i \psi_{01} e^{L_1 t}}{1 - M_2 \psi_{02} e^{L_2 t}} \right]^{\frac{\alpha^i}{1-\alpha^i}} \right] \tag{2.29}$$

For the analysis, assuming behavioural interchange ability between leader and the follower we can expect a corresponding convergence path for both leader and follower. The first observation is that:

- The costate variable of both the leader and the follower increases more rapidly with time.

The marginal utility of a unit increase in (technology) quality, exhibits a convex increasing trajectory. With comparable values of parameters the plot of the costate trajectory of the follower has an upward exponential drift with time. The plot begins at time $t = T_p$, since the follower initiates industry development activities only after the leader has already launched the activity. Regarding the costate trajectory of the leader we see that ψ_l represents marginal utility from a unit increase in quality of the leader's product. The costate variable for both the leader and the follower firm increase for the entire planning horizon. This follows since the leader and follower are competing on the basis of their quality levels. Firms increase their market shares based on their relative quality to that of the competitor's. After launch the product faces its introduction and growth stage.

In these phases, maintaining higher quality becomes even more important since the product sales are directly influenced by product quality. This leads to a convex increasing trajectory for the costate variable. Thus, as a second observation:

- *The investment in innovation made by the follower increases more rapidly with time.*

The investment strategies of the follower are purely a function of its own costate variable; the follower's costate variable increases in a convex fashion. This in turn results in a convex increase in follower's control trajectory. With identical parameter values we can derive that the follower compensates for a delayed entry into the market by increasing its investment intensity. Such an increase in investment results in increased quality and therefore high total revenue for the follower. Thus we observe:

- *The investment in innovation made by the leader initially increases rapidly with time but later increases at a decreasing rate.*

The leader's investment trajectory is sigmoidal or S-shaped. Because of the nature of the game, the leader enters the market before the follower. While formulating his equilibrium investment strategy, the leader takes into account the evolution of his own costate and also the costate of the follower. Being early in the market, the leader takes into account all possible courses of action that a follower may choose.

We note that the leader's rate of investment increases in the initial phase and then starts to decrease. That is, the leader capitalizes on the advantage of early market entry by increasing the intensity of investments and gaining a high market share. Subsequently, after the follower's entry, the leader reduces the intensity of investments and thereby reduces the amount of spillover that is potentially possible.

- *When the parameter values of the leader and follower are identical, the follower invests higher than the leader.*

In the course of time initially the follower maps its investment strategy to that of the leader. However subsequently the leader starts reducing the rate of investments, while the follower continues with the high investment rate based strategy.

As a further observation:

- *The rate of increase of the follower's product quality increases with time.*

The quality of follower's product increases for the entire time-horizon. Moreover, this increase is a convex function. As can be inferred from the problem formulation, the quality level of the follower is a function of investments made by the leader and the follower. Specifically, the quality trajectory is influenced by both the convex profile of investments made by the follower and also by the spillover effect of the investments made by the leader. This results in a convex increase in quality improvements. The state trajectory is therefore upward sloping in convex form.

The follower starts accruing revenue only after $T_p + \tau$, where T_p is the date of launch of the leader. In the game context of quality-based competition, the follower compensates for the delayed entry by increasing the quality levels at a fast rate.

- *The rate of increase of the leader's technology quality decreases with time.*

The leader's investment trajectory follows an S-shaped trajectory. In the problem formulation the leader's quality improvement is only a function of its own investments. Moreover, it is assumed that the leader doesn't obtain the advantages of spillover of knowledge gained by the follower's investments. Furthermore, the leader needs to deliberately avoid maintaining very high investments to ensure that the follower doesn't achieve huge gains from spillovers. Under such a setup it must be noted that the leader chooses an S-shaped trajectory for investments. With this kind of investment profile the investment increases rapidly in the initial phase but then eventually tapers off. Corresponding to this investment profile, the rate of quality improvement is high in the initial phase but then eventually the rate of improvement starts decreasing. Thus, the quality trajectory of the leader is concave. This leads to another observation.

- *When the parameter values of the leader and follower are identical, the quality increase of the follower's technology is higher than that of the leader's technology.*

With identical parameter values the follower and leader are perfectly symmetric in their capabilities. Moreover, the leader has the advantage of earlier market entry, whereas the follower obtains the gains of information asymmetry and the associated knowledge spillovers from the leader. It is reasonable to assume that the follower employs his inherent competence and the benefit of spillover of knowledge from the leader's investments to increase quality at a much faster rate. Under such circumstances the overall gain and loss in the competitive game is dictated by the relative revenues achieved and the costs incurred by the two players. With higher investments than the leader the follower incurs higher costs. At the same time these investments also lead to higher quality levels and therefore revenues for the follower. In the event of the value of R_1 being very high the follower wins the game while the results favour the leader if R_1 is low.

2.5. Asymmetries in Firm Capabilities

We now turn to industry asymmetries and their implications. It is likely that industries take up the role of leader and follower based on inherent strengths and weaknesses. In this type of situation, firm asymmetries would turn technically into a non-zero sum differential game whose structure has been studied by Yao and Weyant (2004). Therefore, an explicit consideration of firm asymmetries is very important and could potentially lend more insights in a sequential game setup. In practical terms asymmetries may be addressed in at least four ways: First, it is possible that organizational approaches and techniques (such as total quality management) can be used to make the product development process more cost-efficient and effective. This would influence the value of the resource productivity parameter α. Second, it is possible to have an advantage in product development by making capital investment in technology development. This is equivalent to considering asymmetries in the value of K. Third, it is possible that the obsolescence parameter of industries denoted by L is different. Finally, different values of M suggest different levels of spillover of knowledge from the leader's investments to the follower. The firm with higher value of L has a higher obsolescence or decay in quality. We restrict assessment of asymmetries by considering different values for the parameters: (α^i and α^j), (K_1 and K_2), (L_1 and L_2) and (M_1 and M_2).

Innovation Resource Productivity

Parameters α^i and α^j denote the innovation resource productivity parameter of two industries. An asymmetry could result if the competing industries have differing capabilities in making a productive use of investments. The skill set of employees, training and development activities, the quality culture are some of the reasons for such an asymmetry. For example, ($\alpha^i = 0.2$) > ($\alpha^j = 0.1$) suggest that industry i has a higher innovation productivity over j. An investigation of different values of α suggests that the firm with higher innovation productivity also invests a higher amount in product development. From the results we observe that the follower has a relatively higher level of investments in innovation as compared to the leader. Therefore, an increase in the value of α of the follower will only result in making these investments still higher. Instead, an increase in leader's α would provide some interesting insights in that it will show that the leader sails ahead with the follower having no chance in catching up. It clearly shows that the leader has a higher investment than that of the follower for almost the entire planning horizon. As can also be noted, the quality of the leader's product is always higher than that of the follower. Hence an asymmetry in terms of resource productivity parameters provides a totally different result than what was observed when the competing firms were symmetric. It suggests that the leader with an advantage in terms of early market entry as well as a higher level of resource productivity indeed continues having higher revenues. Under this situation the leader doesn't worry much about the spillover to the follower since its own resource productivity enables attaining higher revenues by increasing quality levels relative to that of the follower. With a high value of R_1 it can be conjectured that the result favors the leader.

Capital Investment Parameters

Industry asymmetries can be analyzed by evaluating different values for K and the implications on control and state trajectories.. K_1 and K_2 are proportional to the level of capital investment in developing technology by the two competing (cross-country) industries. If ($K_1 = 20$) > ($K_2 = 10$), it suggests that the leader i has higher levels of capital investment in developing technology as compared to the follower j. The implications of a higher value of K for the leader can easily be derived. The parameter K exerts a positive effect on innovation investments. Similar to the conjecture regarding different values of α, the intuition behind this effect is that with a higher level of capital investments in development technology, a firm targets the investments towards increasing the product quality. Thus with a higher value of K the investment by the leader is relatively higher than that of the follower for most part of the planning horizon. However, in the latter part of the planning horizon, the follower's investment in fact shoots up while that of the leader tapers off. Such an investment profile would have an impact on the state trajectory..Furthermore, the technology quality of the leader is higher than that of the follower for most part of the planning horizon. Eventually, at the end of the planning horizon, the high growth in the follower's investment results in higher quality than that of the leader. In the model, the relative difference in resources due to strategic investments is captured in asymmetries in the value of K. Given adequately high values of R1, the leader i would have relatively higher profits than the follower j.

The Obsolescence Parameter

L1 and L2 characterize the decay or in other words the obsolescence effect of technology quality. Different values of L1 and L2 help evaluate the difference among the two industries regarding this effect. (L1 = 1) > (L2 = 0.7) suggests that the obsolescence effect for leader i is higher than that for the follower j. An investigation into the dynamics of innovation investments reveals that with higher value of the parameter L, an industry would make higher level of investments. Interestingly, with a difference in L1 and L2 the shape of investment trajectory of the leader is now convex. That is when the leader faces a high obsolescence effect the investments are increased at a faster rate to ensure an increasing state trajectory. However, as opposed to parameter a and K such an increased control trajectory doesn't translate into higher quality. In fact, in this situation, the leader has lower product quality in spite .of higher investments. A high decay effect puts the leader into a disadvantageous position. In such a situation, under equilibrium control the leader always loses the competitive game.

Spillover Factor M_2

M_2 characterizes the amount of spillover from the leader to the follower. In this section the impact of reduction of the spillover factor M_2 is considered. Evidently in this case the leader would be less worried about the amount of advantage the follower obtains from the leader's own investments. If the spillover effect is low, the leader pursues investments more aggressively, consistent with the incentive enhancement of spillover effects in the context of network externalities (Saaskilahti, 2006). Under such circumstances, the control trajectory of the leader is also convexly increasing and is only marginally lower than that of the follower.

Regarding the impact of such investments on the state trajectory, the quality of the follower is higher than that of the leader and both obtain a convex increasing state trajectory. But unlike α, K and L, a different value of M_2 doesn't correspond to any advantage related to resources, core competence or dynamic capabilities. This is purely an exogenously defined variable based on technology and industry types. Under changed circumstances with respect to M_2 the leader doesn't really gain much in the competitive game. The results in fact point to the follower winning the game due to much higher levels of quality and only marginally higher levels of investments.

CONCLUSIONS AND EXTENSIONS

There is apparently a paradox in trying to assess, both empirically and theoretically, the impact of competitive pressure on innovation and growth. On one hand, according to the tradition originating in Schumpeter (1947) the prospective reward provided by monopoly rent to a successful innovator is required to stimulate sufficient R&D investment and technological progress. On the other hand, the incentives to innovate are weaker for an incumbent monopolist than for a firm in a competitive industry (Arrow, 1962). When competition is intense in the product market, innovation may even be seen as the only way for a firm to survive. In neo-Schumpeterian models of endogenous growth (Grossman and Helpman, 1991; Aghion and Howitt, 1998), innovation allows a firm in an industry to take the lead and gain profit. But the monopoly rent enjoyed by the winner is only temporary, and a new innovator, capitalizing on accumulated knowledge, is always able to 'leapfrog' the leader unless the leader is endowed with advantages of industry asymmetries.

In the more recent research literature, Aghion, Harris and Vickers (1997), and Aghion, Harris, Howitt and Vickers (2001), supposing a duopoly in each sector, both, at the research and production levels, have introduced what they call "step-by-step innovation," according to which technological progress allows an industry (firm)to take the lead, but with the lagging industry (firm) remaining active and eventually capable of catching up. This model has been extended by Segerstrom (2005), Zeira (2005) Denicolo and Zanchettin (2006) allowing for the possibility that the lagging industry (firm) leapfrogs the leader, without driving it out of the market. Here we adopt a simplified approach to consider spillover effects. Griliches(1979) lays out the conceptual framework and provides an early discussion of the importance of spillover effects of R&D. Later in 1992, Griliches reviewed the recent empirical evidence on spillovers, and tentatively concluded that spillover effects may be substantial. As we can qualify from Grossman and Helpman's study (1998,Chap.8) that, first, when knowledge spillovers are small and countries are dissimilar in size, the small country may find its world market share declining over time because of economies of scale in research, and second, that technologically backward countries may tend to remain backward.

The model can be extended by evaluating the improvement in technology quality with a learning effect. This effect is very well documented in the literature and thus the extension to incorporate learning effects is straightforward. Specifically, learning can be used to characterize the dynamics of evolution of technology quality and the characterization of costs associated with innovation investments. For analytical simplicity the revenue function is treated as a salvage value. As an extension the incorporation of the dynamics of revenue in the analysis of the model can be explored. In the sequential play game, the state dynamics of the follower can be considered to be dependent on the state of the leader at previous time instant. This modification would allow for analysis of a model in which the leader uses open-loop Nash equilibrium strategy for innovation investments whereas the follower would adopt a Markovian Nash equilibrium strategy. Additional insights can be gained by this modification for leader-follower competitive dynamics in new technology development.

Firm asymmetries can be explored by considering multiple parameters at the same time. This would enable a richer understanding of the strategies that a leader and a follower should adopt based on their strengths and weaknesses. In view of the upcoming discussion (Chap. 3) on the linkage between economic growth and industrial competition we could observe the lower ranked the leading firms of a country are versus rival countries (regions) and the more asymmetric firms are within a country the more challenging it would be to achieve catch-up with leading countries. Thus the industry gap can be reduced not only by strengthening national champions versus global competitors but also by closing the gap between national champions and their domestic followers. This is likely to induce growth and performance. As The Economist (2007, p.4)) reported '… the World Bank has calculated that India could quintuple the size of its economy if it only caught up with itself – that is, if the mediocre firms in its industries closed the gap with the best.'

The conventional approach used in innovation and R&D research viewed the process as one with constant returns, competitive output and factor markets and no externalities. However, such a framework does not offer a full explanation of productivity growth. For a better understanding it therefore becomes very important to consider increasing returns to scale, R&D spillovers and other externalities and disequilibria.

APPENDIX

Mathematical Preliminaries, Definitions and Theorems

This section covers some of the salient analytical aspects specific to a sequential play game. For a finite horizon T let L and F denote the leader and follower respectively. Let x denote the vector of state variables, u^L the vector of control variables of the leader, and u^F the vector of control variables of the follower. Assume $x \in R^n$, $u^L \in R^{mL}$ and $u^F \in R^{mF}$.

Definition 1 The initial value of the, follower's costate variable λ_i is said to be non-controllable if $\lambda_i(0)$ is independent of the leader's control path $u^L(t)$. Otherwise, it is said to be controllable.

The definition suggests that if the costate variable is controllable, the follower's control variable $u^F(t)$ at time t depends also on future values of $u^L(.)$; that is, on values $u^L(s)$ with $s > t$.

Theorems and Proofs

Theorem 1. The maximized costate variables for the follower are a function of time and are given by:

$$\lambda_1^* = \lambda_{01} e^{L_2 t} \tag{A1}$$

$$\lambda_2^* = \lambda_{02} e^{L_1 t} \tag{A2}$$

where λ^*_1 and λ^*_2 are the costate variables reflecting the marginal price for a unit increase in the follower firm's own state and the state of the leader i ; $\lambda_1(0) = \lambda_{01}$, $\lambda_2(0) = \lambda_{02}$ are constants.

Proof: Stackelberg equilibrium conditions are derived by constructing the Hamiltonians. The analytical solution is derived for the follower firm j by writing the Hamiltonian as:

$$H^j = -[u^j(t)] + \lambda_1 [K_2 u^j(t)^{\alpha^j} - L_2 x^j(t) + M_2 u^i(t)] + \lambda_2 [K_1 u^i(t)^{\alpha^i} - L_1 x^i(t)] \tag{A3}$$

The necessary conditions for optimality are:

$$H^j_{u^j} = 0 \tag{A4}$$

$$\lambda_1^* = -H^j_{x^j}; \quad \lambda_2^* = -H^j_{x^i} \tag{A5}$$

$$x^j(0) = x_0^j \tag{A6}$$

From Equation A5:

$$\lambda_1^* = L_2 \lambda_1; \quad \lambda_1^* = \lambda_{01} e^{L_2 t} \tag{A7}$$

$$\lambda_2^* = L_1 \lambda_2; \quad \lambda_2^* = \lambda_{02} e^{L_1 t} \tag{A8}$$

where $\lambda_1(0) = \lambda_{01}$ is the known positive constant denoting the initial value of the costate λ_1 and $\lambda_2(0) = \lambda_{02}$ is a known negative constant denoting the initial value of the costate λ_2.

Theorem 2. The Stackelberg equilibrium investment by the follower in product development is given as:

$$u^j(t)^* = \left[K_2 \alpha^j \lambda_{01} e^{L_2 t}\right]^{\frac{1}{1-\alpha^j}} \tag{A9}$$

Proof: Differentiating Equation A3 with respect to $u^j(t)$, we obtain:

$$H_{uj} = -1 + \lambda_1 \alpha^j K_2 [u^j(t)]^{\alpha^j - 1} \tag{A10}$$

By equating Equation A10 to zero and some algebraic manipulations, the following expression is obtained for optimal effort in product development:

$$u^j(t)^* = \left[K_2 \alpha^j \lambda_1^*\right]^{\frac{1}{1-\alpha^j}} \tag{A11}$$

Substituting the expression for λ_i in Equation A11:

$$u^j(t)^* = \left[K_2 \alpha^j \lambda_{01} e^{L_2 t}\right]^{\frac{1}{1-\alpha^j}} \tag{A12}$$

Theorem 3. The maximized costate variables for the leader are given by:

$$\psi_1^* = \psi_{01} e^{L_1 t} \tag{A13}$$

$$\psi_2^* = \psi_{02} e^{L_2 t} \tag{A14}$$

$$\psi_3^* = -\psi_{03} e^{-L_2 t} \tag{A15}$$

where ψ_1^*, ψ_2^* and ψ_3^* are the costate variables reflecting the marginal price for a unit increase in the leader's own state, the state of the follower and the costate of the follower; ψ_{01}, ψ_{02} and ψ_{03} are constants.

Proof. The Stackelberg equilibrium conditions are derived by constructing the Hamiltonian. An analytical solution is derived for the leader firm i by writing the Hamiltonian as:

$$H^i = -\left[u^i(t)\right] + \emptyset \left[K_1 u^i(t)^{\alpha^i} - L_1 x^i(t)\right] + \\ + \emptyset_2 \left[K_2 u^j(t)^{\alpha^j} - L_2 x^j(t) + M_2 u^i(t)\right] + \emptyset_3 \left[\lambda_1 L_2\right] \tag{A16}$$

The necessary conditions for optimality are:

$$H^i_{u^i} = 0 \tag{A17}$$

$$\psi_1^* = -H^i_{x^i}; \quad \psi_2^* = -H^i_{x^j}; \quad \psi_3^* = -H^i_{\lambda_1}; \tag{A18}$$

$$x^i(0) = x_0^i \tag{A19}$$

From Equation A18:

$$\psi_1^* = L_1 \psi_1; \qquad \psi_1^* = \psi_{01} e^{L_1 t} \tag{A20}$$

$$\psi_2^* = L_2 \psi_2; \qquad \psi_2^* = \psi_{02} e^{L_2 t} \tag{A21}$$

$$\psi_3^* = -\psi_3 L_2; \qquad \psi_3^* = -\psi_{03} e^{-L_2 t} \tag{A22}$$

where ψ_1^*, ψ_2^* and ψ_3^* are the costate variables reflecting the marginal price for a unit increase in the leader's own state, the state of the follower and the costate of the follower; ψ_{01}, ψ_{02} and ψ_{03} are constants.

Technology and Industrial Races

Theorem 4. The Stackelberg equilibrium investment by the leader in product development is given as:

$$u^i(t)^* = \left[\frac{K_1 \alpha^i \psi_{01} e^{L_1 t}}{1 - M_2 \psi_{02} e^{L_2 t}}\right]^{\frac{1}{1-\alpha^i}} \tag{A23}$$

Proof: Differentiating (A.3) with respect to $u_i(t)$, we obtain:

$$H_{u^i} = -1 + \psi_1 \alpha^i K_1 [u^i(t)]^{\alpha^i - 1} + \psi_2 M_2 \tag{A24}$$

By equating Equation A24 to zero and some algebraic manipulations, the following is expression is obtained for optimal effort in product development:

$$u^i(t)^* = \left[\frac{K_1 \alpha^i \psi_1^*}{1 - M_2 \psi_2^*}\right]^{\frac{1}{1-\alpha^i}} \tag{A25}$$

Substituting the expression for $\psi 1*$ and $\psi 2*$ in Equation A25 yields:

$$u^i(t)^* = \left[\frac{K_1 \alpha^i \psi_{01} e^{L_1 t}}{1 - M_2 \psi_{02} e^{L_2 t}}\right]^{\frac{1}{1-\alpha^i}} \tag{A26}$$

Theorem 5. The equilibrium state trajectory of performance improvement of the follower is given as:

$$x^j(t) = \frac{e^{-L_2 t}}{L_2} \left[L_2 x_0^j + (-1 + e^{L_2 t}) M_2 \left[\frac{K_1 \alpha^i \psi_{01} e^{L_1 t}}{1 - M_2 \psi_{02} e^{L_2 t}}\right]^{\frac{1}{1-\alpha^i}} + \right.$$
$$\left. + (-1 + e^{L_2 t}) K_2 (K_2 \alpha^j \lambda_{01} e^{L_2 t})^{\frac{\alpha^j}{(1-\alpha^j)^2}} \right] \tag{A27}$$

Proof: The expression for the optimal state trajectory can be obtained by considering the state dynamics given in Equation (A11). Substituting $u^i(t) = u^i(t)^*$ and $u^j(t) = u^j(t)^*$ in Equation A11 the following first-order differential equation can be obtained:

$$x^j(t) = \frac{e^{-L_2 t}}{L_2} \left[L_2 x_0^j + (-1 + e^{L_2 t}) M_2 \left[\frac{K_1 \alpha^i \psi_{01} e^{L_1 t}}{1 - M_2 \psi_{02} e^{L_2 t}}\right]^{\frac{1}{1-\alpha^i}} + \right.$$
$$\left. + (-1 + e^{L_2 t}) K_2 (K_2 \alpha^j \lambda_{01} e^{L_2 t})^{\frac{\alpha^j}{(1-\alpha^j)^2}} \right] \tag{A29}$$

Theorem 6. The equilibrium state trajectory of performance improvement of the leader is given as:

$$x^i(t) = \frac{e^{-L_1 t}}{L_1}\left[L_1 x_0^i + (-1 + e^{L_1 t}) K_1 \left[\frac{K_1 \alpha^i \psi_{01} e^{L_1 t}}{1 - M_2 \psi_{02} e^{L_2 t}}\right]^{\frac{\alpha^i}{1-\alpha^i}}\right] \quad (A30)$$

Proof: The expression for the optimal state trajectory can be obtained by considering the state dynamics given in equation (14). Substituting $u^i(t) = u^i(t)^*$ in (14) the following first-order differential equation can be obtained:

$$x^j(t) = K_1 \left[\frac{K_1 \alpha^i \psi_1^*}{1 - M_2 \psi 2^*}\right]^{\frac{\alpha^i}{1-\alpha^i}} - L_1 x^i(t) \quad (A.31)$$

The first order differential equation can be solved with the initial condition $x^i(0) = x_0^i$. The resulting expression for $x^i(t)^*$ is:

$$x^i(t) = \frac{e^{-L_1 t}}{L_1}\left[L_1 x_0^i + (-1 + e^{L_1 t}) K_1 \left[\frac{K_1 \alpha^i \psi_{01} e^{L_1 t}}{1 - M_2 \psi_{02} e^{L_2 t}}\right]^{\frac{\alpha^i}{1-\alpha^i}}\right] \quad (A.32)$$

REFERENCES

Aghion,P., Harris, C. and J. Vickers (1997), 'Competition and Growth with Step-by-Step Innovation: An Example', *Review of Economic Studies* 41, 771-782

Aghion,P. and P. Howitt (1998), Endogeneous Growth Theory, Cambridge,Ma., MIT Press

Aghion,P., Harris, C., Howitt, P.. and J. Vickers (2001), 'Competition, Imitation and Growth with Step-by-Step Innovation', *Review of Economic Studies* 68, 467-492

Arrow,K.J. (1962), '*The Economic Implications of Learning by Doing*'. Review of Economic Studies 29, 155-173

Denicolo,V. and P. Zanchettin (2006),'Competition, Darwinian Selection and Growth', mimeo, Univ. of Bologna, May 26

Dockner,E., Jorgensen, S., Van Long, N. and G. Sorger (2000), Differential Games in Economics and Management Science, Cambridge, Cambridge Univ. Press

Francois,P. and H. Lloyd-Ellis (2002), 'Animal Spirits through Creative Destruction', mimeo, CentER and Dept. of Economics, Tilburg University, Holland

Friedman, A. (1971), Differential Games, New York, Wiley

Griliches,Z.(1979), 'Issues in Assessing the Contribution of Research and Development to Productivity Growth', *The Bell Journal of Economics* 10(1), 92-116

Griliches,Z.(1992), 'The Search of R&D Spillovers', *The Scandinavian Journal of Economics* 94, S29-S47

Grossman,G. and E. Helpman (1993), *Innovation and Growth in the Global Economy*, Cambridge, Ma., MIT Press

Isaacs,R. (1965), Differential Games, New York, Dover

Moss Kanter,R.(2006), 'Innovation: The Classical Traps', Harvard Business Review, Nov. 2006, 72-83

Robson,A.J.(1990),'Duopoly with Endogenous Strategic Timing: Stackelberg Regained', *International Economic Review* 31, 25-35

Saaskilahti,P. (2006),'Strategic R&D and Network Compatibility', *Economics of Innovation and New Technology* 15(8), 711-733

Schumpeter, J.A.(1947), Capitalism, Socialism and Democracy, , New York: Harper

Segerstrom,P.S. (2005), 'Intel Economics', mimeo, Stockholm School of Economics,

Stockholm, August 22

Teece, D.J., Pisano, G. and A. Shuen (1997), 'Dynamic Capabilities and Strategic Management', *Strategic Management Journal* 18(7), 509-533

The Economist (2007), 'High Tech Hopefuls, *A Special Report on Technology in India and China*', Nov. 10

Varian,H R., Farrell,J. and Shapiro,C. (2004),*The Economics of Information Technology*, Cambridge, Cambridge Univ. Press

Yao,T. and J. Weyant (2004), 'Strategic R&D Investments under Uncertainty in Information Technology' , Working Paper, Dept. of Management Science and Engineering, Stanford University, Palo Alto, Ca.,

Zeira,J. (2005),'Innovations, Patent Races and Endogenous Growth', mimeo, Dept. of Economics, Hebrew Univ. of Jerusalem, July

Chapter 3

OVERVIEW OF ECONOMIC GROWTH AND DEVELOPMENT

Hans W. Gottinger

3.1. INTRODUCTION

Economic growth in a cross country context could be sourced by three distinct theoretical explanations: the first is the neoclassical growth model which predicts country convergence among diverse states striving for economic growth through industrialization; the second is the endogenous growth model which, in general, predicts country divergence; and the third is the cliometric approach to economic development which takes a more historical perspective on the growth of nations. The neoclassical model is based on diminishing returns to factor inputs and views the long-run rate of growth as being exogenous. Endogenous [or New] growth theory considers constant or increasing returns to factor inputs and attempts to explain the forces that give rise to technological change.

Cliometric approaches to development include a wide variety of approaches to economic catch-up including technological change (Gerschenkron, 1962; Abramovitz, 1986; Mokyr, 1990), neo-institutional economics (North, 1990; Eggertsson, 1990) and theories of institutional sclerosis (Olson, 1982). These three theoretical explanations are not mutually exclusive categories and some sources discussed belong to more than one category. For example, Abramovitz (1986) fits also within the neoclassical explanation, but one can place him more in the third category due to his more historical approach. Our modeling of economic growth and development is a mix of all these approaches (Chap. 4).

We explore whether the neoclassical model can explain the empirical finding of relative income shifts. When finding the standard neoclassical model insufficient, we extend it using ideas from common development theory, thus adding some endogeneity to the resulting model. This work synthesizes previous approaches for a better explanation of the sources and cycles of economic growth with specific reference to Asian economies. Since the nineteen-eighties, there has been a flood of literature which deals with the growth of nations, catch-up, and transfer of technology. We first briefly review the essentials of the growth literature as we see it.

3.2. FACTOR ACCUMULATION

The neoclassical approach obtained its theoretical foundations with Solow's seminal papers (1956, 1957) which put down the framework of neoclassical growth theory. Solow (1960) cites Harrod (1939) and Domar (1946) as the forces leading up to his 1956 article. For completeness, we should also mention that Swan (1956) independently developed a model similar to Solow (1956), so that the basic neoclassical model is often referred to as the Solow-Swan model. These papers are perhaps not the origin of modern growth theory, but they are the important contributors to it as well as the foundations of much of growth theory. theory. It is common to date the origin of modern optimal growth theory to Ramsey (1928), but his approach was not widely used until the 1960's and is different from a more empirically relevant approach. In particular, Cass (1965) and Koopmans (1965) introduce Ramsey's consumer optimization analysis into the neoclassical growth model to achieve an endogenous determination of the savings rate.

The Solow model predicts, in general, that countries converge to their own steady states; it assumes identical technologies in all countries and concludes that exogenous differences in saving and education are the cause of all observed disparity in levels of income and rates of growth. The mechanism behind convergence is the diminishing return to capital; poor nations have a smaller capital stock which implies that the marginal returns to capital investment are higher than in capital-rich nations. Thus growth is self-limiting, and in the end all per capita variables will grow at the rate of the exogenous technological progress. Consequently, initial conditions or current disturbances have no long-run effects on the steady state level of output. Hence, long-term growth is exogenous and not explained in the model, this is the distinguishing characteristic between the neoclassical model and the endogenous growth model [to be discussed below]. The Solow model is best discussed in terms of mathematics, which is one reason for its lasting popularity, but we will not put down the equations here since Chapter 4 will provide an extension and discussion of the standard model.

3.3. TECHNOLOGY AND INSTITUTIONS

The cliometric approach to growth and development attempts, at least conceptually, to recognize that the growth of nations depend on factors such as technology and institutions. The importance of a nation's institutional framework [such as government regulation and laws] to growth is probably shared by most, if not all, people and economists. Surely the existence of positive and negative externalities, the legal environment, transaction costs, culture, etc. will affect the growth of a nation. However, the neoclassical model chooses to ignore these factors in an effort to clearly show the implications of a competitive market structure. This exercise is of course very important and the approach has been analytically and empirically very fruitful. Eggertsson (1990,p.4) states that its contributions 'overshadows all other theoretical systems in economics and the social sciences' . But the neoclassical model has reached diminishing returns and it might therefore be time to try to extend it.

Of course this could be done while keeping the sound economic principles intact, such as stable preferences, rational choice, and equilibria. One such effort can be found in neo-institutional economics which argues for the inclusion of transaction costs in the model. Of course, just as individuals tend to make rational choices given the constraints, economies should choose efficient institutions to minimize its transaction costs. North and Thomas (1973, p.13) state that: "Economic growth will occur if property rights make it worthwhile to undertake socially productive activity. The creating, specifying and enacting of such property rights are costly ....As the potential grows for private gains to exceed transaction costs, efforts will be made to establish such property rights. Governments take over the protection and enforcement of property rights because they can do it at a lower cost than private volunteer groups. However, the fiscal needs of government may induce the protection of certain property rights which hinder rather than promote growth; therefore we have no guarantee that productive institutional arrangements will emerge ".

This implies that institutional inefficiency can persist over time and may differ across economies (Chap. 7). One should also mention that the importance of institutions is something that guides the non-academic profession in its views of economic growth. This is most clearly seen in the World Development Report 1997. The report states in the foreword by the President of the World Bank that; "History and recent experience have also taught us that development is not just about getting the right economic and technical inputs. It is also about the underlying, institutional environment: the rules and customs that determine how those inputs are used".

In addition to factor accumulation and institutional soundness, technology also plays an important role in growth. Thus, another essential ingredient addresses technology diffusion, a concept dating back to Gerschenkron (1962) who proposed in Economic Backwardness in Historical Perspective that a backward country, by the very virtue of its backwardness, will tend to develop very differently from the advanced country. He states that 'industrialization always seemed the more promising the greater the backlog of technological innovations which the backward country could take over from the more advanced country (p. 6).' The important idea that catch-up might occur due to a backlog of technology will not be traced back historically. Suffice it to say that it is an idea which is very much alive as exemplified by more recent papers [Crafts (1997), Romer (1997)]. They have been previously expressed by Abramovitz (1986) from which we derive particular observations.

3.4. CATCH-UP HYPOTHESIS

Abramovitz (1986) asserts that being backward in level of productivity carries a potential for rapid growth [the catch-up hypothesis]. If the level of labor productivity were given by the level of technology embodied in the capital stock, then the 'leading' country's capital stock embodies the frontier technology at the time of investment, therefore, as Abramovitz states 'the technological age of the stock is ...the same as its chronological age'. For a follower country the technological age of its capital stock will be high relative to its chronological age. Therefore, when a leader nation invests in new capital its technology advance is limited by the advance of knowledge. For the follower, however, investments into new capital have the potential of a larger leap as the new capital could embody frontier technology. Thus, the larger the productivity gap the stronger is the potential for growth in productivity, other things held constant. This is the catch-up hypothesis in its simple form. Note its similarity to the factor accumulation argument made earlier.

The argument laid out by Abramovitz does not end here though. Technological backwardness is not usually an historical accident, societal characteristics probably account for a large portion of a country's past failure to achieve a high level of productivity. These same characteristics, or social capabilities, may remain to keep a country from making the full technological leap proposed by the simple hypothesis. This implies that the simple catch-up hypothesis needs some modification. Abramovitz argues that 'a country's potential for rapid growth is strong not when it is backward without qualification, but rather when it is technologically backward but socially advanced.' Thus being technologically backward is a necessary condition for catch-up, but it is not sufficient. A follower nation must also be able to adopt and adapt the technology which is potentially available to it. These intuitively appealing ideas have been largely missing from the empirical growth literature.

Aggregate Leapfrogging explains the central idea of the catch-up hypothesis as the trailing countries' adopting behavior of a 'backlog of unexploited technology'. Supposing that the level of labor productivity were governed entirely by the level of technology embodied in capital stock, one may consider that the differentials in productivities among countries are caused by the 'technological age' of the stock used by a country relative to its 'chronological age'. While a leader is restricted in increasing its productivity by the advance of new technology, trailing countries 'have the potential to make a larger leap' as they are provided with the privilege of exploiting the backlog in addition of the newly developed technology. Hence, followers being behind with a larger gap in technology will have a stronger potential for growth in productivity. The potential, however, will be reduced as the catch-up process goes on because the unexploited stock of technology becomes smaller and smaller.

This hypothesis explains the diffusion process of best-practice technology and gives the same sort of S-curve change in productivity rise of catching-up countries among a group of industrialized countries as that of followers to the leader in an industry. Although this view can explain the tendency to convergence of productivity levels of follower countries, it fails to answer the historical puzzles why a country, the United States, has preserved the standing of the technological leader for a long time since taking over leadership from Britain and Germany in around the end of the 19th century and why the shifts have taken place in the ranks of follower countries in their relative levels of productivity, i.e., technological gaps between them and the leader.

Steering or guiding the process of industrial racing through the pursuit of industrial policies aims to increase competitive advantage of respective industries, as having been practised in Japan and now more prevalent in China in that it stimulates catch-up races but appears to be less effective in promoting frontier racing. A deeper reason lies in the phenomenon of network externalities affecting high-technology industries. That is, racing ahead of rivals in respective industries may create external economies to the effect that such economies within dominant 'increasing returns' industries tend to improve their international market position and therefore pull ahead in competitiveness vis-a-vis their (trading) partners. The point is that racing behavior in leading high technology industries by generating frontier positions create cluster and network externalities pipelining through other sectors of the economy and creating competitive advantages elsewhere, as supported by the 'increasing returns mechanisms' (Chap. 6) In this sense we speak of positive externalities endogenizing growth of these economies and contributing to competitive advantage. While we know historically about catch-up processes since the time of industrial revolution it has become difficult to identify the catalytic factors that contributed to faster economic growth giving rise to growth diagnostics. Let's look at some anecdotal observations from the literature.

Russia' per capita GDP around 1913 was close to the average over other worldwide industrializing countries but then despite the promises of socialism and massive industrialization it fell back in its rank and only in the late 1930s it caught up with Portugal, a then developing economy. Further back into economic history one could observe dramatic structural changes from the beginning of industrialization in the mid 18th century. For example, Russia's GDP per capita in relation to that of the newly industrializing leader (U.K.) in 1820 was 0.44 while the same ratio to the US was 0.25 in 2001, an over 55 percent decline, clearly a structural underperformance. Within a similar timeframe it has been even more dramatic for China which for the same benchmarks shows an even higher decline (Gaidar, 2004). Although previous records may support a contrarian view Huang and Khanna (2003) argue that India may edge up past China in the longer run due to institutional reasons such as more open and competent entrepreneurship in value driving industries, a sound capital markt, an independent legal system, respect for private property due to its democratic heritage, a younger more dynamic urban population and a grass roots approach to industrial development.

3.5. CONVERGENCE AND CONDITIONAL CONVERGENCE

The cross-country convergence literature experienced a re-birth with Baumol (1986). As usual, this paper does not stand alone. Maddison (1987) discusses the growth and slowdown in advanced capitalist economies and his growth accounting approach is similar to Baumol. Baumol showed that convergence could be observed in some 'clubs' of countries [industrialized market economies and planned economies], but not in others [less developed economies]. The groups which displayed convergence were then called "convergence groups". De Long (1988) criticizes Baumol for performing a regression that uses a number of post sample of countries which are rich and developed at the end of the period, and argues for the use of an ex ante sample. De Long then shows that such a sample does not exhibit convergence. The conclusions and results presented in the papers of Baumol and De Long may not be as relevant as their impacts on empirical growth studies. There is a common set of sources that promote economic growth and convergence whereas others don't. (Easterly, 2003, p.64) As it appears the important point for the evolution of growth theory is the fact that convergence clubs as well as divergence clubs had been identified; In particular, the world as a whole showed evidence of divergence. Two theoretical frameworks have been used to explain these results. One attempts to explain convergence [the neoclassical growth model], the other divergence [the endogenous, or new, growth model].

At first, the empirical convergence literature tried to find out what the steady state distribution of world per capita income and productivity would look like. This is the question which motivated Abramovitz (1986) and Baumol (1986). Since then the empirical growth literature has mostly attempted to explain the cross-country data; in particular, to explain convergence and rates of convergence and to interpret the findings in the context of neoclassical and/or endogenous growth theory. However, as mentioned by Romer (1986), cross-country comparisons of growth rates are complicated by the difficulty of controlling for political and social [institutional] variables that strongly influence the growth process. Conditional convergence can be viewed as an attempt to control for these political and social variables (Fukuda and Toya, 2000).

There have been many studies using the neoclassical model and its steady state predictions to obtain the sources of growth. First of all, if all economies have the same steady state then unconditional convergence is expected; that is, economies with low initial incomes should have higher growth rates. If economies differ in their steady states, then conditional convergence should be observed; that is, after controlling for steady state differences, initial incomes should be negatively related to growth rates. Not all convergence studies choose to consider the steady state, some take a more direct growth accounting approach. The end results are essentially the same in terms of sources of growth, but the latter approach is not able to consider the transitional dynamics. The number of convergence studies is very large as we refer to a limited sample in the following list of worldwide scope: Ahn (2005), de la Fuente (2002), Kolodko (2003), Taylor and Rada (2003), Ortiz, Castro, Badillo (2007), Furman, Hayes (2004), Dowrick, DeLong (2001) and Lim, McAleer (2003). The goal of these studies is often to find out whether a particular variable or set of variables is important to the growth of nations. This introduces the question of robustness which will be discussed briefly below. The following review is a partial list of influential convergence studies

Factor Accumulation: Many empirical studies explore whether the cross-country evidence can be explained by different accumulation rates of factor inputs as predicted by the neoclassical model. Most of these studies also include a set of control variables to subtract out the effects of different institutional environments or steady states (see e.g. Dowrick and Nguyen, 1989; De Long and Summers, 1991; Barro, 1991, 1994, 1997; Mankiw et al., 1992; Dowrick, 1992; and Barro and Sala-i-Martin, 1995). Convergence Clubs: Another approach to control for different steady states [or institutions] is to follow Baumol (1986) and seek to find convergence clubs. The idea is that if a homogeneous sample of countries can be found, then according to the neoclassical model unconditional convergence should be observed. (see also Barro and Sala-i-Martin, 1992; Helliwell and Chung, 1995).

Human Capital: Many of the studies mentioned above include human capital as a factor of production. The variable used as a proxy for this is usually educational attainment, such as proportion of total population that attends secondary school. However, contrary to expectations the human capital variable often comes out as being insignificant in the estimations. One explanation for this is that human capital should be included as a level instead of as a growth rate. Benhabib and Spiegel (1994) and Kyriacou (1991) give several reasons why this might be the correct specification, and find human capital in this form as being significant.

Openness: A variable that theoretically should be important for convergence is openness. Several reasons for this exist; for example, exports allows for external capital as a source of growth, imports leads to availability of inputs, dissemination of knowledge etc. These ideas, and many more, are studied in, among others, Dollar (1992), Ben-David (1993), Sachs and Warner (1995, 1997), and Frankel and Romer (1996).

Fundamentals: The importance of the institutional framework has been implicitly assumed when cross-country studies use variables to control for these differences across countries. There exist some studies that more directly attempt to verify the importance of political and civil rights, the legal environment, language, culture etc. (see e.g. Scully, 1988; Knack and Keefer, 1995; Mauro, 1995; Hall and Jones, 1997; and Easton and Walker, 1997).

3.6. ENDOGENOUS GROWTH MODELS

We have argued that the early catch-up literature showed much concern for technological backwardness. It is therefore curious that the empirical growth literature almost completely ignores this part of growth. As spelled out by Bernard and Jones (1996, p. 1038) "Technology, at best, is allowed to index differences in an initial multiplicative factor, and all economies are assumed to accumulate technology at the same rate. In such a capital-based world, differences in growth rates stem from differences in capital accumulation. Technological choices, through adoption and accumulation, are completely assumed away in explaining both relative output levels and growth rates, hence convergence. To the extent that the adoption and accumulation of technologies is important for convergence, the empirical convergence literature to date is misguided." Although the endogenous growth literature does not answer this statement on an empirical level, theoretically the approach highlights the importance of technology.

Endogenous growth theory re-emerged in the mid-1980s out of a dissatisfaction for basically two things: first, some growth theorists were not happy with the exogenously driven explanations of long-run productivity growth, and secondly, the data for large samples of countries did not show convergence. This led to a construction of models where the determinants of growth are endogenous. Romer (1986) and Lucas (1988) are usually mentioned as the instigators of this movement. The Romer (1986) model contains increasing returns as a result of accumulation of knowledge which has a positive external effect on the production possibilities. Lucas (1988) is based on learning-by-doing which lead to [external] increasing returns to scale in the production process (Chap.6). Neither model postulate a theory of technological change. However, research and development, imperfect competition, and internal returns to scale were added to this class of models in Romer (1987, 1990), Grossman and Helpman (1991), Aghion and Howitt (1992), Jones (1995), Aghion and Howitt(2009). Technological advance is the result of R&D activity which is rewarded some ex-post monopoly power. This means that, as long as the economy keeps on being innovation driven, the growth rate can remain positive in the long run. Also, the long-run growth rate is now dependent on government policies (except for Jones, 1995).

3.7. R&D SPILLOVERS

An important and related research area is the effect of research and development [R&D] on productivity growth. Although R&D spillover studies commonly focus on firms and industries, there is an overlap with both the growth accounting research and the new growth models. The basic idea is that firms undertake research to develop new products or processes (extend their technologies) but, as opposed to other forms of investment, the benefits from the research cannot be fully excluded from other firms. The impact of discovered knowledge on the productivity of others (the R&D externality) stems from research being a non-rivalrous good with a higher social than private return. R&D spillovers may have several growth effects; for example, the spillovers may reduce production costs of other firms so that there are industry-wide cost-reduction effects. However, spillovers also generate a free-rider problem which may act to reduce the R&D investment and growth [Good et al. (1997)].

It is of course possible to include either aggregate R&D expenditures or R&D capital (see Griliches (1979, 1992)) for how to construct such variables) in the standard growth accounting framework to explore whether R&D appears to be positively correlated with growth. This econometric production function approach is more general than the alternative case study approach (see Griliches, 1973) as it abandons the details of specific events. The attempt is thus to estimate the part of productivity growth that can be attributed to R&D. The drawback is that this approach suffers from several estimation problems, in particular simultaneity and multicollinearity (see next section)]. Nadiri and Prucha (1992) perform this kind of estimation for six of the major OECD countries. Their results are, briefly, that aggregate R&D expenditures have a modest positive effect on both growth of output and growth of labor productivity. They argue that the modest contribution stems from the small share of R&D investment in total output.

A possible relation between R&D studies and this work is in terms of how well R&D expenditures might proxy for the level of technology. High levels of R&D imply a high level of technological knowledge, whether or not the R&D expenditures go to own research or the incorporation of foreign technology. This result can be seen in Good et al. (1997) and Griliches (1992). It could therefore be argued that past R&D is a candidate for being a proxy for the level of technology in econometric estimation. However, it is perhaps equally likely that R&D should affect the adoption of foreign technology. That is, if an economy has a high level of R&D then it is able to grow quickly by adopting best practice technology.

Next, there is a more direct relation between new growth theory and R&D spillovers and externalities. Many endogenous growth models use R&D externalities as a way to escape the fate of diminishing returns. However, as Griliches (1992) points out whether or not such spillovers lead to increasing returns depend on their empirical magnitude. This is thus related to the many studies that attempt to determine the social return to R&D investments (e.g. Bernstein and Nadiri, 1988, 1989). The general finding of these studies is that the social returns are greater than the private returns, and the productivity of firms or industries is related to both own R&D spending and the R&D of other firms and industries.

To summarize, it is evident that studies of productivity growth and R&D spillovers are related to shaping growth performance and development paths. However, less work has been done on the magnitude of international R&D spillovers; how R&D expenditures in one country affects the growth of other nations. Nadiri and Kim (1996) do provide a study of, among other things, how R&D spillovers have affected the productivity of the G7 countries. International spillovers are shown to significantly affect the growth of total factor productivity for all seven countries. The importance of own R&D to foreign R&D spillovers vary across countries; e.g., for the U.S. own R&D is much more important than foreign spillovers, while for countries like Canada and Italy foreign R&D is more important than own R&D for their productivity growth.

3.8. NEOCLASSICAL VERSUS ENDOGENOUS GROWTH MODELS

As mentioned above there are numerous articles which show the existence of conditional convergence. Some empirical work has been done to either verify the neoclassical model or simply to look whether a particular variable is important for growth. This approach, if not the results, have been criticized on econometric grounds (see below). Other empirical work that attempts to verify the endogenous growth model is relatively few. Until recently, support for this model consisted of regressions showing the non-existence of convergence. The failure of per capita output to equalize across the developed and the developing world economies as well as the failure of growth rates of developing countries to exceed those of the industrialized West were seen as evidence that there is little observable tendency for poor countries to catch up with richer ones [see for example Pritchett (1997)]. Lately there have been time-series studies which more directly attempt to find evidence of endogenous growth. In general, convergence in a time-series approach has the implication that output differences between countries cannot contain unit roots [time trends] and the weak implication that output levels in two economies must be co-integrated [Bernard and Durlauf (1994)]. The results from these time-series models, using a variety of criteria, are mixed. Jones (1995a, 1995b) argues that the scale effect which are predicted by the endogenous growth model is not observed in the data. Lau (1996) also finds evidence unfavorable to the endogenous growth model, while Neusser (1991) finds time-series evidence which is favorable to the exogenous growth models at least for some countries. The results from Lau and Sin (1997) are unfavorable to both classes of growth models. On the other hand, Kocherlakota and Yi(1996, 1997) find time-series evidence slightly more favorable to the endogenous growth model using data from the United States and the United Kingdom.

After having considered the empirical results from both conditional convergence studies and tests of endogenous growth models it is hard to conclude that either of the two models towers over the other in terms of empirical relevance. Thus from this vantage point one may choose to utilize the neoclassical model because of its tractability. However, given this choice of theoretical approach, there are some common objections to the neoclassical growth model as brought forward by Mankiw et al.(1992), Mankiw (1995).

General objections: First and foremost, is the neoclassical model a good theory of economic growth? In particular, can the model shed any light on growth when its steady state growth is only due to exogenous technological progress? The model explains economic growth by simply assuming that there is economic expansion in the form of technological progress which is determined outside of the model. This criticism was partially due to the development of endogenous growth theory. As Mankiw (1995) argues, it depends on what the purpose of growth theory is. If the goal is to explain the existence of growth, then obviously the neoclassical model is uninformative. But if the goal is to explain why there is such variation of economic growth in different countries and at different times, then the neoclassical model's assumption of constant, exogenous technological progress is not a problem. In fact, the neoclassical model is well equipped for shedding light on the cross-country growth experiences.

Another common objection is that the neoclassical model requires an assumption of identical national production functions at any given point in time in order to explain the international variation in growth. This assumption is clearly wrong. The answer to this criticism is that the production function should not be viewed as a literal description of a specific production process; instead it is a mapping from quantities of inputs to quantities of outputs. Thus the assumption of identical production functions merely says that if countries had exactly the same inputs then they would produce the same output. However, different countries with different levels of inputs need not rely on exactly the same production process for producing goods and services.'

Empirical objections: There are three common empirical objections to the neoclassical predictions: (1) The magnitudes of international differences in per capita output are too large compared to the observed differences in savings and population growth, (2) the "observed" rate of convergence is too slow, and (3) rate of return differences between rich and poor countries are too small. Mankiw et al. (1992) argue that these three concerns can be [more or less] addressed by viewing capital more broadly. That is, the definition of capital should include not only physical capital but also- human capital and the effects of externalities.

The neoclassical model would only be inconsistent with divergence if all countries have identical steady states. If poor nations are converging to low steady states while rich nations are converging to even higher steady states, then divergence is a possibility. Also, if all or some of the countries are already in their steady states then no convergence should be observed. In fact, as pointed out by Barro (1997), even if convergence held, the dispersion of per capita output would not necessarily narrow over time. The reason is that this could depend on the weighing of the convergence force relative to the effects from shocks hitting each country. Such shocks, if independent across countries, tend to create dispersion. Leapfrogging on a macro scale can also be similarly explained by differences in steady states. In fact, the next sections explore whether different steady states are sufficient to explain the observed leapfrogging using the neoclassical framework.

Despite all the potential problems of the empirical convergence literature, the cross-sectional evidence leans toward the neoclassical model. For example, a timely paper by Young (1995) looks at the East Asian countries, perhaps the group least likely to fit the neoclassical model, and concludes that their success is explained by the neoclassical model, also the book by Henry Wan (2003) works on variations of the neoclassical model to lend support to the path of East Asian newly industrialized economies (NIEs). This path is further pursued for Japan in Chaps. 8 and 9.

3.9. LEAPFROGGING

As in economic races between corporations or companies on a micro scale (Gottinger, 2006), we will argue that leapfrogging on a macro scale, i.e. shifts of relative aggregate income positions, is important and a significant characteristic of cross-country growth. For large developing economies, such as India and China, 'piggy backing' in their national industries may be an observable phenomenon before acquiring the potential to leapfrog rival industry leaders (The Economist, 2007). The question is whether the growth models discussed above are consistent with leapfrogging. The neoclassical growth model has attempted to explain the cross-country data in terms of convergence and rate of convergence. The Solow model predicts, in general, that countries converge to their own steady states; it assumes identical technologies in all countries and concludes that exogenous differences in saving and education are the cause of all observed disparity in levels of income and rates of growth.

The neoclassical model's predictions with regard to leapfrogging are apparent: in a group of homogeneous countries (as defined by the similarity of steady states) no leapfrogging should be observed. The diminishing return to capital provides a vehicle for convergence, but there is no mechanism for shifts in relative positions. If, however, countries are approaching different steady states, then positions might change due to the transitional effects as shown by Jones (1995). Also, if a random disturbance is added to a model which contains a convergence force, then one would expect shifts in relative income positions. As mentioned in Easterly et al. (1993), if there is a large dispersion of distances between countries' initial incomes and their steady states then the transitional effect will dominate the effect of random shocks.

New growth theory has appeared in reaction to the neoclassical model. These models consider non-convexities and economies of scale, and, in particular, focus on the incremental change in technology. In these models, investments into human and physical capital make either the same or an increasing contribution to output as economies become richer. Hence, the "predictions" of the early endogenous growth models are that technical change proceeds most rapidly in those countries with established advantages in technologically advanced sectors, i.e. the "leaders". This implies economic and technical divergence between nations and no leapfrogging should be observed. If one thinks of the endogenous growth model as the limiting case of the neoclassical model where α approaches 1 (i.e. capital is interpreted very broadly by, say, including knowledge in its definition), then two properties appear: differences in saving rates across countries lead to ever larger differences in income over time, and large differences in income are not related to differences in return to capital. However, in, general, endogenous growth models can lead to a variety of growth experiences.

Different starting conditions and the fact that government policies are allowed to make a difference can lead to leapfrogging. For example, if long-run growth is a function of the amount of R&D conducted in a nation, then a follower could leapfrog by allocating funds to R&D. Lately a few endogenous growth models have in fact approached the issue of overtaking, discussing either growth miracles (Lucas, 1993) or leadership change (Brezis et al., 1993). A more general treatment can be found in Goodfriend and McDermott (1994). Parente and Prescott (1994) provide a pertinent attempt to simultaneously account for disparity in income levels and growth miracles. Their model is based on differences in technology adoption barriers which may lead to both income differences and, if persistently reduced, to development miracles.

The cliometric approach to economic development argues that a technology gap presents an opportunity for rapid growth through technology flows, but a country's ability to absorb the new technology must also be considered. A low absorption capability makes it difficult for a country to take advantage of its opportunity. Since poor developing nations typically suffer from both a large technology gap and a low absorption capacity, the predictions about rate of growth and convergence are ambiguous. However, high indicators of absorption capacity (e.g. high level of education or "good' institutions) imply a faster rate of growth for a country which faces a given technology gap, hence the possibility of leapfrogging.

The focus of the section on leapfrogging is on the neoclassical model and its predictions regarding leapfrogging. In particular, the analysis will incorporate both transitional effects and random shocks when simulating the human capital augmented Solow model. It does not, however, attempt to test an endogenous growth model or one based on technology dispersion.

Why does leapfrogging matter? This is a valid question since it is arguable that the rank of a nation per se is of no importance to that nation. However, politically and also economically this is an important question as exemplified by the fact that the popular press constantly talks about the rank of the U.S or the ranks between the US and the EU, and, in particular in the late 1980s, the 'imminent' loss of that rank to Japan. A fall in relative productivity standing is not incompatible with high growth in productivity as is exemplified by Britain which increased its per capita output by 300 percent over the last 12 decades, but which is still viewed as a failure by the rest of the world (Baumol et al., 1992) and which becomes more evident in times of global economic crises. Baumol et al. also argue that loss of economic leadership implies more than just a relative standard of evaluation. Although the advantages of leadership to the general population are unclear, Baumol et al. mention national pride, military strength, and imperialist adventures. Others have pointed out the traumatic effects inflicted upon those countries that find them being overtaken.

We will, however, stay mostly clear of the political discussion though some specific results relate to historical research as outlined by Kennedy (1987) and a growing literature on this subject. Instead it derives its motivation from the theoretical growth literature, arguing that the mere fact that models have been and are being developed to explain and account for the growth of nations indicates the need to know the empirical facts. The hope is that my study may enhance the understanding of the forces underlying economic growth and show the growth patterns exhibited in the world. As Parente and Prescott (1993, p.3) point out: "Any theory inconsistent with the development facts cannot help us understand the differences in the wealth of nations... (Data can play an important role in the creation and evolution of successful theory. If we know what the development facts are, we (...) have a better idea (of) what features belong and don't belong in a model of economic development".

Thus, if the analysis of a panel of cross-country incomes shows a high amount of overtaking, then perhaps the growth models should attempt to explain this. We believe, however, that growth models should only explain leapfrogging if such rank movements are statistically significant. As will be seen below, countries which are close in per capita income levels tend to gain and lose relative positions frequently; this could be due to randomness. A country which leaps through the ranks over a long time period [e.g. Japan] seems to be a better example of overtaking.

We argue that the available evidence of 'leapfrogging'-shifts of relative per capita income positions between two or more countries-is incomplete. This may account for the fact that little effort has been devoted to endogenizing relative income shifts in standard models of economic growth. Models are being developed in an attempt to justify growth miracles and shifts of productivity leadership. However, extraordinary growth and changes in leadership are subsamples of leapfrogging in general, as has been outlines for industrial racing in Chaps.1 and 2. However, there is no generally agreed upon measure of rank mobility.

One possible explanation for leapfrogging is that the observed economic and technological leapfrogging is random. Some countries are lucky in one period, while others are unlucky. Thus countries close in income levels might shift positions as they are 'hit' by heterogeneous productivity shocks. If this is true, then the research into reasons for overtaking is misguided. If, on the other hand, leapfrogging is a general characteristic of cross-country data, then future models of economic growth should provide an explanation for it.

3.10. RANK MOBILITY MEASURES

The available evidence of shifts in relative income levels is incomplete. Maddison (1982) in 'Phases of Capitalist Development' compiles data on sixteen countries and discusses the dynamics between leader and follower countries. Maddison points out that there have been three "lead" countries since 1700 (the Netherlands, the U.K., and the U.S.). Abramovitz (1986) notes that Maddison's compilation is characterized by rank movements. He states that the general process of convergence is also accompanied by shifts in countries' productivity rankings.

Parente and Prescott (1993) add to existing knowledge by discussing growth miracles and growth disasters. Also, they discuss a rigorous definition of relative wealth mobility using a first-order autoregressive (statistical) process. Even though a distribution of incomes is stable over time, the individual countries within the distribution can move between periods. The same idea of 'dynamically evolving distributions' is used in Quah (1993, 1996). Quah's study uses a Markov transition matrix which allows for more in depth analysis. Quah finds high persistence annually; i.e. countries are not likely to move from one relative income group to another. Over the entire sample period the predominant feature is still persistence, but it is less pronounced. This means that countries are moving between relative income groups. This work was extended by Chari et al. (1996) who document the empirical regularities in the distribution of relative incomes. They also find a significant amount of mobility within the distribution and countries in the 'middle income bracket' show more mobility in relative positions than countries at either extreme. Their paper develops a neoclassical growth model with a broad measure of capital in which investment decisions are affected by stochastic distortions. This model is reasonably successful in replicating their stylized facts.

Jones (1995) considers the steady state distribution of per capita income, showing that the projected future world distribution of per capita income is characterized by shifts in the relative position of countries. His approach is similar in spirit to Quah (1993), but differs in methodology. Jones uses the neoclassical model to obtain the relevant economic determinants of the steady state distribution, and then use estimates of these determinants to predict the steady state distribution. As an exercise we use a model similar to the one in Jones (1995); that is, the human capital augmented Solow model, and it also borrows parameters from that paper. The results are mainly expressed in the form of a Markov transition matrix, similar to Quah (1993) and Chari et al. (1996).

3.11. STYLIZED FACTS OF LEAPFROGGING

Looking at the OECD sample it is apparent that the nations' growth paths cross, as this is shown for East Asia by Lau and Wan (1993) with simple neoclassical type models. It shows the countries' per capita GDP relative to the U.S. over the period 1960-90. The U.S. is the income leader for most of the years [Switzerland obtained the leader position a few times over the sample period]. Three countries in particular shifted income positions. Japan went from being one of the poorest countries in 1960 [rank 19] to become quite wealthy [rank 8] in 1990. Japan appears to be a growth miracle. The same can be said for Norway which advanced from rank 12 to 4 over the sample period. In contrast, New Zealand made a rapid descent through the relative income positions [from 3 to 17], earning the title growth disaster. However, most of the rank movements take place among the middle income countries [those ranked 3 to 16 in 1960] which are close in per capita GDP levels. For these countries leapfrogging could be due to random disturbances or heterogeneous shocks. A closer examination of the rankings reveals that it is very common for two countries to switch positions, only to immediately switch back. A few examples are: Germany and the U.K. from 1961 to 1968, Japan and Italy between 1971 and 1980 [these two countries changed positions six times only to end up at the same place in 1980], and the U.S. and Switzerland up until 1975. This shows that much of the rank dynamics are driven by short-term fluctuations such as exchange rate adjustments.. These rank movements are most likely due to country-specific fluctuations, such as lagged business cycles, and represent what this paper calls randomness. One way to remove this from the data is to consider a longer time period than one year for the analysis. Panel studies, this included, often consider 3-5 year time intervals to side-step the influence of business cycles.

3.12. PROBABILITY OF MOVEMENT

The methodology of Quah (1993) and Chari et al. (1996) presents the evidence in the form of a mobility matrix. Their papers are concerned with the world income distribution and, therefore, group countries in transition states based on their incomes relative to the world average. This approach only indirectly reveals the amount of leapfrogging since the mere fact that one country's income is 1/4 of world average in 1960 but 1/2 of world average in 1990 does not imply a shift in relative position [especially if the sample simultaneously display convergence]. The Markov transition matrix used directly addresses the change in ranks since we group countries according to rank instead of incomes relative to world average.

A mobility matrix in our study represents the average transitions for the sample; for each time period the probability of rank movement is calculated and the average is found for the 30-year period. Each entry in the Markov transition matrix represents the probability of moving from the column rank to the row rank during the specified time period. If there was no leapfrogging at all, then the matrix would be an identity matrix. All off-diagonal entries show a probability of shifts in relative positions, and the more probability mass off the diagonal the more common is rank movement. We consider average annual, 3-year, and 5-year transition matrices in this study.

The main characteristic of the data, whether presented annually or for 3(5)-year intervals is persistence, especially at the extremes. There is more mobility among the 'middle income countries'. These are the countries which are initially close in per capita income levels. As the time interval is extended the mobility matrix shows more and more off-diagonal probability mass, which indicates that these movements are not driven by business cycles alone. The probability of jumping more than one state is also increased, once again indicating sustained movements of countries.

3.13. Conditional Probability

Considering 3- and 5-year intervals is one attempt of removing rank movements caused by cyclicality we also want to get a sense for what the probability of falling back is once a nation has moved ahead. This can be achieved by considering conditional probabilities. First, we find the probability that a nation which gains in ranking will never fall below its original rank. That is, if a nation starts off on an upward movement will it ever reverse direction and actually become worse off? This is done for 1, 3, 5, and 10 year periods, and the results are that no nation which gains a rank this year will ever be ranked lower than originally the next year. However, for 3- and 5-year periods about half of countries forging ahead will be worse off than originally. Over 10 years approximately two thirds of countries on an upward path will reverse their gains.

Another possible measure is the conditional probability that a nation which moves up in rank will never lose a ranking in the next 1, 3, 5, and 10 years; that is, do growth miracles ever look back? This measure is harsh in that a temporary stumble followed by continued advancement will lower the conditional probability. The 1-year probability of losing rank after experiencing a gain is about a third. The probabilities of falling behind after a gain increase as the time period is extended, for the 10-year period this probability reaches 0.90.

These combined results show that countries that are leaping ahead quite often reverse their gains. In the great majority of cases they at least stumble in their paths. These findings imply that a model which yields growth miracles based on their steady states will only be correct in the steady state. It also cast a doubt on measuring leapfrogging over short periods of time. However, it is still true that a third of the nations which leap ahead will not be worse off after 10 years, and one out of ten countries which leap forward will not even stumble in the next 10 years. Also, most of the rank movement reversals take place within 5 years, leaving open the possibility that countries that move ahead for other reasons than cyclicality. may continue their upward trends. It is also possible that countries follow very long cycles of relative income gains and losses somewhat akin to Schumpeter's long waves (Aghion and Howitt, 2009).

It has been shown elsewhere that the OECD countries display both convergence and catch-up. The human capital augmented Solow model, as shown by Mankiw et al. (1992), is able to replicate this stylized fact to a large degree. What is shown, however, is that the Mankiw et al. model remains largely unable to replicate actual growth patterns of the OECD sample in the postwar period. It is my belief that these two points call for a better structural model. Surprisingly, since the whole idea of catch-up started as a discussion of technology differences (see eg. Gerschenkron, 1962), little effort has been devoted to the inquires of how much of the postwar experiences is due to technology catch-up. It seems likely that much less would have to be assigned to randomness and a better explanation of actual growth patterns could be achieved if relative technology levels were considered. The next two chapters combine technology adoption rates with country inefficiency levels in an attempt to better explain the growth process.

REFERENCES

Abramovitz, M. (1986) ,'Catching Up, Forging Ahead, and Falling Behind,' *Journal of Economic History* 46(2), 385-406.

Aghion, P. and P. Howitt, (1992), 'A Model of Growth through Creative Destruction,' Econometrica 60, 323-351.

Aghion, P. and P. Howitt (2009), Economics of Growth, Cambridge, MIT Press

Ahn, C. (2005),'Catchup and Regional Disparity in Economic Growth', *Forum of International Development Studies* 30, Sep., 35-50

Barro,R.J. (1991),'Economic Growth in a Cross Section of Countries', *Quarterly Journal of Economics,* 106, 407-443

Barro,R.J. (1994),'Democracy and Growth', *National Bureau of Economic Research* (NBER) Working Papers 4909

Barro, R. J. (1997) Determinants of Economic Growth: *A Cross-Country Empirical Study*, Cambridge, MIT Press.

Barro, R. J. and X. Sala-i-Martin, (1992) 'Convergence', *Journal of Political Economy*, 100(2), pp. 223-251.

Barro, R. J. and X. Sala-i-Martin, (1995), Economic Growth, New York, McGraw Hill.

Baumol, W.J. (1986) 'Productivity Growth, Convergence and Welfare: What the Long-Term Data Show', *American Economic Review* 76, 1072-1085.

Baumol,W.J., Blackman, S.A.B. and E.N. Wolff (1992),Productivity and American Leadership: The Long View, Cambridge, MIT Press

Ben-David, D. (1993),'Equalizing Exchange: Trade Liberalization and Income Convergence', *Quarterly Journal of Economics* 108, 653-679

Benhabib,J. and M.M. Spiegel (1994),'The Role of Human Capital in Human Development: Evidence from Aggregate Cross-Country Data', *Journal of Monetary Economics* 34, 143-173

Bernhard,A.B. and S.N. Durlauf (1994),'Interpreting Tests of the Convergence Hypothesis', NBER Technical Working Paper 159

Bernhard, A.B. and Ch. I. Jones (1996),'Technology and Convergence', *Economic Journal* 106, 137-1044

Bernstein,J.I. and M.I. Nadiri (1988),'Interindustry R&D Spillovers, Rates of Return, and Production in High Tech Industries', *American Economic Review*, Papers and Proceedings 78, 429-434

Bernstein,J.I. and M.I. Nadiri (1989),'Research and Development and Intraindustry Spillovers: An Empirical Application of Dynamic Duality', *Review of Economic Studies* 56, 249-267

Brezis,E.S., Krugman,P.R. and D. Tsiddon (1993),'Leapfrogging in International Competition: A Theory of Cycles in National Leadership', *American Economic Review* 83, 1211-1219

Cass, D.(1965), 'Optimum Growth in an Aggregative Model of Capital Accumulation', Review of Economic Studies, 32, 233-240.

Chari, V.V, Kehoe, P. J. and E. R. McGrattan (1996), 'The Poverty of Nations: A Quantitative Exploration', Federal Reserve Bank of Minneapolis, Research Department Staff Report 204.

Crafts, N. F R., (1996) ,'The First Industrial Revolution: *A Guided Tour for Growth Economists, American Economic Review*: Papers and Proceedings, 197-201.

De La Fuente, A. (2002), 'Convergence across Countries and Regions: Theory and Empirics', mimeo, Instituto di Analysis Economico (CSIC), Barcelona, Nov., 1-40

De Long, J. B.(1988) ,'Productivity Growth, Convergence, and Welfare: Comment,' American Economic Review, 78(5), 1138-1154.

De Long, J. B. and L. H. Summers (1991), '*Equipment Investment and Economic Growth,*' Quarterly Journal of Economics 106, 445-502.

Dollar, D. (1992), 'Outward-oriented Developing Economies Really Do Grow More Rapidly: Evidence from 95 LDCs, 1976-1985,' *Economic Development and Cultural Change,* 523-546.

Domar, E. D., (1946) '*Capital Expansion, Rate of Growth, and Employment,*' Econometrica, 14, 137-147.

Dowrick,S. and D.-T. Nguyen (1989),'OECD Comparative Economic Growth, 1950-85: Catch-Up and Convergence, American Economic Review 79, 1010-1030

Dowrick, S. (1992) '*Technological Catch Up and Diverging Incomes:* Patterns of Economic Growth 1960-88,' Economic Journal 102, 600-610

Dowrick,S. and J. B. DeLong (2001), 'Globalisation and Convergence', NBER Conf. on Globalisation in Historical Perspective, Santa Barbara,Ca., 1-55

Easton,S. and M.A. Walker (1997),'Income,Growth and Economic Freedom', American Economic Review: Papers and Proceedings 87, 328-332

Easterly, W., Kremer, M., Pritchett, L. and L. H. Summers (1993), 'Good Policy or Good Luck? Country Growth Performance and Temporary Shocks', NBER Working Paper 4474.

Easterly,W (2002) ,The Elusive Quest for Growth, Cambridge, Ma, MIT Press

Eggertsson, T., (1990) ,Economic Behavior and Institutions, Cambridge, Cambridge University Press.

Frankel,J.A. and D. Romer (1996),'Trade and Growth: An Empirical Investigation', NBER Working Paper 5476

Fukuda,S. and H. Toya (2000), 'Conditional Convergence in East Asian Countries: The Role of Exports in Economic Growth' Chap. 10 in T. Ho and Anne E. Krueger eds., East Asian Economic Growth, Cambridge, Ma., Harvard Univ. Press

Furman, J.L. and R. Hayes (2004),'Catching Up or Standing Still? National Innovative Productivity among "Follower" Countries'. Research Policy 33, 1329-1354

Gaidar,E.T.(2004) ,'Modern Economic Growth in Russia and Catch-Up Development', Herald of Europe, Sept., 1-11

Gerschenkron, A., (1962), Economic Backwardness in Historical Perspective, Cambridge, MA, Belknap Press.

Good, D.H., Nadiri, M. I. and R. C. Sickles, (1997), 'Index Number and Factor Demand Approaches to the Estimation of Productivity,' in Peasaran, M. H. and P. Schmidt, eds. Handbook of Applied Econometrics, Vol.. II: Microeconomics, Blackwell

Goodfriend, M. and J. McDermott (1994), 'A Theory of Convergence, Divergence, and Overtaking,' mimeo, Federal Reserve Bank of Richmond.

Gottinger, H.W. (2006), Innovation, Technology and Hypercompetition, London, Routledge

Griliches, Z. (1973), 'Research Expenditures and Growth Accounting', in B.R. Williams, ed., Science and Technology in Economic Growth, London, MacMillan, 59-95.

Griliches, Z. (1979), 'Issues in Assessing the Contribution of Research and Development to Productivity Growth,' *The Bell Journal of Economics,* 10, 92-116.

Griliches, Z. (1992) ,'The Search for R&D Spillovers,' *Scandinavian Journal of Economics* 94 (Supplement), 29-47.

Grossman, G. and E. Helpman (1991) ,Innovation and Growth in the Global Economy, Cambridge, MA: the MIT Press.

Hall, R. E. and Ch. I. Jones (1997), 'The Productivity of Nations' Levels of Economic Activity across Countries', American Economic Review: Papers and Proceedings 85,173-177

Harrod, R. F (1939), 'An Essay in Dynamic Theory', Economic Journal 49, 14-33.

Helliwell, J.F. and A. Chung (1995),'Convergences and Growth Linkages between North and South', in D.Currie and D. Vines, eds., Macroeconomic Linkages between North and South, Cambridge, Cambridge Univ. Press

Huang,Y. and T. Khanna (2003), 'Can India overtake China?', Foreign Policy July-Aug. 2003

Jones, Ch. I.(1997) 'Convergence Revisited,' *Journal of Economic Growth* 2, 131-153

Jones, Ch. I. (1995a) 'R&D-Based Models of Economic Growth,' Journal of Political Economy, 103, 759-784

Jones, Ch. I. (1995b)'Time Series Tests of Endogeneous Growth Models', Quarterly Journal of Economics 110, 495-525

Kennedy,P. (1987), The Rise and Fall of the Great Powers, New York, Vintage

Kolodko,G.W. (2003), 'Globalization and Catching Up in Emerging Market Economies', Mimeo, Academy of Entrepreneuership and Management in Warsaw (WSPiZ), www.tiger.edu.pl , Nov., 1-47

Knack, S. and P. Keefer, (1995) 'Institutions and Economic Performance: Cross-Country Tests Using Alternative Institutional Measures', Economics and Politics 7, 207-227.

Kocherlakota, N. R. and Y. Kei-Mu , (1996) 'A Simple Time Series Test of Endogenous vs. Exogenous Growth Models: An Application to the United States,' *Review of Economics and Statistics,* 126-134.

Kocherlakota, N. R. and K-M. Yi (1997) 'Is There Endogenous Long-Run Growth? Evidence from the United States and the United Kingdom,' *Journal of Money Credit, and Banking*, 29, 235-262.

Koopmans, T. C., (1965) 'On the Concept of Optimal Economic Growth', in The Econometric Approach to Development Planning, Amsterdam, North Holland.

Kyriacou, G. A., (1991) 'Level and Growth Effects of Human Capital: A Cross Country Study of the Convergence Hypothesis,' C.V Starr Working Paper 91-26,New York Univ.

Lau, S-H. P., (1996) 'Testing the Long Run Effect of Investment on Output in the Presence of Cointegration,' Working Paper, Australian National University

Lau, S-H. P. and C-Y.Sin(1997) 'Observational Equivalence and a Stochastic Cointegration Test of the Neoclassical and Romer's Increasing Returns Models', Economic Modelling, 14, 39-60.

Lim,L.K. and M. McAleer (2003), 'Convergence and Catching Up in ASEAN: A Comparative Analysis', mimeo, Dept. of Economics, Univ. of Western Australia, Perth, 1-38

Lucas, R.E. Jr., (1988) 'On the Mechanics of Economic Development', *Journal of Monetary Economics*, 22, 3-42

Lucas, R. E. Jr., (1993) 'Making a Miracle', Econometrica, 61(2): 251-272.

Maddison, A., (1982) Phases of Capitalist Development, New York, Oxford University Press.

Maddison, A.(1987) 'Growth and Slowdown in Advanced Capitalist Economies: Techniques of Quantitative Assessment', *Journal of Economic Literature* 25, 649-698.

Mankiw, N. G., Romer, D. and D. N. Weil, (1992) 'A Contribution to the Empirics of Economic Growth,' *Quarterly Journal of Economics*, 107, 407-437.

Mankiw,N.G.(1995),'The Growth of Nations', Brookings Papers on Economic Activity 1, 275-326

Mauro, Paolo, (1995) 'Corruption and Growth,' *Quarterly Journal of Economics* 110, 681-712.

Mokyr, J. (1990) The Lever of Riches, Oxford, Oxford Univ. Press

Nadiri, M.I. and K. Seongjun (1996) 'International R&D Spillovers, Trade, and Productivity in Major OECD Countries,' C. V. Starr Center for Applied Economics, Research Report 96-35.

Nadiri, M. I. and I. R. Prucha, (1992) 'Sources of Growth of Output and Convergence of Productivity in Major OECD Countries,' Working Paper.

Neusser, K. (1991) 'Testing the Long-Run Implications of the Neoclassical Growth Model', Journal of Monetary Economics 27, 3-37.

North, D. C. and R.P. Thomas (1973), The Rise of the Western World, Cambridge, Cambridge University Press

North, D. C. (1990) Institutions, Institutional Change and Economic Performance, Cambridge: Cambridge University Press.

Olson, M., (1982) The Rise and Decline of Nations: Economic Growth, Stagflation, and Social Rigidities, New Haven, Yale University Press

Ortiz,C.H., Castro, J.A. and E.R. Badillo (2007), 'Industrialization and Growth: Threshold Effects of Technological Integration', mimeo, Universidad del Valle, Departamento de Economía, A.A. 25360, Cali, Colombia, 1-19

Parente, St. L. and E. C. Prescott, (1993) 'Changes in the Wealth of Nations', *Federal Reserve Bank of Minneapolis Quarterly Review*, 17(2),3-16.

Parente, St. L. and E. C. Prescott, (1994) 'Barriers to Technology Adoption and Development', *Journal of Political Economy,* 102(2): 298-321.

Pritchett, L. (1997) 'Divergence, Big Time,' Journal of Economic Perspectives,11, 3-17.

Quah, D., (1993) 'Empirical Cross-Section Dynamics in Economic Growth', *European Economic Review*, 37,426-434.

Quah, D.(1996) 'Empirics for Economic Growth and Convergence', *European Economic Review*, 40, 1353-1375.

Ramsey, F., (1928) 'A Mathematical Theory of Saving,'Economic Journal, 38, 543-559.

Romer, P. M., (1986) 'Increasing Returns and Long-Run Growth', *Journal of Political Economy*, 94, pp. 1002-1037.

Romer, P. M., (l990) 'Endogenous Technological Change', *Journal of Political Economy,* 98, S71-S 102.

Romer, P. M., (1996) 'Why, Indeed, in America? Theory, History, and the Origins of Modern Economic Growth', American Economic Review: Papers and Proceedings, May, 202-206.

Sachs, J. D. and A. M. Warner, (1995) *'Economic Convergence and Economic Policies'*, NBER Working Paper 5039.

Sachs, J. D. and A. Warner, (1997) 'Fundamental Sources of Long-Run Growth', *American Economic Review Papers and Proceedings*, May, 184-188.

Scully, G. W, (1988) 'The Institutional Framework and Economic Development,' *Journal of Political Economy* 92(3), 652-662.

Solow, R. M., (1956) 'A Contribution to the Theory of Economic Growth', *Quarterly Journal of Economics*, 70, 65-94.

Solow, R. M. (1957) 'Technical Change and the Aggregate Production Function,' Review of Economics and Statistics, 39, 312-320.

Solow, R. M., (1960) 'Investment and Technical Progress', in K. Arrow, S. Karlin, and P. Suppes, eds., Mathematical Methods in the Social Sciences, Stanford, Ca: Stanford University Press, 89-104.

Swan, T. M., (1956) 'Economic Growth and Capital Accumulation', *Economic Record*, 32, 334-361.

Taylor,L. and C. Rada (2003), 'Can the Poor Countries Catch Up? Sources of Growth Accounting Gives Weak Convergence for the Early 21st Century', mimeo, Center for Economic Policy Analysis, New School University, New York, June, 1-45

The Economist (2007), 'High Tech Hopefuls, *A Special Report on Technology in India and China*', Nov. 10

Wan, H.Y. and M-L Lau (1993), 'On the Mechanism of Catching up', *European Economic Review* 38, 952-963

Wan, H.Y. (2004), Economic Development in a Globalized Environment, East Asian Evidence, Dordrecht, Kluwer

World Bank (1997), World Development Report 1997. New York, Oxford University Press

Young, A., (1995) 'The Tyranny of Numbers: Confronting the Statistical Realities of the East Asian Growth Experience,' *Quarterly Journal of Economics*, August, 641-680.

Chapter 4

MODELLING AGGREGATE TECHNOLOGICAL RACING: CATCHING UP, FALLING BEHIND AND GETTING AHEAD

Hans W. Gottinger

4.1. INTRODUCTION

Moving beyond the firm- and industry-led racing patterns evolving in a particular industry to a clustering of racing on an industry level is putting industry in different geo-economic zones against each other as they are becoming dominant in strategic product/process technologies. Here racing patterns among industries in a relatively free trade environment could lead to competitive advantages, more wealth creating and accumulating skill dominance in key product / process technologies in one region at the expense of others. The question is whether individual races on the firm level likewise induce races on the industry level and if so what controlling effects may be rendered by regional or multilateral policies on regulatory, trade and investment matters.

Similar catch-up processes are taking place between leaders and followers within a group of industrialized countries (or even emerging economies) in pursuit of higher levels of productivity. Moses Abramovitz (1986) explains the central idea of the catch-up hypothesis as the trailing countries' adopting behavior of a 'backlog of unexploited technology'. Supposing that the level of labor productivity were governed entirely by the level of technology embodied in capital stock, one may consider that the differentials in productivities among countries are caused by the 'technological age' of the stock used by a country relative to its 'chronological age'. The technological age of capital is an age of technology at the time of investment plus years elapsing from that time. Since a leading country may be supposed to be furnished with the capital stock embodying, in each vintage, technology which was 'at the very frontier' at the time of investment, the technological age of the stock is, so to speak, the same as its chronological age.

While a leader is restricted in increasing its productivity by the advance of new technology, trailing countries have the potential to make a larger leap as they are provided with the privilege of exploiting the backlog in addition of the newly developed technology. Hence, followers being behind with a larger gap in technology will have a stronger potential for growth in productivity. The potential, however, will be reduced as the catch-up process goes on because the unexploited stock of technology becomes smaller and smaller. This hypothesis explains the diffusion process of best-practice technology and gives the same sort of S-curve change in productivity rise of catching-up countries among a group of industrialized countries as that of followers to the leader in an industry. Although this view can explain the tendency to convergence of productivity levels of follower countries, it fails to answer the historical puzzle why a country, the United States--though with a structural advantage of being on the winning side of two world wars--has preserved the standing of the technological leader for a long time since taking over leadership from Britain in around the end of the last century and why the shifts have taken place in the ranks of follower countries in their relative levels of productivity, i.e., technological gaps between them and the leader. Abramovitz poses some extensions and qualifications on this simple catch-up hypothesis in the attempt to explain these facts.

Among other factors than technological backwardness, he lays stress on a country's social capability, i.e., years of education as a proxy of technical competence and its political, commercial, industrial, and financial institutions. The social capability of a country may become stronger or weaker as technological gaps close and thus, he states, the actual catch-up process 'does not lend itself to simple formulation'. This view has a common understanding to what Mancur Olson (1996) expresses to be 'public policies and institutions' as his explanation of the great differences in per capita income across countries, stating that any poorer countries that adopt relatively good economic policies and institutions enjoy rapid catch-up growth' (see also Chap. 7). The suggestion should be taken seriously when we wish to understand the technological challenge to American leadership by Japan, the continuous strong position of Germany in selective technologies and the 'Rise of the Rest' late industrializers in East Asia (Amsden, 2001) following the lead of Japan in the post-war period and the potential of a shift in standing between these countries. Amsden (2001) argues that late industrialization often provided a significant advantage of backwardness in particular for East Asian economies with Japan as an early pathfinder. Thus with a similar cultural background the East Asians NIEs closely followed Japan's development pattern with an initial strong emphasis on heavy industries and manufacturing, and special features of industrial targeting (Wan, 2004).This consideration will directly bear on the future trend of the state of the art which exerts a crucial influence on the development of the world economy.

Steering or guiding the process of racing through the pursuit of industrial policies aims to increase competitive advantage of respective industries, as having been practiced in Japan, in that it stimulates catch-up races but appears to be less effective in promoting frontier racing. A deeper reason lies in the phenomenon of network externalities affecting high-technology industries. That is, racing ahead of rivals in respective industries may create external economies to the effect that such economies within dominant 'increasing returns' industries tend to improve their international market position and therefore pull ahead in competitiveness vis-a-vis their (trading) partners (Krugman, 1997). The point is that racing behavior in leading high technology industries by generating frontier positions create cluster and network externalities pipelining through other sectors of the economy and creating competitive advantages elsewhere, as supported by the 'increasing returns' debate (Chap.6).

In this sense we speak of positive externalities endogenizing growth of these economies and contributing to competitive advantage (Grossman and Helpman, 1991, Chap.4).

Let us briefly recall the pattern of industrial racing and the implications of the way the firms in major high technology markets, such as telecommunications, split cleanly into the two major technology races, with one set of firms clearly lagging the other technologically. The trajectories of technological evolution certainly seem to suggest that firms from one frontier cannot simply jump to another trajectory. Witness, in this regard, the gradual process necessary for the firm in the catch-up race to approach those in the frontier race. There appears to be a frontier 'lock-in' in that once a firm is part of a race, the group of rivals within that same race are the ones whose actions influence the firm's strategy the most. Advancing technological capability is a cumulative process. The ability to advance to a given level of technical capability appears to be a function of existing technical capability. Given this 'path dependence', the question remains: why do some firms apparently choose a path of technological evolution that is less rapid than others. Two sets of possible explanations could be inferred from our case analysis, which need not be mutually exclusive. The first explanation lingers primarily on the expensive nature of R&D in ICT industries which rely on novel discovery for their advancement. Firms choosing the catch-up race will gain access to a particular technical level later than those choosing the frontier, but will do so at a lower cost.

How does this process on the micro level correspond to the one on a macro level? Sec. 4.2 provides a broad review in the literature on balanced vs. unbalanced economic growth in the context of industrialization strategies of developing economies. In Sec. 4.3 we expand a Solow type growth model toward endogenization in a knowledge economy, identify its steady state and its natural path of convergence. Sec. 4.4 connects the model to a broader set of recent endogenous growth models on R&D based growth and highlights some econometric issues. Sec. 4.5 gives some rough aggregate technology adoption rates for larger regions concerned and 4.6 tables some efficiency/inefficiency rates for particular countries in those regions. Sec. 4.7 explains how efficiency could be determined in the model for being useful in an international policy context while 4.8 provides some empirical results to shed more light on the catch-up potential.

4.2. INDUSTRIAL RACING BETWEEN NATIONS OR NATION GROUPS

The cumulative literature on industrialization has formalized the long standing idea that development traps are the result of a failure of economic organization rather than a lack of resources or other technological constraints. The so-called 'big push' models of industrialization have shown how, in the presence of increasing returns, see Chap. 6, there can exist preferable states to advance the economic states of countries in contest with other countries. Such a view not only provides an explanation for the co-existence of industrialized and non-industrialized economies, but also a rationale for government intervention to coordinate investment in a 'big-push' toward industrialization. Moreover, unlike competing theories, these models emphasize the temporary nature of any policy. Thus, industrialization policy involves facilitating an adjustment from one equilibrium to another rather than any change in the nature of the set of equilibria per se.

While recent formalisation makes clear the possible role for the government in coordinating economic activity, little has been said about the form such policy should take. Is there a conceptual model to analyse the question: what precise form should the 'big push' take? It is argued that while many different industrialization policies can be successful in generating escapes from development traps, the form of the policy that minimizes the costs of this transition depends on the characteristics of the economic situation at hand. Factors such as the strength of the complementarities, externalities and increasing returns, among others, all play a role in influencing the nature of a 'getting- ahead' industrialization policy. Such ideas were present in the debates on development economics in the 1940s and 1950s regarding the form of industrialization policy. The models underlying these less formal debates inspired the recent more formal research but the policy elements of these have not been addressed, to date, in any substantive way.

Principal among the earlier policy debates was that surrounding the efficacy and costs involved in the alternative strategies of 'balanced' versus 'unbalanced growth'. Rosenstein-Rodan (1943, 1961) and Nurkse(1952, 1953) provided the rationale for the notion that the adoption of modern technologies must proceed across a wide range of industries more or less simultaneously. It was argued that the neglect of investment in a sector (or sectors) could undermine any industrialization strategy. Reacting to this policy prescription was the 'unbalanced growth' school led by Hirschman (1958) and Streeten (1956, 1963). Both saw the balanced strategy as far too costly. The advantages of multiple developments may make interesting reading for economists, but they are gloomy news indeed for the underdeveloped countries.

The initial resources for simultaneous developments on many fronts are generally lacking. By targeting many sectors, it was argued that scarce resources would be spread too thin- so thin, that industrialisation would be thwarted. It seemed more fruitful to target a small number of "leading sectors." (Rostow, 1960) Then those investments would "....call forth complementary investments in the next period with a will and logic of their own: they block out a part of the road that lies ahead and virtually compel certain additional investment decisions." (Hirschman, 1958, p.42) Thus, the existence of complementarities between investments and increasing returns motivated an unbalanced approach. Consequently, at the same time, "complementarity of industries provides the most important set of arguments in favour of a large-scale planned industrialization" (Rosenstein-Rodan, 1943, p. 205).

Both sides appeared to have agreed that a 'big push' was warranted, but they disagreed as to its composition. Our purpose here is to use the guidelines provided by the recent formalization of the 'big push' theory of industrialization to clarify the earlier debate of the appropriate degree of focus for industrialization policy. After all, the recent literature has stressed the roles of complementarities and increasing returns that both schools saw lying at the heart of their policy prescriptions. The seminal article formalising the 'big push' theory of industrialisation is that of Murphy, Shleifer and Vishney (1989). In their model, firms choose between a constant returns and an increasing returns of technology based on their expectations of demand. However, these choices spill over into aggregate demand creating a strategic interaction among sectors in their technology adoption decisions. Thus, under certain conditions, there exist two equilibria: with all firms choosing the constant returns or all choosing the increasing returns technology. Clearly, in the latter equilibrium, all households are better off.

While the Murphy, Shleifer and Vishny model shows how increasing returns (and a wage effect) aggregate to strategic complementarities among sectors, it does not lend itself readily to the debate concerning the degree of balance in industrialization policy. First, the static content leaves open the question of whether the intervention should take the form of anything more than indicative planning. Second, the most commonly discussed policy instrument in the industrialization debate is the subsidization of investments. However, in the Murphy, Shleifer and Vishny example, use of this instrument biases one toward a more unbalanced policy. To see this, observe that it is the role of the government to facilitate a move to the industrializing equilibrium. This means that the government must subsidize a sufficient amount of investment to make it profitable for all sectors to adopt the modern technology.

Given the binary choice set, there then exists some minimum critical mass of sectors that must be targeted to achieve a successful transition. A greater range of successful industrialisation policies might be more plausible, however, if firms had the choice of a wider variety of technology to choose from. One might suppose that targeting a large number of sectors to modernise a little and targeting a small number of sectors for more radical modernisation might both generate a big push. Thus, to consider the balanced approach properly, a greater technological choice space is required.

4.3. MODELLING TECHNOLOGY ADOPTION IN AN ENDOGENIZED GROWTH MODEL

Prerequisites

We endogenize a Solow type growth model to allow for the transmission of technological knowledge across national borders. The standard neoclassical model assumes a closed economy and an exogenous constant saving rate to predict that countries converge to their own steady states determined by rates of accumulation and the depreciation rate. However, in addition to having different accumulation rates, economies also differ in levels of technology. This introduces the possibility that flows of technology may present an additional opportunity for growth. Thus, adoption of technology from abroad (for example, through foreign direct investment) is one possible mechanism through which the capital stock of a nation increases, as better technology improves the productivity of the existing stock of capital. The receiving nation would therefore appear to have more capital if better capital is equivalent to more capital. The possibility of adoption of knowledge and ideas is especially clear if we take a very broad view of capital by including both human and physical capital in its definition. Flows of technology are analogous to capital mobility and labour mobility (if each migrant carries some amount of capital) since the capital stock is in effect augmented. The extension to incorporate cross-national technology flows implies that economies are open to some extent, that is, at least ideas and technical knowledge are able to travel across national borders.

Whereas physical capital tends to flow from economies with low rates of return to those with high rates of return and labour tends to travel from low wage to high wage nations, technology flows from very productive economies with high levels of technology to the technological laggards. The model with technology flows will differ from a model with labour or capital mobility in that technology flows are nonexclusive; i.e., flows of technology benefit the receiving economy without hurting the source economy. In contrast, for labour and capital migration the gains in population and capital stock for the destination economy represent corresponding losses for the source economy.

Replacing the closed economy nature of the traditional Solow model by a partially open economy potentially affect a nation's steady state and transitional dynamics. The results are similar to those derived for capital and labor mobility, which are that mobility tend to speed up an economy's convergence toward its steady state. It will also come out that technology flows might augment the level of that steady state. We enhance the possibility of technology adoption in the Solow model of a closed economy by allowing a cross national flow of knowledge but assume that the economy is closed with respect to foreign assets and foreign labor. Thus in this setup ideas and knowledge can flow across national borders independently of capital and labor migration. The assumption of immobility of physical capital and labor is strong, but it serves for analytical purpose to single out some effects of technology on the growth process

The Model

The model is for the most part identical to the standard neoclassical model which assumes a Cobb-Douglas production function:

$$Q_t = K_t^{\alpha}(A_t L_t)^{1-\alpha} \qquad (4.1)$$

and exogenous growth for population and technological progress:

$$L_t = L_0 e^{nt} \qquad (4.2)$$

and

$$A_t = A_0 e^{g \cdot t} \qquad (4.3)$$

The only difference from the standard model appears in the equation for the evolution of capital. The capital evolution depends on an exogenous savings rate, the depreciation rate, and a technology catch-up term, $\gamma(T, T^*)$, with a benchmark term T^* of the technological leading country (region) so that:

$$\dot{K}_t = sQ_t - \delta K_t + \gamma(T, T^*)_t K_t. \qquad (4.4a)$$

It is instructive to point out the difference to models of purely disembodied technical change. These models specify capital evolution as:

$$\dot{K}_{it} = sQ_{it} - \delta K_{it} \qquad (4.4b)$$

so that the stock K_t can be interpreted as new-machine equivalents implied by the stream of past investments (and δ, depreciation, is the weight that transforms each vintage investment into new-machine equivalents). We assume, in contradistinction, that new investment might also embody differences in technical design. Thus a new 'machine' may be more efficient than an old 'machine' even if there is no difference in physical capacity. The standard capital evolution Equation 4.4b will then tend to understate the true productivity of the capital stock. In this setup, technology from abroad may make the existing and new capital stock more productive and therefore increase the capital stock (a resource is measured in efficiency units).

Transforming the model into an 'intensive form' model so that all variables are divided by $A_t L_t$, the Cobb-Douglas production function becomes:

$$y_t = f(k_t) = k_t^\alpha \tag{4.5}$$

and the capital evolution Equation 4a becomes:

$$\dot{k}_t = s\, k_t^\alpha - (\delta + n + g)\, k_t + \gamma\, (T, T^*)_t\, k_t \tag{4.6}$$

This means that the growth rate of capital intensity, k, is given by:

$$\dot{k}/k = c_k = s k^{\alpha - 1} - (\delta + n + g)\, k_t - \gamma\, (T, T^*)), \tag{4.7}$$

so the effective depreciation rate $(\delta + n + g)\, k_t - \gamma\, (T, T^*)$ includes the term $\gamma\, (T, T^*)$. Thus the adoption of foreign technology acts to reduce the rate of effective depreciation. In the standard Solow-model a lower rate of effective depreciation yields a higher steady state, so one expects this to be true in the present model as well.

Technology Adoption Function and Knowledge Gap

The new results derive from the technology adoption function, $\gamma\, (T, T^*)$. Assume that the adoption of technology is a function of an economy's technology gap to the leader, defined as the nation with the highest level of technology. The economy is then able to adopt some fraction of this gap every time period. The simplest definition of the technology adoption function would then be:

$$\gamma\, (T, T^*)_t = \rho\, (T^*_t - T_t) \tag{4.8}$$

where ρ denotes the technology adoption rate.

The measurement of technology is difficult, as no variable captures it perfectly. Possible candidates such as number of patents or number of Ph.Ds. are elusive. As a possible proxy one can make the assumption that technology is a function of the economy's capital intensity. In particular, technology will be a logarithmic function of the intensive:

$$T_t = \ln(k_t) \tag{4.9}$$

This implies that technology is a positive, diminishing function of capital intensity (see Figure 4.1). From these assumptions one obtains:

$$\gamma(T, T^*)_t = \gamma(\ln(k), \ln(k^*))_t = \rho[\ln(k_t^*), \ln(k_t)], \qquad (4.10)$$

or equivalently:

$$\gamma(\ln(k), \ln(k^*))_t = -\rho \ln(k_t/k_t^*) \qquad (4.11)$$

and the technology adoption function is decreasing in k.

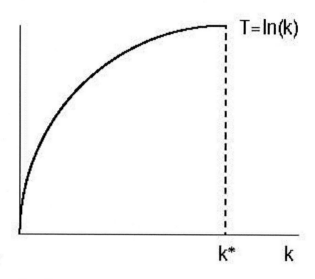

Figure 4.1. Technology Function.

The technology gap could be put in terms of $ln(k/k^*)$, convex decreasing with larger k, k^*. Also, an important characteristic of the technology function is that it is bounded below by zero; that is, having a higher level of technology than the "leader" will never hurt you. This point goes back to the nonexclusive character of technology so that the leader nation's rate of growth is never hurt by the fact that the economy has the highest level of expertise. Another crucial characteristic of the adoption function is that technology flows are one-directional. That is, technology only flows from the leader to the followers. This is an assumption which would likely be violated in a multi-sectoral world, but perhaps can be justified in terms of net flows.

The Steady State

Figure 4.2 is the standard Solow growth diagram augmented by the technology adoption function. The $sf(k)/k$ curve is downward-sloping as usual because of the diminishing average product of capital. The commonly horizontal line at $(\delta + n + g)$ has been replaced by the upward-sloping curve $(\delta + n + g - \gamma(T, T^*))$. The height of the effective-depreciation curve is $(\delta + n + g)$

at $k > k^* = k^w$ since at these capital intensity levels the technology gap facing the economy is removed (i.e. zero). The steady state corresponds to the intersection of the $sf(k)/k$ and $(\delta+n+g-\gamma(T, T^*))$ curves at the point k^*.

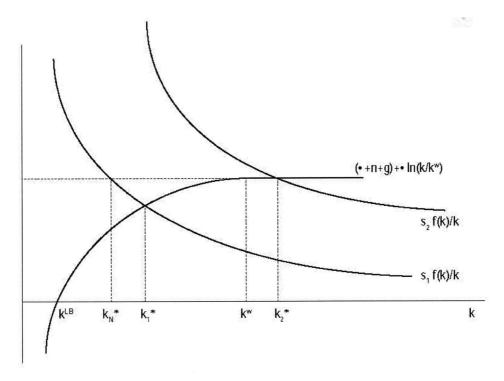

Figure 4.2. Steady State Growth.

In the diagram we have drawn two possible $sf(k)/k$ curves depending on the saving rate. The obvious result is that a higher saving rate ($s_2 > s_1$) will lead to a higher steady state, but more interestingly the saving rate will also determine whether this steady state will differ from the standard Solow steady state. In the figure, the higher saving rate corresponds to a steady state outcome which is identical to the one expected from the Solow-model (as case 2). On the other hand, the lower saving rate (s_1) leads to a steady state greater than predicted by the standard neoclassical model since k^* now corresponds to a point where the follower economy is a recipient of technology in its steady state. That is, the economy will remain in steady state as a perpetual receiver of technology (as case 1). This reception of technology allows the economy to reach a steady state which is above the one predicted by its saving rate and $(\delta+ n + g)$. An implication of the model is that steady state capital intensity is bounded below since $sf(k)/k$ is non-negative. Its lower bound is given by k^{LB} in Figure 4.2 and is equal to $k^w / \exp(\delta+n+g)/\rho$.

We can also use Figure 4.2 to assess the effects of changes in the model's various parameters on the steady state values. As seen above, the effect from an increase in the saving rate is a higher steady state. The same is true if the production function were to shift outwards from an increase in the capital-share coefficient, α. This result stems from the fact that the rate of diminishing returns from capital decreases as α increases. The other possibility is a changing effective-depreciation rate. The rate of depreciation will increase from a boost in either δ, n, or g, or from a decrease in the technology adoption function resulting from either a lower ρ or a lower k*, for any given k. The decrease in the effective-depreciation rate results from the obvious (reversed) changes of parameters. An increase (decrease) of the effective-depreciation rate leads to a lower (higher) steady state. One does not have to refer to this picture in order to find the steady state; this point can also be derived.

The definition of the steady state is that the capital intensity does not change; that is, k = 0. This implies that:

$$\dot{k}_t = 0 = s\, k_t^\alpha - (\delta + n + g)\, k_t + \gamma(T, T^*)_t\, k_t \tag{4.12}$$

The solution of Equation 12 for case 2 when there is no technology gap in the steady state [i.e. $\gamma(T, T^*) = 0$] is given by:

$$k^* = [\, s/(\delta + n + g)\,]^{1/1-\alpha} \tag{4.13}$$

The corresponding steady state output per effective unit of labour is given by:

$$y^* = [\, s/(\delta + n + g)\,]^{\alpha/1-\alpha} \tag{4.14}$$

For case 1 when the economy is a perpetual recipient of technology, the steady state solution is given by:

$$k^* = [\, s/(\delta + n + g) - \gamma(T, T^*)\,]^{1/1-\alpha} \tag{4.15}$$

or similarly:

$$k^* = [\, s/(\delta + n + g) + \rho \ln(k^*/k')\,]^{1/1-\alpha} \tag{4.16}$$

where $k^*/k' \leq 1$. Hence, if $k^* < k'$, then the economy's steady state will be affected by the technology gap. Correspondingly, the steady state output per effective labour for case 1 is given by:

$$y^* = [\, s/(\delta + n + g) + \rho \ln(k^*/k')\,]^{\alpha/1-\alpha} \tag{4.17}$$

Transitional Dynamics and Rate of Convergence

To assess the speed of convergence we log-linearize Equation 4.12 around its steady state. Since there are two kinds of steady states, there will also be two distinct convergence rates. The derivations yield that the rate of convergence for case 1 is equal to:

$$\beta = (1 - \alpha)(\delta + n + g) \tag{4.18}$$

which is exactly the same as for the standard Solow model. However, although the rate of convergence is identical and the economy reaches its steady state in the same amount of time, the actual growth path will be very different with the present model compared to the standard Solow model.

For case 2, the rate of convergence is also determined by the rate of technology adoption, ρ, and is given by:

$$\beta = (1 - \alpha)(\delta + n + g) + \rho [1 + (1 - \alpha) \ln(k^*/k^w)] \qquad (4.19)$$

where the first term is the rate of convergence which is obtained from the standard Solow model and the second term is a non-negative additional convergence factor stemming from the adoption of foreign expertise. The latter term as non-negative stems from the fact that $sf(k)/k$ is always a positive number and, hence, steady state capital has a lower bound, as described above. Thus, the "typical" economy for which $k^* = k^w$, that is all economies have identical steady states, and when assuming that $\rho > 0$, then the above Equation 19 shows that the potential for technology adoption raises the convergence coefficient, β, above the Solow value by the amount of ρ.

An interesting finding which differs from the standard model is that the rate of convergence will now depend on the steady state position, k^*. In the standard model the rate of convergence only depends on $(1 - \alpha)(\delta + n + g)$, thus the saving rate does not affect the speed of convergence and neither does the level of technology, A. These results stem from the reality that in the Cobb-Douglas cases A produces two offsetting forces which exactly cancel each other. The two forces are: (1) given k, a higher saving rate leads to greater investment and therefore higher speed of convergence and (2) a higher saving rate raises the steady-state capital-intensity, and thereby lowers the average product of capital in the vicinity of the steady state. Again, these two forces exactly cancel in the Cobb-Douglas case. In this model, however, when $\rho > 0$, β increases with the steady state capital-intensity. Of course, this is only true as long as $k^* < k^w$ and the reason is that a higher k* implies a higher steady state technology adoption.

A permanent improvement in the production function or a higher level of saving raises the steady state as well as increasing the rate of convergence. A final point is that the standard result that an increase in the capital-share, α, leads to lower convergence speed is possibly compromised since a higher α lowers the convergence effect from technology adoption (if $k^* < k^w$).

Convergence Path

Technology adoption introduces the possibility of rapid growth in addition to being below the steady state position. However, once the technology gap has been exploited, the economy is left with the traditional source of growth, namely the difference $sf(k)/k - (\delta + n + g)$. This is the reason why the convergence rate only depends on these factors for the case when steady state is independent of the technology gap. However, this does not mean that an economy whose steady state is above the leader's cannot take advantage of a technology gap when such an opportunity is presented. Instead, the follower economy will be able to grow rapidly in the early stages of its catch-up due to both the diminishing return to capital effect and the adoption of foreign technology. Yet, once the technology gap has been bridged, the economy's capital growth is reduced to that predicted by the diminishing returns effect. Figure 4.3 shows that the rate of growth can be split up into its standard part (γ_1) and the technology adoption effect (γ_2), and that γ_2 may eventually become zero. The fact that the convergence time will be identical to the Solow model, but that the convergence path is very different can be seen in simulations of the model. This indicates the effect on the convergence path when a market does or does not adopt technology when assuming identical steady states for all economies (i.e. identical saving rates). Simulations can be run for various economies which differ in initial capital stock, as well as with different adoption rates and efficiency levels of adoption (E).

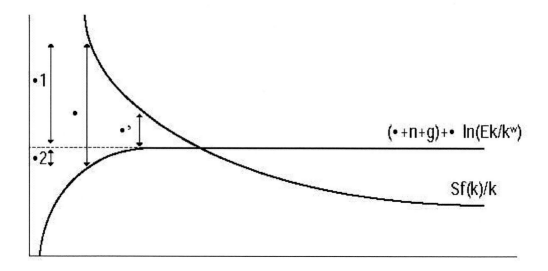

Figure 4.3. Rate of Growth.

To contrast the present model with the standard, it would make sense in simulations to add technology adoption to one of the follower countries and to assume the income leader also to be the technological leader. It shows that this shifts the convergence paths significantly without changing the economies' steady states. However, although the same steady state is reached, the market which adopts technology will have a higher level of income at any point. Furthermore, a flow of disembodied technology across economies may modify the neoclassical model's steady state and rate of convergence. One also needs to consider an economy's ability to adopt and absorb this new knowledge. One reason why economies may differ in their ability to take advantage of the technology gap is through the rate of adoption, ρ. As referred to earlier, Abramovitz (1986) proposes that the abilities of countries to take advantage of the catching-up potential depend on their respective "social capabilities;" i.e. that systematic variation in social institutions and processes make some countries better or worse at catching-up.

Since 'follower' countries typically suffer from both a large technology gap and a low absorption capacity, the predictions about the growth effects from the technology gap are ambiguous. As Abramovitz (1986) stated 'a country's potential for rapid growth is strong not when it is backward without qualification, but rather when it is technologically backward but socially advanced.' In other words, a technologically backward country is more likely to catch up or even get ahead if its social institutions (predominantly, education, entrepreneurship, economic freedom) have lower absorption barriers. How fast the adoption rate will be, the speed of adoption for catching up, will clearly depend on its adoption capacity, its adoption learning, and its strategic selection and following through all of those clearly shaped by institutional mechanisms. Of particular interest would be the efficiency (E) level of an economy to adopt, an important ingredient of Abramovitz' 'social capability', that is an inefficient economy may be very slow to adopt and spread available technology through institutional inertia, lack of complementary competence and inability to digest. Thus, we may empirically identify countries though having high adoption rates but low levels of efficiencies that lag significantly in their potential of catch-up.

4.4. EXTENSION OF TECHNOLOGY MODEL AND EXPLANATIONS

In addition to having different accumulation rates, economies also differ in levels of technology. This introduces the possibility that flows of skill may present an additional opportunity for growth. Thus, adoption of technology from abroad, through know-how transfer in physical capital or human capital influx, is one possible mechanism through which the assets stock of a nation increases, as better technology and its exploitation improves the productivity of the existing stock of capital fostered by competitive institutions in the importing economy (Aghion and Griffith, 2005). Thus we can view growth of a nation as being based on this nation's deviation from the overall technological leader, plus different rates of factor accumulation rather than deviation from a hypothetical steady state. Furthermore, R&D based economic growth models are pushing for a large industry segment applying advanced technology achieving ever higher increasing returns industries for overall enhanced economic growth as in models by Denicolo (2006), Segerstrom (2007), Etro (2008), Chen and Kee (2005) and Zeira (2007), and building on previous work of Romer (1986,1990) and Lucas (1988).

Let us see how the ideas that there exist technology gaps and differing abilities to take advantage of this catch-up potential, play out in the standard neoclassical framework. The possibility of technology adoption from countries ahead is included by adding a catch-up term. This adoption potential is allowed to be compromised by varying political and social institutions as estimated by a measure of efficiency." This chapter's focus lies in the introduction of a rate of adoption of technology and the consideration of relative efficiency of nations. The empirical exploration relates to three samples of countries: Europe, Latin America and East Asia. For the three regions the U.S. is assumed to be the leader nation in key technology industries (ICT, medical, pharmaceutical). This assumption is based on the fact that the U.S. is both the leader in terms of per worker GDP and that it has a relatively efficient institutional framework. For each region, the general growth process is similar across countries.

The estimation sheds some light on the reasons behind the varied performance of the regions relative to the United States. We attempt to find what the cross-regional similarities and differences have been in the post-war period (i.e. 1960-1985) using two regions which have been successful in catching up with the U.S., Europe and East Asia, and one region which has not, Latin America (Fagerberg and Godinho, 2004). Significant results are obtained for regional adoption rates and country-specific inefficiency levels. An interesting finding is

Latin America's high rate of technology adoption (higher than Europe and East Asia) indicating that the region should have taken advantage of its catch-up potential. However, once levels of inefficiency are considered it is apparent why Latin America has in fact failed to do so.

Once the relative efficiency levels of the sample countries are obtained we look for the factors that determine the observed differences. Consider a set of variables related to a nation's social and political institutions. We take the standard model with a Cobb-Douglas production function:

$$Q_{it} = A_{it} K_{it}^{\beta_1} L_{it}^{\beta_2} H_{it}^{\beta_3} \qquad (4.20a)$$

where Q depends on technology A, physical capital stock K, employment L and human capital H. All countries are represented by i, i = 1, ..., N, in each time period t, t = 1, ..., T. Use the common specification of the evolution of exogeneous world technology and number of workers so that:

$$L_t = L_0 e^{nt} \qquad (4.20b)$$

and

$$A_{it} = A_{i0} e^{gt}. \qquad (4.20c)$$

The only difference from the standard model appears in our Equation 4a for the evolution of capital. The capital evolution depends on an exogenous saving rate, the depreciation rate, and a technology catch-up term, $\gamma(T, T^*)$, so that:

$$\dot{K}_t = sQ_{it} - \delta K_{it} + \gamma(T, T^*)_{it} K_{it}. \qquad (4.21)$$

In this setup, technology from abroad may make the existing and new capital stock more productive and therefore increase the capital stock (capital is measured in efficiency units). The catch-up term is specified as a logarithmic function of the inverse ratio of labor productivity:

$$Y_i = Q_{it} / L_{it} \qquad (4.22)$$

the 'desired' level of labor productivity, Y_i^*, which may differ between countries:

$$\gamma(T, T^*)_{it} = \rho_i \ln(Y^*_{i,t-1} / Y_{i,t-1}) \qquad (4.23)$$

Using a desired level of labor productivity reflects our belief that all countries are not able to obtain the same level of productivity. For example, the Latin American nations may not be able to adopt the entire technology gap between themselves and the U.S. because of institutional inefficiencies except that the U.S. will by itself deteriorate.

Log linearizing and differencing the production function and substituting for the growth rate of capital yields that the growth rate of per worker output depends on the growth of factor inputs as well as the productivity gap:

$$y_{it} = \phi + \beta_1 k_{it} + \beta_2 l_{it} + \beta_3 h_{it} + \rho_i \ln(Y^*_{i,t-1}/Y_{i,t-1}) \qquad (4.24)$$

where $\rho_i = \beta_1 \theta_i$ is the country-specific technology adoption rate and $\phi = (\gamma - \beta_1 \delta)$ is net exogenous technology growth. Empirical growth studies (e.g Mankiw et al., 1992) usually assume that all countries have experienced the same rate of technological progress, which is highly unlikely (see Grossman and Helpman, 1991, p.29). The above specification does not impose such a strong assumption.

Next, to capture some of Abramovitz (1986) ideas on "social capabilities", we suggest that in addition to economies' varied abilities to adopt the technology gap, they may also differ in ability to recognize or exploit the available technology. To incorporate this into the model, a term labeled inefficiency, is included which acts to reduce the available technology gap to economies. To account for varied institutional rigidities, the desired or maximum, controlling for institutional features, level of labor productivity is some fraction of the leader's productivity, and that fraction is determined by the nation's level of inefficiency:

$$Y^*_{it} = (Y^L_i / E_{it}) \Rightarrow \ln Y^*_{it} = \ln Y^L_i - \ln E_{it} \qquad (4.25)$$

where YiL is the leader's labor productivity and Eit is the inefficiency parameter. Substituting into the growth rate of capital and rearranging we obtain:

$$y_{it} = \phi - \rho_i \ln E_{i,t-1} + \beta_1 k_{it} + \beta_2 l_{it} + \beta_3 h_{it} + \rho_i \ln(Y^*_{i,t-1}/Y_{i,t-1}) \qquad (4.26)$$

That is, the growth rate of GDP per worker for country i depends on the rate of growth of factor inputs, the common rate of exogenous technological change minus capital depreciation, country-specific inefficiency, and the technology gap between the leader and the follower countries lagged one period. Interpretation of the parameters are straightforward:

β_1, β_2, and β_3 show the elasticity of per worker GDP to a change in the growth of factor inputs, ρ_i is the adoption of available technology from abroad and the estimated inefficiency measure, $\rho_I \ln E_{i,t-1}$, shows the reduction in growth of labor productivity due to political and social factors which reduce the available technology gap.

Econometric Issues

In view of estimation procedures one can frame the growth model in terms of dynamic frontier production functions. Along this line we consider the case when countries adopt all technical innovations in a timely manner and let a random variable η_{it} (>0) denote country i's inefficiency score induced by a technology that has diffused to country i at time t. Assume that the η_{it} are independently distributed over different i and t. Further, assume:

$$E(\eta_{it} \mid W_{i,t-1}) = \omega_I \geq 0 \qquad (4.27)$$

is the 'knowledge' set available to country i at the beginning of time t. Next define:

$$\alpha^*_{it} = \alpha_t^C - \eta_{it} = \beta_0 + \gamma t - \eta_{it} \qquad (4.28)$$

where α^*_{it} is country i's productivity level if it adopted technology innovations timely and $\alpha_t C$ denotes the time-varying component of 'common' technology which is commonly accessible to all countries. Deterministic frontier production is given by:

$$y_{it}^C = x_{it}\beta + \alpha_t^C \qquad (4.29)$$

while stochastic frontier production is:

$$y_{it}^C = x_{it}\beta + \alpha_t^C + \mu_{it} \qquad (4.30)$$

where the μ_{it} are assumed to be independently distributed over different i and t with zero mean. Actual production is given by:

$$y_{it} = x_{it}\beta + \alpha_{it} = x_{it}\beta + \beta_0 + \gamma - u_{it} + b\mu_{it} \qquad (4.31)$$

where b is zero or one depending on whether the production frontier is deterministic or stochastic. The actual productivity level is given by:

$$\alpha_{it} = \alpha_t^C - u_{it} \qquad (4.32a)$$

where u_{it} (≥ 0) is country i's technical inefficiency level at time t.

Another possible source of technical inefficiency in addition to terms such as μ_{it} is a country's sluggish adoption of technical innovations. An implicit assumption in the bulk of the production frontier literature, as well as the growth literature, is that adjustment rates are instantaneous so that the data is generated from a country in long-run static equilibrium (steady state). If there are costs that inhibit instantaneous adjustment, inefficiency measures developed by the dynamic frontier literature may be proxies for differing adjustment costs and misspecification of the long-run/short-run dynamics. Consider, therefore, the possibility that countries adopt technology only slowly over time. Specifically, assume that technical innovations introduced at the beginning of time t are only partially adopted and the adoption speed, ρ_i may differ across countries:

$$\alpha_{it} = (1 - \rho_i)\alpha_{I,t-1} + \rho_I \alpha_{it}^* \qquad (4.32b)$$

where $0 < \rho_i < 1$. When a firm adjusts its production technology in this fashion, the inefficiency level must be correlated with its lagged levels. Substituting:

$$\alpha_{it} = \alpha_t^C - u_{it} \qquad (4.33)$$

into Equation 4.32b one can show that the long-run average technical inefficiency level of country i is given by:

$$u_i^{LR} \equiv \lambda_I / \rho_i = \omega_I + (1 - \rho_i) \gamma / \rho_I \qquad (4.34)$$

The first component of u_i^{LR}, ω_i measures the long-run inefficiency due to country i's inability to comprehend and fully utilize newly introduced production technologies while the second component, $(1 - \rho_i) \gamma / \rho_i$ captures the long-run efficiency loss due to the country's sluggish adoption of technological innovations, which are negatively related with the adjustment speed ρ_i.

Grossman and Helpman (1991) argue that a positive coefficient on the investment ratio may be picking up the effects of disparate technological progress on the growth rate. That is, if investment rates are high where productivity growth is fast, then the coefficient on the investment ratio should also pick up variation in per capita incomes due to countries different experiences with technological progress as in Baumol et al. (1992), and Baumol (2002). Similar results are obtained when splitting the sample into three regions, Europe, East Asia and Latin America. Including initial wealth, the investment ratio is significantly positive for all regions, but of a lesser magnitude in Europe, perhaps indicating diminishing returns (that is, the investment ratio might be negatively correlated with the capital-labor ratio). Employment growth affects growth of per worker income negatively in Europe, but positively, although insignificantly so, in East Asia and Latin America. The growth of human capital is insignificant and negative for all regions. The average level of human capital has a positive coefficient, but is significant only for East Asia. Both results for human capital are similar to the ones obtained in Benhabib and Spiegel (1994). In all cases, initial per worker income is significantly negative, which indicates conditional convergence.

4.5. TECHNOLOGY ADOPTION RATES

Looking at 5-year adoption rates in the 1990s for Europe (0.36), East Asia (0.32), and Latin America (0.59), calculated from OECD statistics and Young (1995) before considering institutional inefficiencies, Europe closes about 36 percent of the initial technology gap every five years. Of course, this should be taken with a grain of salt; the higher the adoption rates, the bigger the technology gap, the lower the technological competence of a country and region against a top benchmark. It shows built-in convergence revealed by the underlying model.

In a dynamic context over a longer run what should really count is the relative change of adoption rates for one or any region and comparatively among regions. Furthermore, the numbers indicate that Latin America has been more successful at adopting foreign technology than Europe and East Asia, a perhaps surprising result. However, recall that we have separated out the technology adoption which presumably is included in the growth of physical and human capital. Also, we can likely infer that a possible reason why Latin America has adopted technology faster than Europe might be that they are further behind and "older" technologies might be easier to adopt whereas more effort is needed to adopt new reduction techniques. This does not, however, explain why Latin America has a greater adoption rate than East Asia. Here we are pointing to observations in Chapter 8, East Asia's technology adoption is to a larger degree embodied in new capital, and the large amount of foreign direct investment to Latin America might have contributed significantly to the region's technology adoption. The amount of foreign direct investment is less for the East Asian countries.

4.6. Efficiency

Next we explore the inefficiency of the follower nations; i.e., the negative effect on the potential technology gap stemming from inefficient social and institutional factors. Increasing efficiencies deblock catch-up in lagging countries (Juma and Clark, 2002). Efficiency is found by dividing a nation's estimated fixed effect by the regional adoption rate. As defined here, it is quite robust to different estimations and samples. The relative efficiencies of the nations within regions appear to conform to common beliefs. For example, in Europe, the Netherlands, Belgium and Switzerland are the most efficient while Turkey, Portugal and Greece are the least efficient. In East Asia, Hong Kong is the most efficient while Indonesia and Thailand are the least efficient. Finally, in Latin America, Mexico and Argentina are at the top and Honduras and Bolivia at the bottom. Another way to discuss the findings is to consider the time required to catch-up. Previously, Parente and Prescott (2004) showed that countries with lower levels of relative efficiency will adopt modern technologies at much later dates. Conversely, one could argue that if those countries adopt modern technologies concurrently with their low level of relative efficiency then their rates of growth would stay at a subpar level of their potential.

One major source of efficiency generation for a country, according to Parente and Prescott (2004), is belonging to a 'free trade club' that improves efficiency through greater industrial competition. We calculate the required time period until the nations reach their frontier when only the catch-up term and inefficiency are allowed to vary across regions and countries. Two frontiers are considered: nations' inefficiency frontier and the leader nation's frontier. The latter requires that the inefficiency levels fade away in time which we assume occurs at the rate of ρ. The European countries, with the exception of Turkey, all seem to have reached their inefficiency reduced frontier. The same is true for most of the East Asian countries. Thus, these nations will not catch-up with the U.S. without higher accumulation rates or improved efficiency. For Latin America, most countries are still catching-up with their inefficiency frontier, so that if accumulation rates were the same catch-up would still take place through diffusion of disembodied technology. Of course, if inefficiency levels remain then a follower could never completely catch-up with the leader by taking advantage of the technology gap alone. As an illustrative example, for the required time to catch-up with the leader if inefficiency levels were improving at the rate ρ much of Europe and Latin America could then approach the frontier faster than East Asia on account of East Asia's lower rate of technology adoption. This begs the question of what determines these (in)efficiencies?

It is reasonable to expect a tradeoff between a general technology level (GTL) of a nation's leading industries and its institutional efficiencies (IE). Thus, using an aggregate score, (GTL,IE), say, a country may be in the top rank of GTL but weak on IE which may be surpassed in growth by one which is lower in GTL rank but strong on IE.

4.7. Determinants of Efficiency

Subsequently we endeavor to find the determinants of the nations differing in efficiency levels. An econometric approach would consider a set of measurable variables related to nations' social and political institutions including public (economic) policies with tax transparency, low business taxes, minimal corruption and upholding (intellectual) property rights. The variables relate to government market supporting and fairness sustainable policies, implementing the rules of law, political and civil rights, levels of education and openness to international trade. Earlier studies which consider the determinants of country efficiency include Scully (1988) and when considering productivity Hall and Jones (1996). Scully defines efficiency by per capita income relative to the leader and finds that the institutional environment as proxied by political and civil rights indices, are significant in determining levels of efficiency and growth. Hall and Jones regress total factor productivity on a set of variables. They find that countries which are close to the equator, do not speak an international language, have ineffective market supporting policies or are not open to international trade have low productivity. Let us consider some of the variables.

Government market supporting policies: Previous studies have used several variables to capture this aspect of nations' institutional framework. Barro (1991) used two variables measuring political instability: revolutions and coups, and assassinations. However, as discussed in Knack and Keefer (1995), these variables might not measure what we have in mind since they are only loosely correlated to the more general institutional environment. Instead we use other institutional indices: such as institutional variables from Business International as reported in the The Economist Intelligence Unit. In general, the effect of government policies can be of two kinds; either the government provides growth promoting public goods and designs taxes which close the gap between private and social costs, or, alternatively, the government waste funds and impose taxes and regulations that distort private decisions. Hence, the government may not only suppress diversion but often acts as the most effective diverter.

The indices from Business International (BI) are thought to proxy some general institutional variables. The numbers are obtained from Mauro (1995) who restricts his attention to nine different indicators of institutional efficiency which are all independent of macroeconomic variables and apply to both domestic and foreign firms. The BI indices range between 0 and 10, where a high value signifies "good" institutions. These nine indicators are grouped into two categories: political stability and bureaucratic efficiency. The political stability index contains the following six indicators: political change-institutional, political stability-social, probability of takeover by opposition group, stability of labor, relationship with neighboring countries, and terrorism. The bureaucratic efficiency index consists of three variables: judiciary system, red tape and bureaucracy, and corruption.

Openness: We include openness to international trade for two reasons; its relation to the diversion of resources from their free market allocation, and because international trade is a leading source of technology diffusion (Brakman et. al., 2006, Chap. 11). Levine and Renelt (1992) find that the relationship between trade and growth is mostly based on enhanced resource accumulation and not as much on improved resource allocation. Since we already include accumulation rates in the determination of efficiency levels, one might expect that openness will not be a significant determinant of relative productivity. Two measures of openness are used, the index compiled by Sachs and Warner (1997) and the measure of openness obtained from Summers and Heston(1991). The Sachs-Warner index measures the fraction of years during the period 1950 to 1994 that an economy has been considered open. A country is open if five criteria are satisfied: (1) non-tariff barriers cover less than 40 percent of trade, (2) average tariff rates are less than 40 percent, (3) any black market premium was less than 20 percent during the 1970s and 1980s, (4) the country is not socialist in its economy and (5) the government does not monopolize major exports (Sachs and Warner, 1997). As a simple index we only consider whether the country was classified as being open or closed during the 1960-85 period. The variable is numbers of years open during the sample period. The Summers and Heston openness variable is simply the fraction of imports and exports summed to GDP

Education: Since countries may be unproductive because their level of education does not allow for efficient use of resources and the adoption of new technology, we also include it in the regression. The significance of the level of education is likely to be affected by its use in the estimation of efficiency levels.

4.8. SOME RESULTS ON DETERMINANTS OF EFFICIENCY

We initially find the simple Pearson correlation coefficient of different indices to the levels of efficiency across countries (Table 4.1). The Economic Freedom index has a correlation of -0.77 to efficiency. Thus, as political and civil freedoms deteriorate (Freedom increases) efficiency falls. The political stability (PS) and bureaucratic efficiency (BE) indices have correlation coefficients of 0.72 and 0.80, respectively, which tells the same story. Regarding openness, the Sachs-Warner index has a correlation of 0.72, while the Summers-Heston index only has a correlation of 0.33. The openness result is therefore ambiguous. The average level of education is also highly correlated with efficiency having a correlation coefficient of 0.60. One problem with the simple correlations is that both the indices and my efficiency measures are highly correlated to log of per worker income.

After that we regress the institutional indices on efficiency. When regressing efficiency against average education and Freedom, highly significant positive and negative coefficients are obtained indicating again, that more human capital and political and civil rights make a country more efficient. When a measure of openness is added to the regression the same holds true. However, both the Sachs-Warner (S-W) and Summers-Heston (S-H) openness measures are insignificant but positive. Hence, the openness of a nation does not seem to make it significantly more efficient. As we add other institutional measures the level of education loses all its significance. Also, the BE variable is more significant than the Freedom index. The coefficient on political stability (PS) is not significantly different from zero. The reason why human capital acted as a proxy for bureaucratic efficiency is unclear.

A regression of all indices on efficiency gives the following result (numbers in parentheses are t-statistics and R^2 is 0.71) (Table 1).

$$\text{eff 1} = -1.40 + 0.0016\text{ED} - 0.95\text{FREED} + 0.009\text{PS} + 0.10\text{BE} + 0.004\text{SW} \qquad (4.35)$$
$$(-2.98) \quad (0.12) \quad (-3.03) \quad (0.14) \quad (2.39) \quad (0.69)$$

Table 4.1. Pearson Correlation Coefficient

	eff 1	eff 2	eff 3	eff4	Freed.	BE	PS	Educ	S-W	S-H
eff 1	1.00									
eff 2	0.97•	1.00								
eff 3	0.98•	0.96•	1.0							
eff4	0.97•	0.90	0.99•	1.00						
Freed.	-0.73•	-0.69•	-0.76•	-0.73•	1.00					
BE	0.78•	0.73•	0.82•	0.78•	-0.48•	1.00				
PS	0.63•	0.56'	0.75'	0.63•	-0.33•••	0.90•	1.00			
Educ.	0.61•	0.54•	0.60	0.61•	-0.48*	0.66•	0.48•	1.00		
5-W	0.62	0.47•	0.73•	0.62^1	-0.56•	0.58	0.52*	0.49•	1.0	
S-H	0.18**•	0.15	0.32*	0.18	0.01	0.33	0.24	0.22	0.29•	1.00

Note: * = significant at 1 percent level, ** = significant at 5 percent level, and *** = significant at 10 percent level. effl = estimated efficiencies using 5-year pooled data in regional estimations, eff2 = 5-year pooled data in estimation of entire sample, eff3 = annual data and entire sample, and eff4 = annual data in regional estimations. EM and eff4 exclude East Asia. Freedom = weighted average of Gastil's political and civil rights indices, BE = Bureaucratic efficiency, PS = Political stability, Educ. = Average Education, S-W = Sachs-Warner index of openness, S-H = Summers and Heston openness variable.

Discussion

Performing growth accounting with only the common factors of production is not sufficient to explain the growth process. This may not be true in the long-run, if we define the long-run to be when technology has diffused to all nations, and countries' rates of growth are functions of input accumulation. However, this steady state story does not hold presently as countries are different in levels of technology. We therefore see a need to model these heterogeneities. The model derived contains three growth effects in addition to varying accumulation rates. Each nation is faced with a technology gap approximated by the difference to the leader in per worker output which can increase the productivity of capital. This is interpreted as the catching-up potential described in Abramovitz (1986). Also, we include heterogeneous absorption capacities, e, and adoption rates, ρ, in the growth term:
$\rho[\ln Y^L - \ln Y - e]$. Thus a nation might not take advantage of the catch-up potential if it either fails to adopt foreign technology ($\rho = 0$) or technology absorption is seriously compromised due to the nation's level of inefficiency. The new model provides a mechanism for explaining why some countries forge ahead while others fall behind, while maintaining all the steady state predictions of the neoclassical model.

Estimations of the model developed here yields results comparable to previous research as well as significant country heterogeneities and regional adoption rates. Consider, as a rough example, average results for our three regions. Europe, Latin America, and East Asia faced on average a technology gap, $\ln Y^L - \ln Y$, of 0.58, 0.71 and 0.82, respectively, over the 1960-2000 period. These catch-up potentials are compromised by inefficiencies. From this adjusted catch-up potential, $Y^L - \ln Y - e$, the region's countries benefit according to their adoption rates. In terms of annual growth over this period, East Asia has taken advantage of its catch-up potential even with its lower technology adoption rates, while EU -Europe and Latin America have done less well. Also, East Asia had higher accumulation rates than Europe, while Latin America struggled in this aspect as well. This could explain the regions varied post-war performance.

Another way to discuss the findings is in terms of catch-up times. We found the required times for the nations to catch-up with both their inefficiency frontier and to the leader's frontier, the latter requiring declining inefficiency levels. Europe and East Asia have mostly caught up with their inefficiency frontier, while Latin America is still approaching theirs. Thus, unless Europe and East Asia reduce their inefficiency levels, they must rely on higher accumulation rates to continue to catch-up with the United States. Another option for the regions is to become relatively more efficient. We show that the institutional framework is likely to be important in achieving this improved efficiency. In particular, it was found that the bureaucratic efficiency index and the index of political and civil rights are the main explanations for nation's different levels of productivity. However, political stability and levels of education do not seem to be as important for the determining efficiency, although they are certainly crucial in the overall growth process as shown elsewhere.

We should be sensitive to the fact that the results one obtains from the aggregated data can only point toward possible explanations for the fundamental reasons behind cross-country growth differences. Given this disclaimer, there emerge some clear policy implications. First of all, technology diffusion is an important source of growth of follower nations. Furthermore, countries seem to differ significantly in their ability to take advantage of newer and better technology. Thus, in general, any policy that allows follower nations to better adopt foreign technology should increase their growth rate, at least in the short-run. Since the difference in technology adoption appears to be related to a nation's institutional efficiency, observations suggest that governments are well-advised to pursue policies that increase the efficiency of markets. That is, improved technology adoption is an added motivation for the pursuit of efficient institutions. For example, consider two follower nations that face identical initial technology gaps. Their growth paths will be very different according to their ability to close this technology gap. If a nation does not incorporate foreign technology into their production it will have to rely solely on accumulation of factor inputs as a source of growth. If, on the other hand, the economy adopts better technology, then rapid growth is expected until the technology gap is removed, at which time the nation is left with factor accumulation or the coming up with new ideas as the sources of growth. However, the latter state will be richer (i.e. more productive) at all points in time.

To conclude this argument, higher income can be achieved not only from increases in the savings rate, the neoclassical prediction, but also from institutional change. The institutional framework of countries cannot be ignored in any attempt to explain cross-country growth. But little could be said in the aggregate about the role of each specific institution. One interesting line of exploring would be, if specific institutional rigidities lead to inefficiencies which cause heterogeneous rates to catch-up. Thus, if several countries with a similar resource endowments and technical capabilities would have similar growth, and some country would introduce a lower tax regime and effective anti-corruption instruments , will then this country outperform its peers by how much and on a sustainable basis? Thus, given the available technology, the efficient use of factor inputs will depend on tax structure, regulations, education, infrastructure, and political and social rights. In addition, given the institutional environment, adoption of more productive technologies increases the production efficiency of nations and this diffusion of expertise depends on factors such as distance from the source country, language, as well as trade barriers.

This chapter has addressed several important issues related to the growth and performance of nations. We discussed and provided tools to analyze patterns of catching up, falling behind and getting ahead that are identified with aggregate technological racing among nations or regional economic entities. In Section 4.3 a structural model was constructed of the Solow type based on capital accumulation rates but extended to include the impact of technology adoption. In the model adoption of technology becomes one possible mechanism through which the effective capital stock may increase.

The impact of social institutions arises by allowing the potential technology gap to be modified by them. The resulting model only slightly modifies the steady state and rates of convergence predicted by a conventional neoclassical model. However, it allows for more complex growth dynamics, including non-random relative income shifts while maintaining a high degree of tractability. This model accomplishes the goal of reconciling the neoclassical model with slow technology diffusion and institutional variations as outlined in approaches to economic development. In identifying technological racing among countries, model predictions and empirical observations indicate that follower countries, in striving for catching up, significantly benefit from the technology gap to the leader and that adoption rates vary between them. This variance could be mostly contributed to the 'social capabilities' of those countries that demonstrate various 'efficiency levels' of adoption promoted by bureaucratic efficiency (including a low level of corruption) and democratic rights (Economist, 2005) though it is naturally difficult and needs further research to pinpoint the specific types of institutions that act 'as driving forces behind countries' inefficiencies and some of the institutional factors may show some tradeoff pattern between them, thus limiting the net impact of each of them. A good case in point is Latin America which carries relatively high adoption rates but overall the region fails to take advantage of its potential because of poor political and social institutions. Other interesting cases relate to Japan, Korea and the emergence of economic rivalry between China and India (Economist, 2005; North, 2005). A similar case pointing to institutional inertia relates to divergences in EU Europe (Baily and Kirkegaard, 2004).

Unlike tracing technological rivalry among corporations and industrial entities with clearly defined market conditions the results one obtains from the aggregated data can only point toward 'more aggregate' explanations for the factors behind cross-country growth processes. Yet, a few key factors could be singled out. First of all, we can conclude that technology diffusion is an important source of growth of follower nations. Furthermore, countries seem to differ significantly in their ability to take advantage of newer and better technology. Thus, in general, any policy that allows follower nations to better adopt foreign technology should increase their growth rate, at least in the short-run. Since the difference in technology adoption appears to be related to a nation's institutional efficiency, research suggests that governments are well-advised to pursue policies that increase the efficiency of markets, i.e. foster competition, combat corruption, decrease the extent of regulation in full compliance with true market externalities, through improvement of the quality of enforcement and low income (private and corporate) taxation. Further, we would subscribe to Barro's (1997) cross country survey showing that democracy is positively correlated with growth at low levels of development, negatively correlated with growth of transitory economies, and again highly correlated with advanced, high level per capita GDP economies.

Improved technology adoption is an added motivation for the pursuit of efficient institutions. For example, consider two follower nations that face identical initial technology gaps. Their growth paths will be very different according to their ability to close this technology gap. If a nation does not incorporate foreign technology into their production it will have to rely solely on accumulation of factor inputs as a source of growth. If, on the other hand, the economy adopts better technology, then rapid growth is expected until the technology gap is removed, at which time the nation is left with factor accumulation or the coming up with new ideas as the sources of growth. However, the latter nation will be richer and more productive at all points in time. To conclude this argument, higher income can be achieved not only from increases in the savings rate, the neoclassical prediction, but also from institutional change.

REFERENCES

Abramovitz, M. (1986), 'Catching Up, Forging Ahead, and Falling Behind' „Journal of Economic History, 46, 385-406

Amsden, A.H. (2001), 'The Rise of "The Rest" . Challenges to the West from Late Industrializing Economies', Oxford, Oxford Univ. Press

Aghion, P. and R.Griffith (2005), Competition and Growth, Cambridge, MIT Press

Bailey, M. and J. Kirkegaard (2004), 'The Landlocked Continent', *The Wall Street Journal* , December 6

Barro, R.J., (1991) 'Economic Growth in A Cross Section of Countries,' *Quarterly Journal of Economics*, 106, 407-443

Barro, R. J., (1994) 'Democracy and Growth', NBER Working Papers # 4909

Barro, R.J. (1997), Determinants of Economic Growth: A Cross-Country Empirical Study, Cambridge, Ma: The MIT Press

Baumol,W.J., Blackman, S.A. and E.N. Wolff (1992), Productivity and American Leadership: The Long View, Cambridge, MIT Press

Baumol, W. (2002), The Free Market Innovation Machine , Analyzing the Growth Miracle of Capitalism, Princeton, Princeton Univ. Press

Benhabib,J. and M.M. Spiegel (1994), 'The Role of Human Capital in Economic Development: Evidence from Aggregate Cross-Country Data', *Journal of Monetary Economics* 34, 143-173

Brakman,St., Garretsen,H., Van Marrewijk,Ch. And A. van Witteloostuijn (2006), Nations and Firms in the Global Economy, Cambridge, Cambridge Univ. Press

Chen, Derek H.C. and H.L. Kee (2005),' A Model on Knowledge and Endogenous Growth', World Bank Policy Research Working Paper 3539, March, 1-24

Denicolo,V. and P. Zanchettin (2006), 'Competition, Darwinian Selection and Growth', mimeo, Dept. of Economics, Univ. of Bologna, May 26, 1-47

Economist, The (2005), 'The tiger in front. A Survey of India and China., March 5 , 3-16

Eggertsson, Th., (1990) Economic Behavior and Institutions, Cambridge: Cambridge University Press

Etro,F. (2008), 'Growth Leaders', Journal of Macroeconomics 30, 1148-1172

Fagerberg,J. and M.M. Godinho (2004), 'Innovation and Catching-Up', Chap. 20 in Handbook of Innovation, Oxford, Blackwell

Grossman, Gene and Elhanan Helpman, (1991) Innovation and Growth in the Global Economy, Cambridge, Ma: MIT Press

Hall, R. E. and Ch. I. Jones, (1996) ,'The Productivity of Nations,' NBER Working Papers #5812

Hirschman,A.O. (1958), The Strategy of Economic Development, New Haven: Yale Univ.Press

Knack, S. and P. Keefer, (1995) 'Institutions and Economic Performance: Cross-Country Tests Using Alternative Institutional Measures', *Economics and Politics* 7, 207-227

Juma,C. and N. Clark (2002),'Technological Catch-Up: Opportunities and Challenges for Developing Countries', SUPRA Occasional Paper, Research Centre for the Social Sciences, University of Edinburgh ,February

Krugman, P. (1997), 'Myths and Realities of U.S. Competitiveness', Chap. 6 in P. Krugman, Pop Internationalism, Cambridge, MA: MIT Press

Levine, R. and D. Renelt, (1992) 'A Sensitivity Analysis of Cross-Country Growth Regressions', American Economic Review 82(4), 942-963

Lucas, R. E. Jr., (1988) 'On the Mechanics of Economic Development', *Journal of Monetary Economics*, 22, 3-42.

Lucas, R. E. Jr., (1993) 'Making a Miracle', Econometrica, 61(2), 251-272

Mankiw, N. Gregory, Romer, David and David N. Weil, (1992) 'A Contribution to the Empirics of Economic Growth', *Quarterly Journal of Economics*, 107, 407-437.

Mauro, P. (1995) 'Corruption and Growth', *Quarterly Journal of Economics*,110, . 681-712.

Murphy, K.M., A. Shleifer, and R.W. Vishny (1989), 'Industrialization and the Big Push', *Journal of Political Economy* 97, pp.1003-1026

North, D. C. (2005), 'The Chinese Menu (for Development)', *The Wall Street Journal* , April 7

Nurkse,R. (1952), 'Some International Aspects of the Problem of Economic Development', American Economic Review, 42, 571-583

Nurkse, R.(1953), Problems of Capital Formation in Underdeveloped Countries, Oxford: Basil Blackwell

Olson, M. (1996), The Rise and Decline of Nations: Economic Growth, Stagflation, and Social Rigidities, New Haven: Yale University Press.

Parente, St.L. and E. C. Prescott, (2004) ,'What a Country Must Do to Catch-Up to the Industrial Leaders', mimeo, Federal Reserve Bank of Minneapolis

Parente, St.L. and E. C. Prescott, (1994) 'Barriers to Technology Adoption and Development', *Journal of Political Economy*, 102(2), 298-321.

Pritchett, L.(1997) 'Divergence, Big Time', Journal of Economic Perspectives, 11, 3-17.

Romer, P. M., (1986) 'Increasing Returns and Long-Run Growth', *Journal of Political Economy*, 94, 1002-1037.

Romer, P. M.,(1990)'Endogenous Technological Change', *Journal of Political Economy*, 98, S71-S 102.

Rosenstein-Rodan,P.N. (1943), 'Problems of Industrialisation of Eastern and Southeastern Europe', *Economic Journal* 53, 202-211

Rosenstein-Rodan, P.N.(1961),'Notes on the Theory of the "Big Push" ', in Economic Development for Latin America, H.S. Ellis and H.C.Wallich, eds, New York: St. Martin's

Rostow, W. W. (1960), The Stages of Economic Growth, Cambridge: Cambridge Univ. Press

Sachs, J. D. and A. Warner, (1997) 'Fundamental Sources of Long-Run Growth,'American Economic Review Papers and Proceedings, May,184-188.

Segerstrom, P.S. (2007), 'Intel Economics', *International Economic Review* 48(1), 247–280.

Scully, G. W, (1988) 'The Institutional Framework and Economic Development', *Journal of Political Economy*, 92(3), 652-662.

Solow, Robert M., (1956) 'A Contribution to the Theory of Economic Growth', *Quarterly Journal of Economics*, 70, 65-94.

Solow, Robert M. (1957) 'Technical Change and the Aggregate Production Function', Review of Economics and Statistics, 39, 312-320.

Summers, R. and A. Heston, (1991) 'The Penn World Table (Mark 5.0): Expanded Set of International Comparisons, 1950-1988,' *Quarterly Journal of Economics,* 106(2),327-368.

Streeten, P.,(1956), 'Unbalanced Growth', Oxford Economic Papers,167-190

Wan, H.Y. (2004), Economic Development in a Globalized Environment, East Asian Evidence, Dordrecht, Kluwer

Young, A. (1995) 'The Tyranny of Numbers: Confronting the Statistical Realities of the East Asian Growth Experience', *Quarterly Journal of Economics*, 110, 641-680.

Zeira, J. (2005), 'Innovations, Patents and Economic Growth', mimeo, Hebrew Univ. of Jerusalem and CEPR, July, 1-34

Chapter 5

URBAN ECONOMIC GROWTH AND DEVELOPMENT

Hans W. Gottinger

5.1. INTRODUCTION

Theories of economic growth highlight the forces considered important for characterizing relative aggregate growth. In addition to the more traditional adjustment factors such as changes in relative prices, the capital-labor ratio and productivity, more recent economic theories have emphasised the importance of externalities in driving economic expansion. In particular, externalities may arise from the geographic proximity of production centers (Krugman, 2007). Empirical analysis attempting to understand the role of any of these factors in growth must control for the effect of other externality-based sources in addition to the more traditional adjustment factors.

In this chapter issues are addressed in analyzing relative aggregate (i.e. city based) growth for a cross section of East/South-East Asian cities. A methodology is employed by which the patterns of correlation can be described between individual growth sources and measures of aggregate growth. An analysis is made of how potential interactions between individual sources alter the observed correlations. Since externalities can be considered explicity, both negative and positive, i.e. those that are likely to constrain the city's growth as environmental pressures, demographic changes and congestion, as compared to those that promote them through positive network effects of scale and scope. Making this tradeoff would enable a community to strive for 'sustainable'growth, as growth internalized by externalities (Gottinger, 1998).

The methodology employed in this chapter was to categorise the sources that are predicted to vary with growth and to establish empirical proxies for these variables. Then, in order to consider properly the effects of externality-based variables, an explicit distinction was made in the empirical analysis between productivity, labor and capital growth. In so doing, it was possible to identify whether particular externality-based variables influence aggregate growth through specific pathways rather than focussing on output per capita only.

In departing from much of the conventional growth literature the city was chosen as the relevant unit of observation, in fact, we consider urban growth as a major precursor to national GDP growth in fast growing East Asian economies. There is clear empirical evidence in the contemporary Chinese economy that coastal city growth had a deep impact on accelerating national income growth .Wei (2000), and Young (1992) considered city growth as a precursor to national growth. In the present case data was used from the period from 1960 to 2000, which was marked by significant change and intercity variation among towns, to estimate a multiple equation growth system

This chapter focusses on sustainable growth of contemporary large major Asian cities from several East Asian and South-East Asisian countries: Japan, China, Korea, Malaysia, Singapore, and Thailand. The study covers factors of growth in a multiequation econometric (regression) model, subject to sensitivity analysis. The cities covered were: Tokyo, Seoul, Osaka (as North); Beijing, Shanghai, Hongkong (as Central); and Kuala Lumpur, Singapore, Bangkok (as South). This initial first choice was made foremost on consideration of the need for a geographical balance and comparable size where those cities created regional/national centers. Also accessibility of sufficient data on a time frame of 40 years was a consideration. In a first examination census data were taken for every ten years so that with a selection of 9 cities 36 observations were made. Additional census years were incorporated to improve forecasting ability. No single theory appeared to explain, in a consistent way, the observed growth in the period.

This chapter is organized as follows. The next section, Sec. 5.2, puts the methodology in context with other empirical approaches , categorizes these sources and link them to various empirical proxies. These categories include aggregates for geographic externalities such as urbanization, localization and specialization. Sec. 5.3 develops a classification scheme for the various sources of growth as predicted by existing theories. The econometric framework is laid out in Sec. 5.4. Next Secs. 5.5 and 5.6 discuss empirical results. We find that several traditional and geographic externalities as well as socio-political factors all covary significantly with aggregate growth though in very specific ways. For example, the size of a city (a measure of the degree of urbanization) is uncorrelated with output growth, positively correlated with labor growth and negatively correlated with capital growth.

5.2. Growth in Cities: Methodology and Approach

A first important feature of our approach was to concentrate on cities per se as a driver of growth rather than as derivative features of the economies of each national state. Metropolitan regions are a natural geographic unit for fiscal analysis as regional economic life is primarily organized around city centers. In choosing this focus we follow a group of researchers who have argued that economic development can be better understood by examining cities independent of their cultural, ethnic and national background. Earlier, Jacobs (1969, 1984) and Porter (1990) both presented strong historical cases for the appropriateness of studying cities as opposed to nations in exploring the sources of growth. This emphasis has also emerged in more formal empirical studies. For example, Glaeser et al (1992, 1994) focused on the role of dynamic externalities, including measures of competition, urbanization and diversity, in explaining the growth of city-industry labor demand. Other studies have examined aggregate regional or city growth (Blanchard and Katz, 1992; Henderson, 1994, 2005; Barro and Sala-i-Martin, 2003, Henderson and Thisse, 2004), further in a cross-atlantic comparative framework by Savitch and Kantor (2004). Cuberes (2004) developed a growth model with increasing returns to scale that showed evidence of leapfrogging. More recently, Cuberes (2008), termed 'Sequential City Growth', showed convincingly that catch-up and jumps sequentially also apply to cities and metropolitan regions across country and cultural boundaries. Statistical representations of cities' growth rates derive from the effective growth potential of their countries' development path.

The starting point of our investigation is two fundamental pathways by which aggregate growth can occur: factor accumulation (increases in the levels of capital and labor operating within a region) and productivity growth (increases in the production capabilities of given levels of capital and labor). These pathways can be written down in the following form:

$$g_{Q,t} = \phi_c (g_{A,t}, g_{K,t}, g_{L,t}) \tag{5.1}$$

or

$$\ln [Q_{c,t+1}/Q_{c,t}] = \phi_c \{ \ln [A_{c,t+1}/A_{c,t}], \ln [K_{c,t+1}/K_{c,t}], \ln [L_{c,t+1}/L_{c,t}] \} \tag{5.2}$$

where $Q_{c,t}$, $A_{c,t}$, $K_{c,t}$ and $L_{c,t}$ denote the levels of output, productivity, capital and labor, respectively, in region c, at time t, and ϕ_c is a nondecreasing function of the growth rates in capital, labor and productivity. Differences in growth rates will therefore be a function of the magnitudes of factor accumulation and productivity growth rates in each region. That is:

$$g_{Q,1} - g_{Q,2} = \phi_1(g_{A,1}, g_{K,1}, g_{L,1}) - \phi_2(g_{A,2}, g_{K,2}, g_{L,2}) \tag{5.3}$$

The growth rates of capital, labor and productivity growth may themselves be functions of economic variables. Identifying those variables which affect factor accumulation and productivity expansion is the primary step. Relative labour and capital growth are functions of the incentives for movement that face workers and investors and, also, of the incentives to supply more of those factors. A first item to recognize is that labor and capital growth is interdependent.

Labor and capital may be technological complements in production and the incentives facing decision-makers may be highly correlated (e.g., a region which experiences a positive shock may become more attractive to both workers and investors even if there are technological substitutes in production). Also, prices will induce movements of capital and labor to the highest rents and wages, respectively. The relative factor mix (the capital-labor ratio) might reflect the relative marginal productivities of capital and labor, and thus the incentives for factor movements. Finally, a variety of production externalities may operate at the industry, regional, or economy-wide level that affect incentives influencing the location of factors (agglomeration economies) as well as their qualities (social externalities) all as part of increasing returns mechanisms as identified and further explored in Chap. 6. The growth of labor or capital, then, is potentially dependent on input prices, the factor mix, and the presence of particular externalities.

After controlling for input growth, the remaining share of output growth can be attributed to output development. Productivity growth arises from technical and organisational change as well as the exploitation of economies of scale or scope. A principal means by which regional productivity expansion may occur is through the adoption of more fruitful techniques from other regions. With ongoing interaction among regions the implication is that there is a tendency for productivity growth rates across regions to converge. Correspondingly, there may be a tendency toward 'adaptive efficiency' in economic institutions (North, 2004). Adoption may also occur within regions and within regional industries. Furthermore, local knowledge spillovers can result in a positive relationship between the growth rate of productivity and these local externalities.

5.3. Empirical Relations in Urban Growth

In modeling the sources of urban growth one would like to include as many theoretical correlative predictions as possible under an empirical framework. To this end it is useful, by reviewing the literature, to group the phenomena we want to address into three categories: traditional economic factors, geographic production externalities, and other external factors.

Traditional Economic Factors

From its early origins the neoclassical growth model has provided sharp predictions on the effects that relative factor prices, factor utilization and productivity levels have on relative growth rates (Solow, 1957; King and Rebelo, 1993). Factor prices and factor accumulation should be positively correlated, as higher wages and rents attract more labor and capital. Relative factor utilization should engender opposing effects on relative labour and capital growth. Capital-intensive cities will induce more labour inflows than less capital-intensive cities. The primary reason for this is that the marginal productivity of labor is higher in a capital-intensive area. Conversely, cities which are highly labor-intensive will attract more new capital. Finally, there is a tendency for productivity growth rates across regions to converge (Barro and Sala-i-Martin, 2003, Rhode and Toniolo, 2006). The principal empirical implication of the traditional convergence hypothesis is that the relative level of productivity is negatively correlated with the growth rate in productivity.

These traditional economic variables are easily represented by city level aggregate measures. The average prices of labor and capital and the aggregate capital-labour ratio can proxy for the factor prices and the factor utilization level which affect individual incentives for movement and accumulation of assets and labour. Also, measures of productivity, such as output per worker, provide empirical representations for productivity differentials. These aggregate measures are employed in empirical work.

Geographic Production Externalities

Additional determinants of the rate of input and productivity growth emerge when one considers the potential role of externalities that resemble 'networks' (Gottinger, 2003). Relative urban growth can be tied to production externalities that arise from geographical proximity and a variety of approaches have been used to characterize them. These varied approaches have been compressed into three general categories: urbanization (URB), localization (LOC), and specialization (SPEC).

Economies of Urbanization: Size and breadth of urban regions have been thought to generate potentially important externalities that affect the growth of both inputs and productivity. Economic theories based on such ideas predict positive correlations between relative growth rates and relative measures of city size. For example, the decision to immigrate to a town may be affected by expected fluctuations in the employment environment. It has been widely recognized that larger urban areas are more attractive to immigrants because they offer a reduced risk of unemployment during downturns. A large local economy may also stabilise the demand for intermediate goods, thereby providing additional investment incentives for suppliers of these goods. Furthermore, others have argued that the size of an urban region may affect productivity in one of two ways. First, the potential for local interindustry knowledge spillovers may cause the rate of technological change and adoption to be positively related to the size of an urban region. Second, a dense economy may reduce production costs directly through the proximity of producers to inputs and a large market. All externality-based effects that result from city size can be classified as urbanization economies.

As with the traditional variables, there exist obvious aggregate city-level variables which measure a city's degree of urbanization. In fact, various measures of aggregate economic activity in our estimations were utilized. These included total population, total levels of output and employment, and past population growth (to capture expected local demand) with a particular city.

Economies of Localization: Localization is the degree to which an industry's economic activity takes place in one or a small number of geographical areas. Under this notion, some high technology industry has been linked to externalities which operate at the city-industry level. It has been long thought that productivity growth in a city-industry is positively correlated with the degree of localization in that city industry. As the share of an industry's employment in a particular location increases, intraindustry knowledge spillovers also increase (Porter, 1990). Since local intraindustry knowledge spillovers are a source of industry productivity growth (Beckmann, 1999), localization thus promotes such growth. Factor input growth is also predicted to be positively related with localisation. By lowering the unemployment risk of specialised workers and reducing employer monopsony (i.e. single buyer) power over wages, localized industries foster labour force growth as part of an increasing returns mechanism (Krugman, 2007). Furthermore, specialized capital, as supplied by nontradable intermediate input and service providers, is attracted to localized industries because of the advantageous bargaining position resulting from numerous potential outside opportunities. Each of these effects can be classified as an 'economy of localization'.

Localization's impact upon aggregate city level variables differs qualitatively from that of urbanization or the traditional variables in that its force upon the economy results from its effects upon those industries which are localized. As the number of city-industries which are localised increases, and as the relative size of those industries increases, the aggregate growth benefits to localization will increase. To capture this empirically, it is useful to distinguish those city-industries which are localized from those that are not. This is accomplished by determining some threshold share of national employment a city-industry would need to utilize to be considered localised. For example, if the threshold share for industry X is 10 percent of employment nationally, industry X would need to employ more than 10 percent of national employment in its industry to be considered localized. A city's measure of localization, then, would be the share of its employment contained in localized industries.

Economies of Specialization: This type of economy refers to the degree to which a city's output is dominated by a single or a number of closely related sectors. Specialization, a city-level concept, differs from localization in that it deals directly with a city's sectoral composition. The largest ties to factor growth come through its effects on risk. Specialized cities are especially vulnerable to business cycles – particularly on the downside. When a negative shock occurs in a dominant city-industry, these cities do not have the industrial diversity to absorb labour and capital losses in the dominant industry.

During downturns specialized cities may be subject to particularly high rates of capital and labour outflows and relative productivity decreases (Jacobs, 1984) In addition, the level (as opposed to the growth) of productivity has been positively linked to specialisation. As the division of labour between cities increases, productivity can be increased through trade. Such cities may have higher levels of productivity due to their exploitation of comparative advantage. Moreover, these cities will likely have public infrastructure tailored to serve dominant industries, decreasing production costs and increasing the level of productivity (Arthur, 1988). As these are levels rather than growth effects, though, they suggest no relation between specialisation and productivity growth given our growth equation framwork. We classify the effects on growth which result directly from a city's sectoral composition as economies of specialization.

Empirical measures of specialization must capture the degree to which a city is concentrated in a small number of sectors. A slightly modified Herfindahl index, widely used in the industrial organization literature to measure the level of concentration of a particular industry, is well suited to measure the business concentration of a particular city. The Herfindahl index for urban specialization utilized in the empirical work is given by:

$$SPEC_{c,t} = \Sigma_i^I (L_{i,t} / L_{c,t}) \qquad (5.4)$$

where I is the total number of industries. It is useful to note that we can measure specialization with respect to inputs or outputs (i.e., the specialization of output, employment, or the capital stock). To measure the specialization of output or the capital stock, the city-share of each industry's employment in the specialization equation would be replaced by the city-share of each industry's output or the industry's capital stock, respectively.

Other External Effects

There are a number of other external effects that can potentially influence expansion. As previously reviewed in Chapters 3 and 4, the growth and development literature (Van den Berg, 2001) has focussed on a number of other externalities that potentially affect growth. We examine briefly three types of externalities that have been extensively discussed among those effects considered important for aggregate development. First, the positive role that the level of human capital plays in spurring growth has been emphasized by Lucas (1988) and Romer (1990, 1992); Human capital investment can be leveraged into knowledge spillovers which lead to higher productivity growth. Second, the presence of appropriable returns from innovation has been identified as a critical, though controversial, ingredient in fostering factor input and productivity increase.

Finally, there is a focus on the role of political and social variables in growth. Government expenditure and taxation produce important shifts of incentives for factor input movement through tax policy and the like, (Barro, 1990), and the level and growth of productivity through the provision of public goods and the coordination of legal norms and standards. The precise direction of these shifts is dependent on the nature of the policy provision in question. The most negative ones could be described by transportation congestion, various sorts of pollution, and degradation effects through overbuilding and degenerated land use. Such effects can be parametrized as critical levels for an aggregate (SOC). It is difficult to attain aggregate empirical proxies for many of these variables or, in some cases, to even predict their aggregate impact.

Educational expenditures (or achievement) are potentially empirical proxies for human capital accumulation. Unfortunately, such expenditure information on a city basis is not available over this time period for quite a number of cities. Competition, in contrast, is difficult to characterize empirically, even at the industry level. Government policy proxies, on the other hand, are readily available. City-level data for government expenditures, revenues, and tax rates, can be obtained so the impact of these policies can be evaluated statistically.

5.4. ECONOMETRIC FRAMEWORK

This brief review and empirical classification of the urban growth debate serves as source and motivation for the econometric-statistical framework. The potential role of each of these variables on both input and productivity growth is emphasized. An attempt is made to be as inclusive and as precise as possible in the construction of empirical measures for the underlying effects in the study. The empirical framework assumes that for a particular city, the increase in output is a nondecreasing function of the growth rates of each of the determinants of total output in each period. Additionally, each of the variables on the right-hand side of the growth Equation (1) is potentially governed by the other economic variables which have been identified earlier. In other words, the growth system can be summarized by foccusing on the following four equation system for each c:

$$g_{Q(t)} = \phi_c (g_{A(t)}, g_{K(t)}, g_{L(t)}) \tag{5.5}$$

$$g_{K(t)} = G_K (g_{A(t)}, g_{L(t)}, K(t)/L(t), SPEC(t), LOC(t), URB(t), SOC(t), \text{interest rate, others}, \varepsilon_{K(t)}) \tag{5.6}$$

$$g_{L(t)} = G_L (g_{K(t)}, g_{A(t)}, K(t)/L(t), SPEC(t), LOC(t), URB(t), SOC(t), \text{wages, others}, \varepsilon_{L(t)}) \tag{5.7}$$

$$g_{A(t)} = G_A (Q(t)/L(t), SPEC(t), LOC(t), URB(t), SOC(t), \text{scale economies, others}, \varepsilon_{A(t)}) \quad (5.8)$$

Unfortunately, even if the precise functional form for each of Equations 5.5 to 5.8 was known, this system is underidentified due to the absence of a direct measure of productivity or productivity growth. However, the system can be rewritten as a structural model of city growth in the absence of direct information on productivity growth:

$$g_{Q(t)} = \phi_c (g_{K(t)}, g_{L(t)} , Q(t)/L(t), SPEC(t), LOC(t), URB(t), SOC(t), \text{scale economies, others}, \varepsilon_{A(t)}) \quad (5.9)$$

$$g_{K(t)} = G_K (g_{A(t)}, g_{L(t)} , K(t)/L(t), SPEC(t), LOC(t), URB(t), SOC(t), \text{interest rate, others}, \varepsilon_{K(t)}) \quad (5.10)$$

$$g_{L(t)} = G_L (g_{K(t)}, g_{A(t)}, K(t)/L(t), SPEC(t), LOC(t), URB(t), SOC(t), \text{wages, others}, \varepsilon_{L(t)}) \quad (5.11)$$

The main task is then to adjust the data set in the context of this three equation system; Equations 5.9 – 5.11. Within this system we are interested in identifying the most salient and robust multivariate correlations which exist in the data. From this identification, initial evaluations can be made of individual theories of growth. This will provide insights into the creation of a unified framework for understanding and discussing growth. In consideration of the small sample size, each of the equations can be estimated separately. This increases the precision, allowing for a sharper examination of the main sources of variation. In addition, to make the exposition of the econometric work a little easier, the presentation was restricted to growth measures which utilise first differences of the log of output, capital, and labour as dependent variables.

The above equation system will proceed along a broad Ordinary Least Squares (OLS) specification. There will be a number of alternate regression specifications, including both instrumental variable and reduced form estimates to explore important potential regularities more closely. These additional tests also serve to demonstrate the degree to which qualitative results concerning the conditional correlation are robust to numerous functional forms.

5.5. EMPIRICAL EVIDENCE

The relevant observables and proxies for the variables discussed in the previous section were constructed from datasets of national as well as OECD statistics, covering the period 1960 to 2000, and recent data-analytic research on East Asian cities by Asian Development Bank (2008) and World Bank (Shahid and Nabashima, 2006). The statistics for the countries concerned, allowed for a compilation of a breakdown of manufacturing inputs and outputs by city industry. The number of operating firms was obtained and the recalculated dollar value of output for every city-industry was included. It was thus possible to compute value-added per city industry. The aggregate statistics for the manufacturing sector for each year included the levels of capital, employment, total labour income, and value added. From this information various agregate city statistics were constructed for the levels and growth rates of value-added, capital, employment and wages. The city output, employment and capital-labour ratios were also computed. Additionally, measures of geographic externality variables were constructed, as described previously. Finally, city-level data were gathered on population (Pop), population growth (PopG), government expenditures (GovEx) and taxation rates.

All regression results referred to are summarized in Tables 5.1 to 5.4 which show the results of regressions for Equations 5.9 to 5.11 using various combinations of right-hand side variables. We begin by presenting a broad Ordinary Least Squares (OLS) specification. The task is to explore, first in a preliminary way, the three equation system. Each equation is estimated separately to increase the precision. So that the general structure of conditional correlation is clear, OLS estimates are presented initially from exhaustive linear specifications of the output, capital, and labour growth equations (Table 5.1). Not surprisingly, these rich specifications account for much of the growth variance in the sample (adjusted $R^2 > 0.84$ in each equation). However, only a few variables in each equation are statistically significant. This is partially due to high correlations among regressors, as discussed above (Table 5.2), suggesting that approximately the same amount of variance could be captured by a drastically reduced set of regressors.

Table 5.1. OLS Estimates from exhaustive linear specifications of the Output, Capital and Labour Growth Equations (standard errors in parentheses)

	Output Growth	Dependent Variables (log) Capital Growth	Labour Growth
North	3.2985	3.4415	2.5141
	(0.6845)	(0.8248)	(0.75551)
Central	3.3325	3.4756	3.5251
	(0.6905)	(0.8300)	(0.7595)
South	3.1856	3.5236	3.3864
	(0.6919)	(0.8187)	(0.7613)
LG (log)	0.7878	0.8820	
	(0.0857)	(0.0623)	
CG (log)	0.1894		0.7927
	(0.0850)		(0.0650)
OLR(log)	−0.8552		
	(0.1614)		
CLR(log)		−0.5483	0.4623
		(0.0782)	(0.0798)
RelW(log)	0.2060	0.0560	0.1009
	(0.1667)	(0.1202)	(0.1135)
LOC.	0.0529	0.2691	−0.2838
	(0.1294)	(0.1387)	(0.1306)
SPEC.	−0.5088	−0.4626	0.4027
	(0.2262)	(0.2388)	(0.2275)
Pop.(log)	0.0199	−0.0586	0.0576
	(0.0242)	(0.0275)	(0.0265)
PopG(log)	0.1200	0.2164	−0.0944
	(0.0752)	(0.0790)	(0.0783)
GovEx(log)	0.0164	0.0611	−0.0888
	(0.0410)	(0.0453)	(0.0422)
Ttax	0.0274	0.0033	0.0215
	(0.0250)	(0.0281)	(0.0265)
AdjR2	0.857351	0.856247	0.842605

Significance at 5 pc. level

Table 5.2. Covariance Matrix

	Outp.Gth	Cap.Gth	Lab.Gth	OLR	CLR	Local.	Pop	Spec	PopG	Wage	Gov.Exp.
Outp.Gth	1.000										
Cap.Gth	0.8642	1.000									
Lab.Gth	0.8941	0.8638	1.000								
OLR	0.1966	0.4290	0.4316	1.000							
CLR	−0.0845	−0.1863	0.0609	0.3416	1.000						
LOC.	−0.2769	−0.2594	−0.3245	−0.1155	0.0506	1.000					
Pop.	−0.0524	−0.0656	−0.1098	0.0722	−0.0881	0.5000	1.000				
SPEC.	−0.1701	−0.1942	−0.1884	−0.3560	0.0721	0.5018.	−0.1471	1.000			
PopG	0.2196	0.3653	0.2300	0.3228	0.0021	−0.0396	−0.0448	0.0264	1.000		
Wage	0.1949	0.3671	0.3779	0.8644	0.2461	−0.1052	0.0874	−0.3420	0.2575	1.000	
Gov.Ex.	−0.2435	−0.2201	−0.2834	−0.0543	−0.0767	0.4238	0.4139	0.0624	−0.1008	0.0753	1.000

Table 5.3. Exclusion of Externality Based Variables (standard errors in parentheses)

	Output Growth	Capital Growth	Labour Growth
North	2.9102	4.5702	−3.9684
	(0.5624)	(0.6596)	(0.7657)
Central	2.9100	4.5816	−3.9756
	(0.5689)	(0.6633)	(0.7860)
South	2.8409	4.8341	−3.9979
	(0.5641)	(0.6688)	(0.7860)
West	2.8966	4.5907	−3.9151
	(0.5826)	(0.6618)	(0.7785)
LG (log)	0.7371	0.8981	
	(0.0920)	(0.0673)	
CG(log)	0.2767	0.7684	
	(0.0819)	(0.0591)	
CLR (log)		−0.5555	0.4785
		(0.763)	(0.0782)
RelW			0.0350
			(0.1074)
OLR(log)	−0.5233		
	(0.0884)		
LOC.	−0.1448	0.0951	−0.1655
	(0.0957)	(0.1073)	(0.0993)
Spec.	−0.4874	−0.5138	0.3095
	(0.2287)	(0.2180)	(0.2158)
Pop.(log)	0.0332	−0.0547	0.0381
	(0.0232)	(0.0260)	(0.0224)
PopG(log)	0.1113	0.1868	
	(0.0763)	(0.0778)	
GovEx.			−0.0672
			(0.0324)
AdjR2	0.844363	0.849948	0.841473

Significance at 5 pc. Level.

In examining the output growth equation (Table 5.1), the most striking finding is the strong positive significance of capital and labour growth. Furthermore, output per worker (a measure of labor productivity) is negatively correlated with output growth. Finally, the only other economic variable significantly correlated with output growth is the specialization measure, which has a negative coefficient. The localization and urbanization measures are not significantly correlated with output growth. The output growth equation can be summarized by noting that the traditional factors enter with the expected signs, while those variables associated with geographic production externalities do not demonstrate a strong statistical correlation with output growth. The output growth equation (Equation 5.9) can be summarized by noting that the traditional factors enter with the expected signs, while those variables associated with geographic production externalities do not demonstrate a strong statistical correlation with output growth.

As in the output growth equation, the highly positive simple correlation coefficient between capital and labour growth is borne out in both input growth regressions (Table 5.1). Additionally, the capital-labour ratio comes in as expected in both equations. Further, localization and urbanization are significant in both input growth equations, though not always with the expected sign. The specialization measure is correlated with capital growth, and, as in the output equation, its coefficient is negative. Finally, the share of immigrants in a city is significantly related to both capital and labour growth rates, while government expenditure only enters the labor growth equation and with a negative coefficient.

Table 5.4. Interaction Effects (standard errrors in parentheses)

	Output Growth	Dependent Variables (log) Capital Growth	Labour Growth
North	**3.9036**	**4.8093**	− 4.0948
	(0.7164)	(0.6677)	(0.8336)
Central	**3.9209**	**4.8394**	− 4.1244
	(0.7311)	(0.6715)	(0.8360)
South	**3.8806**	**5.1107**	− 4.1668
	(0.6919)	(0.6787)	(0.8543)
LG (log)	**0.2423**	**0.8939**	
	(0.0848)	(0.0652)	
CG (log)	**0.2423**	**0.7777**	
	(0.0848)	(0.0576)	
OLR(log)	− 0.6309		
	(0.1013)		
CLR(log)		− 0.5506	**0.4704**
		(0.0732)	(0.0757)
RelW(log)			0.0553
			(0.1107)
LOC	− 0.0978	**1.4672**	−1.8807
	(0.8918)	(0.9305)	(0.8712)
SPEC	− 0.6060	− 0.1913	− 0.0145
	(0.2262)	(0.2913)	(0.2868)
Pop.(log)	0.0349	− 0.0501	**0.0472**
	(0.0262)	(0.0290)	(0.0280)
PopG(log)	0.1114	−0.0501	− 0.0944
	(0.0772)	(0.0290)	(0.0783)
GovEx(log)			−0.0708
			(0.0315)
Immigr(log)		0.1718	− 0.1164
		(0.0484)	(0.0486)
SPEC∗LOC.	0.3192	−1.0937	1.1970
	(0.5224)	(0.5596)	(0.5347)
URB∗LOC.	0.0069	−0.0798	0.1141
	(0.0680)	(0.0716)	(0.0672)
AdjR2	0.871770	0.884089	0.851824

Significance at 5 pc. Level.

Earlier the potential and previously unexplored interrelatedness of different externalities was noted. Each of the externality measures was correlated with each other (Table 5.2). To see the effect of this upon the estimation, Table 5.3 re-estimates each of the preferred OLS regressions including the localization, specialization, and urbanization variables in turn.

The most salient insight in Table 5.3 is that exclusion of one of the measures leads to different patterns of correlation than had been observed earlier. For example, by excluding specialization from the output growth equation, a positive correlation between output growth and urbanization was observed. In other words, a theoretical model which suggested inclusion of the localization and urbanization variables, but which ignored specialization, would lead to different conclusions concerning the validity of the theory than the regression which does include specialization.

The interrelatedness and the importance of interactions were demonstrated directly by including interaction terms in the regressions. Table 5.4 shows the results of regression runs that include two reinforcing interaction terms, such as 'specialization jointly with (*) localization' and 'urbanization jointly with (*) localization'. The small sample size does not allow us to fully disentangle interaction effects with the direct effects of geographic proximity variables. Due to this, we do not focus on the implications of particular coefficients. Nor was there an emphasis on how the introduction of these interactions alters the magnitudes and precision of the estimates. Instead, it was noted that in both the capital and labor equations (5.10) and (5.11), respectively, no coefficients changed sign while the interaction term specialization with localization appears to be at least as important a covariate of capital and labor growth as others. In contrast, and conforming to an earlier finding, interaction terms are not significant in the productivity equation.

CONCLUSIONS

The empirical results support the perspective that geographic externalities together with their negative correlates must be considered in a dynamic setting of city based growth paying attention to the interactions between different variables. The importance of omitting individual variables was demonstrated as well as interacting variables. This is in contrast to current theoretical literature on such externalities, which indicates variables as operating in isolation from other forces. The one-variable theory, by construction, cannot account for the role of externalities in urban growth. This is also, of course, of significance for urban policy analysis.

A broader estimation approach is recommended, using three equations to characterise the growth process rather than just a single equation, as in conventional approaches. This allows for a better understanding of the systemic nature of aggregate growth. Hence, for example, the impact of particular variables differs according to whether one considers productivity, capital, or labour growth. In addition, city size, a proxy for urbanization, can be found to be positively correlated with labor growth, negatively correlated with capital growth, and uncorrelated with productivity growth. A significant implication of this is that, by solely estimating a single equation, whether it is productivity, capital, or labor, in trying to characterise aggregate growth, many interesting and significant effects are not recognized. If the common procedure is employed of examining only productivity output per capita, the important relationship would be missed between city size and input factor growth.

Another significant finding involves the ties between capital growth and each of the externality-based variables, in particular, the potential role of the SOC–type externalities on city size and growth. This needs further exploration.

In closing, analyzing statistical results, reinforced by sensitivity analysis, provides a better framework for policy analysis and public policy in the urban arena. With a significantly enlarged database the model clearly has the potential of forming the core of a decision support system for urban policy.

REFERENCES

Arthur, W.B. `(1988) .'Urban Systems and Historical Path Dependence,' in Cities and their Vital Systems, J.H. Ausubel and R. Herman, eds., Washington: National Academy Press

Asian Development Bank (2008), Managing Asian Cities, ADB, Manila, June

Barro,R.J. and X. Sala-i-Martin(2003), Economic Growth, Cambridge: MIT Press

Barro,R.J. (1990), Government Spending in a Simple Model of Economic Growth, *Journal of Political Economy* 95, S103-S125

Beckmann, M. (1999), Lectures on Location Theory, Berlin, Springer

Blanchard, O.J. and L.F. Katz (1992),'Regional Evolutions', Brookings Paper in Economic Activity 1, 1-75

Cuberes, D.(2004),'The Rise and Decline of Cities', mimeo,Univ. of Chicago, Sept., 1-36

Cuberes, D.(2008),'Sequential City Growth: Empirical Evidence', mimeo, Clemson University,Nov. ,1-22

Glaeser, E.L., H.D. Kallal, J.A. Scheinkman, and A. Shleifer (1992), 'Growth in Cities,' *Journal of Political Economy* 100 (6), 1126-1152

Glaeser, E.L.(1994),'Cities, Information and Economic Growth', mimeo,Dept. of Economics, Harvard University, City Scape 9-47

Gottinger, H.W. (1998) ,Global Environmental Economics, Dordrecht, Kluwer

Gottinger, H.W. (2003) . Economies of Network Industries, London, Routledge

Henderson, J.V.(1994) ,'Externalities and Industrial Development,' mimeo, Brown University

Henderson, J.V. and J.F. Thisse (eds.) (2004), Handbook of Regional and Urban Economics, Vol.4, Amsterdam, North Holland

Henderson,J.V. (2005),'Urbanization and Growth', *Handbook of Economic Growth*, Vol.1, P.Aghion and S. Durlauf eds., Amsterdam: North Holland

Jacobs, J. (1969). The Economy of Cities, New York: Random House

Jacobs, J. (1984) . Cities and the Wealth of Nations: Principles of Economic Life, New York, Random House

King, R.G. and S. Rebelo (1993) 'Transitional Dynamics and Economic Growth in the Basic Neoclassical Model,' American Economic Review 83, pp. 908 – 931

Krugman,P.R. (1991), 'Increasing Returns and Economic Geography,'*Journal of Political Economy* 99 (3), 483-499

Krugman, P.(2007), Development ,Geography and Economic Theory ,Cambridge ,Ma, MIT Press

Lucas, Robert E. Jr., (1988), 'On the Mechanics of Economic Development,' *Journal of Monetary Economics*, 22, 3-42.

North, D.C.(2004),Understanding the Process of Economic Change, Princeton: Princeton Univ. Press

Porter, M.E. (1990), The Competitive Advantage of Nations, New York, Free Press

Rhode, P.W. and G. Toniolo (eds.) (2006), The Global Economy in the 1990s, A Long-Run Perspective, Cambridge, Cambridge Univ. Press

Romer, P. M. (1990),'Endogenous Technological Change,' *Journal of Political Economy*, 98, S71-S 102.

Romer,P.M. (1992) 'Human Capital and Growth: Theory and Evidence,' Carnegie – Rochester Conference Series on Public Policy, 32 (1), 251-291

Savitch, H.V. and P. Kantor (2004) Cities in the International Marketplace: The Political Economy of Urban Development in North America and Western Europe, Princeton, Princeton Univ. Press

Shahid,Y. and K. Nabashima (2006), Postindustrial East Asian Cities, Stanford, Stanford Univ. Press

Solow, R. (1957), Technical Change and the Aggregate Production Function , Review of Economics and Statistics 30, 312-320

Van den Berg, H. (2001), Economic Growth and Development, New York, McGraw-Hill

Wei,S.-J. (2000),'The Open Door Policy and China's Rapid Growth: Evidence from City-Level Data', in Ito,T. and A.O. Krueger (eds.), East Asian Economic Growth, Cambidge, Ma., Harvard Univ. Press, 73 - 104

Young, A. (1992), 'A Tale of Two Cities: Factor Accumulation and Technical Change in Hong Kong and Singapore,' in NBER Macroeconomics Annual, O.J. Blanchard and S. Fisher, eds., Cambridge, MIT Press

Chapter 6

INCREASING RETURNS MECHANISM AND ECONOMIC GROWTH

Hans W. Gottinger

6.1. INTRODUCTION

Most built-up sectors of highly industrialized economies are not perfectly competitive. They are usually formed by a small number of big firms with non-negligible market share; besides being prevalent in the economy, big firms cluster around concentrated industrial structures which exhibit a skewed distribution of firm size and market share (Gottinger, 2003). This situation may be brought about by the intrinsic potential of dynamic technological competition to end up in (temporary) technological monopoly, so in those cases industrial competition may start out symmetric but end up asymmetric. We show how the competitive process proliferates in increasing returns industries (IRIs) where the total of all unit activities linked together yield a higher return than the sum of the individual unit activities operating separately. For this to happen it is necessary to show that a variety of increasing returns mechanisms combine to enable the effect of an escalating income industry.

We propose an integrated framework to provide tools and insights for explaining competition among skewed industrial structures. However, it is only a tentative step toward attempting to explain the path-dependent, indeterminate, suboptimal, locking-in nature of technological competition under increasing returns. Due to this we partially review the literature on the dynamics of technological diffusion, substitution, and competition. The purpose is to show that a person cannot accurately understand industrial competition without taking into account the self-reinforcing nature of commercial success in most emerging markets. The increasing returns mechanism is enriched by incorporating a set of stronger, yet neglected, increasing returns mechanisms -reputation effects, infrastructure effects and positive network externalities into a preliminary framework model. The resulting theoretical structure captures the interdependent and cumulative character of the three aspects of industrial competition: the number and size of firms, skewed industrial structures, and the nature of technological competition.

The increasing returns discussion in economics has provided important insights into the characteristics and dynamics of modern industrial economies. However, the discussion on policy applications had some misleading features in the past to conclude that a completely new economy is emerging and that it obeys a set of rules, which are totally different from those that apply to traditional sectors of the economy. While it is undeniable that the increasing returns paradigm remains fairly new and revolutionary and while there is no doubt that this paradigm is key to our understanding of new industrial sectors, and their sustaining role in productivity growth, we should clarify its proper role in industrial structure and growth of the economy.

At this stage we are most concerned about the catalytic role of technological competition in increasing returns industries. Increasing returns industries are nowadays most likely to be identified with high technology industries, in particular with information, communication and health care related industries. It is further enhanced by (foreign) trade related industries. As an example, in a corporate context, how to unlock increasing returns in its global operations; consider General Electric (GE). It constantly evolves its portfolio to drive long-run growth in diversification despite its large size and already significant presence in major markets. It encourages its executives and business units to take an expansive view of its markets as a means of unlocking growth initiatives that a product centric view would miss.

Often, when its market share exceeds 10 percent, it seeks to redefine the market more broadly to include adjacent products or services; this continual questing lies behind successful moves from manufacturing to services that has allowed it to keep growing in complementing given industrial markets. This even remains true, as nowadays, in financial distress situations where complementing growth activities could accelerate a downward cycle. In growth processes we observe the quest for market dominance , expansion through mergers and acquisitions, diversification and integration, investment constraints and 'barriers to entry' : all of those traits fostering or hindering the growth of firms which also prevail in the competitiveness between nations (Penrose, 1995)

For those industries Shapiro and Varian (1999) have suggested a combination of supply-side scale economies and demand-side scale economies to explain the intrinsic aspects of technological competition. It appears however that this way of seeing technological competition is too simple to capture the variety and complexity of real-world businesses. Thus we suggest a general framework to describe technological competition in what can be called the *increasing returns economy*.

6.2. SUPPLY-SIDE SCALE ECONOMIES

A first source of increasing returns assuming constant technology identifies a concentrated industry structure as a result of supply-side scale economies. In many cases large firms are more efficient than smaller companies because of their scale: larger corporations tend to have lower unit costs. This efficiency in turn further fuels their growth. However, positive feedbacks based on supply-side economies of scale usually run into natural limits. Past a certain size companies find growth difficult owing to the increasing complexity of managing a large organizational structure. From then on, negative feedback takes over. As traditional supply-side economies of scale generally become exhausted at a scale well below total market dominance, large firms, burdened with high costs, never grow to take the entire market and smaller, more nimble firms can find profitable niches. Shapiro and Varian (1999) conclude that because of this most industrial markets are oligopolies rather than monopolies.

Negative feedback generated by the difficulties of managing large organizations (i.e. scale diseconomies) indeed interrupts the growth of a firm and the level of industrial concentration. This situation, nevertheless, may be transient, because firms may be subject to other sources of increasing returns. Large companies that go through increasing returns mechanisms (IRMs) other than scale economies may increase their efficiency and overcome the negative aspects of overgrown organizations. Industries in which scale diseconomies are counterbalanced by other IRMs, then, may begin to head toward the extreme of 'winner-takes-most' situation. The IRMs capable to offset scale diseconomies are usually related to technological progress, so in the following sections we analyze other major causes of the growth of a firm, namely, the Schumpeterian loop, cost reducing learning, learning-by-doing, learning-by-using, and demand-side increasing returns.

6.3. SCHUMPETERIAN MECHANISM

The most widely accepted theory of technological change in modern economics is Schumpeter's (1942). In the Schumpeterian world, scale economies are present as well, but technology is not a constant. Here the creative role of the entrepreneur, endogenously driven by 'animal spirits' allows for the introduction of new technologies capable of displacing the established ones (Francois and Lloyd-Ellis, 2002). In the context of IRIs, Schumpeter's main point has been that innovation competition leads to increasing returns economies triggering serial innovations inducing more IRIs (Freeman, 2003). Most of Schumpeter's discussion stresses the advantages of concentrated market structures involving large firms with considerable market share. In his view, it is more probable that the necessary scale economies in R&D needed to develop new technologies can be achieved by a monopolist or by a few big firms of a concentrated industry. Large size firms, besides, may increase their rate of innovation by reducing the speed at which their transient rents and entrepreneurial advantage are eroded away by imitators. In the absence of patent protection large firms may exploit their innovations on a large scale over relatively short periods of time and in this way avoid rapid imitation by competitors by deploying their productive, marketing and financial capabilities. Large firms may also expand their rate of innovation by imitating and commercializing other firms' technologies.

Schumpeter's thesis encouraged a large body of empirical literature in the field of industrial organization. Most of this literature focused on two hypotheses associated with Schumpeter's assertion: (1) innovation increases more than proportionally with firm size and (2) innovation increases with market concentration. The most comprehensive review of the empirical evidence of the relationship between innovation and firm size and market structure dates back to Cohen and Levin (1989) who observed that the empirical results on the Schumpeterian relation are accurately described as fragile. They note that the lack of robust results seems to arise in part from the inappropriate attention to the dependence of these relationships on more fundamental conditions. From their overview Cohen and Levin draw the basic methodological lesson that the omission of important and potentially correlated variables that influence innovation can lead to misleading inferences concerning firm size and concentration.

Following Schumpeter's lead, Richard Nelson and Sidney Winter (1982) stand out for having formalized and completed many of Schumpeter's original intuitions. Whereas the connection between industrial structure and innovation has been viewed by Schumpeter as going primarily from the former to the latter, in Nelson and Winter (1982) there is a reverse causal flow, too. That is, there is clearly a circular causality suggesting a self-reinforcing mechanism between innovations and a firm's growth. Nelson and Winter (1982) stand out not only for having recognized the endogeneous character of innovation and market structure, but also for having pointed out and modeled the mutual causality between technical change and market structure (Nelson, 1986).

Evolutionary economists like Nelson and Winter define innovation very broadly, encompassing product and process innovation, opening up new markets, and acquisition of new sources of raw material. They also describe the nature of technical progress as a succession of major discontinuities detached from the past and with quite a transitory life span. This process of change is characteristic of certain industries, but it is not the sole kind of technological change. Technological change can also be continuous. That is to say, technologies improve constantly in absolute terms after their introduction.

The view of technological progress as a continuing, steady accumulation of innumerable minor improvements and modifications, with only very infrequent major innovations, has two sources: the accumulation of knowledge that makes possible to produce a greater volume of output from a given amount of resources, and the accumulation of knowledge that allows the production of a qualitatively superior output from a given amount of resources. The former source of technological progress is the result of a cost reducing learning process, while the second category is the result of what is known as learning-by-doing and learning-by-using. Given that both categories of technological progress are important determinants of the number and size of firms in a given industry, we analyze them in the next sections.

Cost Reducing Learning

An important aspect of technological change is cost reduction. As we saw before, Porter (1980) and Henderson (1975), in the strategic field, pioneered the notion of experience curve as a source of cost reductions. In economics, Hirsch (1956) has underlined the importance of repetitive manufacturing operations as a way of reducing direct labor requirements, while Arrow (1962) has explored the consequences of learning by-doing (measured by the cumulative gross investment, which produces a steady rate of growth in productivity) on profits, investment, and economic growth. However, the historical study on the patters of growth and competitiveness of large corporations by Alfred Chandler (1990) is a major and detailed contribution to our understanding of the way firms grow by diminishing costs. Large corporations, according to Chandler, along with the few challengers that subsequently enter the industry, do not compete primarily on the basis of price. Instead they compete for market share and profits through functional and strategic effectiveness. They compete functionally by improving their products, their processes of production, their marketing, their purchasing, and their labor relations. Big corporations compete strategically by moving into growing markets more rapidly and effectively than do their competitors. Such rivalry for market share and profits make more effective the enterprise's functional and strategic capabilities, which, in turn, provide the internal dynamics for continuing growth of the enterprise. In particular, it stimulates its owners and managers to expand into distant markets in its own country and then to become multinational by moving abroad. It also encourages the firm to diversify and become multiproduct by developing and introducing products in markets other than the original ones.

Learning-by-Doing

Some of the writings on industrial competition assumes that firms compete mainly in cost-reducing competitive advantages, especially those achieved through scale economies, scope economies (economies of joint production and distribution), and innovation in production and organizational processes. Here technical progress is implicitly treated as the introduction of new processes that reduce costs of producing essentially unchanging products. Beyond, there is a category of learning known as 'learning-by-doing' (Rosenberg, 1982) which enhances the qualitative aspects of final products. Western industrial societies today, Rosenberg (1982) argues, enjoy a higher level of material welfare not merely because they consume larger per capita amounts of the goods available, they have also made available improving forms of rapid transportation, instant communication, powerful energy sources, life-saving and pain-reducing medications, and other goods that were undreamed of one or two centuries ago. Therefore, ignoring incremental merchandise innovation and quality improvements is to overlook what has been one of the most important long-term contributions of technical progress to human welfare. Many products, such as beverages, toothpaste, soap, clothing, VCRs, TV sets can be subject to improvements. Such improvements, however, are marginal when compared with the amazing rate of development that other products and technologies can reach. Automobiles, aircraft, flight simulators, computers, and nuclear reactors are very complex technologies and, as a consequence of this, have a tremendous capacity of being enhanced. Consequently, the competitive behavior of the firms that produce these technologies consists not only of the innovative acts they perform to improve production, organizational, and distribution processes, but also from the efforts to improve constantly their products.

Learning-by-Using

With respect to a given product, Rosenberg (1982) distinguishes between the kind of learning that is internal to the production process (i.e. learning-by-doing) and that which is generated as a result of subsequent use of that product (i.e. learning-by-using). The latter category of learning begins only after a certain new product is used. In an economy where complex new technologies are common, there are essential aspects of learning that are a function not of the experience involved in producing a product but of its use by the final consumer.

The optimal performance of durable goods (especially complex systems of interacting components) often is achieved only after intensive and prolonged use. In the aircraft industry, for instance, the attainment of high standards of reliability is a major concern, in particular during the development stage. But it is only through extensive use of aircraft by airlines that faults are discovered and eliminated and detailed knowledge is gained about such things as metal fatigue, weight capacity, fuel consumption of engines, fuselage durability, minimum servicing, overhaul requirements, and maintenance costs.

Demand Side Increasing Returns

In the economy there are increasing returns mechanisms that come from the demand side of the market, not just from the supply side. For the average (risk adverse and imperfectly informed) consumer it becomes more attractive to adopt a widespread technology or product. A consumer, for example, may wait a year before purchasing a new car model, just to minimize the risk of buying a flawed product. Minimizing the risk of purchasing a defective technology or the cost of searching for an adequate one introduces a reputation or informational feedback that may produce a disproportionately high selection of the best-selling option. Informational or reputational feedback effects occur in various situations that could be reinforced through network externalities. First, when the complexity of the technology or product in question is such that consumers try to reduce uncertainty by asking previous purchasers about their experience with these technologies (Arthur and Lane, 1993). Second, in other situations the source of uncertainty is not the complexity of the technology, but the large quantity of options the consumers face. One is bound to choose, and the best way to do so is by confining one's attention to the best-assessed items in the consumer report. Third, in a market where the quality or value of a product is defined on the basis of arbitrary and short-living conventions, rather than strictly on the basis of lasting objective value, consumers usually tend to follow the expert's opinion. This kind of easy-to-manipulate, reputation-driven market success is typical of markets for highly symbolic products (e.g. art markets, fashion wear and luxury items), which also will result in a disproportionately high selection of one of the options. Finally, the most preeminent and common kind of reputation effects in the economy, arise plainly as a result of a well-timed and very aggressive advertising campaign. This self-reinforcing mechanism, and the lasting market dominance that it causes, might be quite unrelated to relative added value, but it certainly might produce an excessive predilection for one of the options.

By moving beyond the Schumpeterian hypotheses and focus on a more complete model of industrial competition we have identified other fundamental determinants of technological change that affect the mutual link between firm size and market structure (Aghion and Howitt, 1998). These determinants, which in our analysis take the form of increasing returns mechanisms, are usually studied as if they work independently from the other. Nevertheless, there are not many cases of industries where one single mechanism acts in isolation from the other sources of increasing returns. Therefore, the growth of the firm and the evolution of skewed industrial structure, more than the result of a single self-reinforcing mechanism, are the effect of the combination of several sources of increasing returns, which overlap and feed back upon one another. The unification of the resource-based loop, the Schumpeterian loop, scale economies, the different categories of learning, and demand-side increasing returns (reputation) loops A, B, and C, respectively, in Figure 6.1, constitutes a simple but useful model capable to explain endogenously the number and growth of firms in a given business, and in a wider context, the gap of economic performance in a given industrial sector.

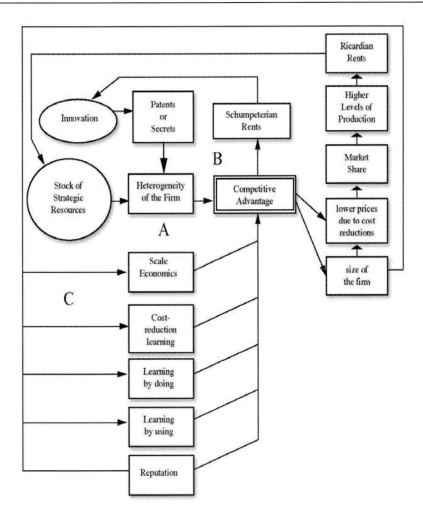

Figure 6.1. Increasing Returns Mechanism: A Qualitative Model of Industrial Competition.

In the model sketched in Figure 6.1 the positive relationship that runs from industrial structure to efficiency operates through the accumulation of rare resources, innovations, scale economies, reputation, and the different aspects of learning. These dynamics, over time, make costs fall as learning accumulates, new technologies are developed and improved, and firm-specific factors are amassed and exploited due to output increases. As a result of this mutual causality, market share and production levels increase, price falls, profitability rises, and with which relatively profitable firms expand continually while unprofitable ones contract uninterruptedly.

A relevant aspect of the structural determinants of the number and size of firms in an industry suggested in the model is that, when one of them is exhausted, causing a slowdown in the growth of the firm, the other mechanisms may be activated, which may allow for a further period of continued rapid growth. When the firms of a given industry are capable to accumulate firm-specific resources, innovations, cost reducing learning, qualitative product innovation based on learning-by-doing and learning-by-using, and reputation, these firms usually use them as a strategic weapon. In doing so, they are capable not only of neutralizing but also of overwhelming the negative effects of complex, overgrown, hard-to-manage organizational structures that arise from their constant expansion. The process can take a long period of time, but eventually the sources of mounting returns can drive markets toward ever more skewed industrial structures. For instance, in the commercial aircraft industry competition principally involves considerable development costs, continuous improvements in aircraft models, technology and product support, so this industry exhibits substantial scale economies, large scope for learning-by-doing, learning-by-using, and reputation effects. As a result of this, the commercial aircraft industry has been characterized by an increasing skewed industrial structure. Recently, the structure of this industry, after the acquisition of McDonnell Douglas by Boeing, was reduced to a monopoly in the United States. In the world aircraft market Boeing only competes with European Airbus. It is obvious that the merger of the two main manufacturers of the American aircraft industry should have brought about some gain in efficiency, which counterbalanced the diseconomies owing to the managing a more complex organization. Otherwise, the merger would not have taken place or would have been the result of irrational behavior.

The structure of some industries does not seem to head toward monopoly. However, over time, their level of concentration has increased substantially. The world automobile industry, for instance, in 1970 was composed of at least forty major competitors. In 1998, with some mergers and acquisitions, the number of main manufacturers was reduced to seventeen. Due to the great possibilities to accumulate cost reducing learning and the large scope for qualitative product improvements in the world automobile industry, both the number and the homogeneity of the firms competing in this industry are expected to decrease even further in the future. Here, again, benefits due to both costs reducing learning and qualitative product innovations brought about by mergers and acquisitions are larger than any cost created by scale diseconomies. Another interesting aspect of this model is that it also offers an endogenous explanation of the number and size of firms. In contrast with the traditional economic views that see industrial structure (number of firms) as an exogenous variable and assume homogenous firms, and the strategic paradigms which are focused first and foremost in explaining heterogeneity among firms within an industry, this model recognizes that the strategic choices and acts of the firms have an effect not only on the performance and size of the firm itself, but also on the structure of the market.

In summary, industrial structure is caused by a combination of various increasing returns mechanisms. Here, then, the combination of accumulation of resources, product innovation, scale economies, cost reducing learning, learning-by-doing, learning-by-using or reputation enhances the performance of the firm and determines, to a great extent, the level of skewness of the structure of the industry where it competes.

6.4. INCREASING RETURNS AND ERGODIC MARKETS

Traditional neoclassical economics has tended to portray most fiscal situations as something analogous to a large Newtonian system, with a unique and stable equilibrium solution predetermined by a given pattern of resources, preferences, and technological possibilities. Brian Arthur and his group (Arthur, 1994, 1990b; Arthur et al., 1987), however, have shown that this conventional way of seeing economic reality overlooks important and frequent economic situations where increasing returns are conspicuous.

Matsuyama (1991,1992) showed that IRMs induced by dynamic industrialization yields superior and sustainable growth paths though attaining multiple equilibria that in a comparative perspective are more likely to lead to a catch-up process and convergence over time. Then, if a switch toward an IRM regime occurs, the history of the economy as times goes on loses in weight and significance. In order to distinguish economic situations characterized by decreasing returns from those where increasing returns are dominant, Arthur et al., (1987) developed the theory of non-linear Polya processes, which describes the long-run self-organizing structures that emerge from dynamic processes where proportions are involved. The general non-linear Polya scheme can be pictured by imaging an urn of infinite capacity to which balls of several colors are added. In the simplest case, where decreasing and constant returns prevail, the probability of a ball of a given color to be chosen the next time is independent of the proportions of colors at the moment of the addition. In this simple sequential process, the strong law of large numbers predicts that, over time, the proportion of balls of color i has a fixed probability, where $\Sigma_i q(i) = 1$. Therefore, it has a unique, predetermined outcome.

Sequences of choices in these simple cases are important at the beginning of the process. However, as the process advances, different sequences of choices are averaged away by the economic forces, which are subject to constant or decreasing returns. So, no matter what the sequences of choices, the system will always end up with the same pattern. For instance, in a coin-tossing experiment the event 'head' is independent of previous tosses, then the expectation of a 'head' in each toss is 0.5 no matter how many times the experiment is repeated. Likewise, the proportion of 6's in a dice-casting experiment will tend to 1/6. The process by which firms in an industry concentrate in different regions is like the coin-tossing or the dice-casting experiment, if the geographic preferences of each firm is not modified by the preferences of the other firms. In more general cases, where increasing returns are present, the dynamics is completely different and the standard strong law is inapplicable. In this regime, the next ball to be added into the urn is not known, but the probability of adding one ball of a specific color depends on the present proportions of colors in the urn. In other words, the probability of an addition of the colors becomes a function of the proportions of balls of each color at each time of choice.

The case of firms deciding where to settle down illustrates this kind of non-linear Polya processes. Here increasing returns can be incorporated within the model by introducing agglomeration effects. As a result of agglomeration effects, additions to a specific region are not independent of previous location choices, and firms are added incrementally to regions with probability exactly equal to the proportions of firms in each region at the time. Under increasing returns, then, the process becomes path- dependent. Arthur et al. (1987) show that at the outset of the process proportions are not stable, but once the industry settles into a vector of proportions, locational patterns become constant at that vector with probability one. However, the constant vector is selected randomly from uniform distribution over all possible shares that sum to 1.0. This means that each time this locational process is rerun under different historical events, it will in all likelihood settle into a different pattern. Therefore, it is possible to predict that the locational pattern will tend toward a constant proportion, but it cannot be foreseen at which proportion it will settle down.

The interpretation of economic history is different under different regimes. Under constant and diminishing returns, the evolution of the system is ergodic (i.e. tending in probability to a limiting form that is independent of the initial conditions). Ergodic structures emerge when repeated random events, that are drawn from the same distribution and are independent from previous ones, have a long-term average that approach their expected value, which is a long-run persistent random cycle (Feller, 1957, p410). The typical example of an ergodic system is coin tossing. If a fair coin is tossed indefinitely, the proportions of heads varies considerably at the outset, but settles down to 50 per cent with probability one. The evolution of an ergodic system, therefore, follows a convex probability function, which has expected motions that lead toward a unique, determinate outcome. In this regime "historical chance" cannot influence the evolution of the systems so history is reduced to a mere deliverer of the inevitable and the known.

Under increasing returns, by contrasts, the process is nonergodic, because small historical events become magnified by positive feedback. A nonergodic system follows a nonconvex probability function, so two or more outcomes are possible and 'historical chance' determines which of these is ultimately selected. History becomes all-important (North, 2005, Chap.2). There are some cases of nonergodic systems in which, from the multiplicity of structures that may emerge, there are some 'corner solutions' with a single option monopolizing the choices. In this specific kind of nonergodic systems, while information on preferences, endowments and transformation possibilities allows locating and describing the various possible corner equilibria, it is usually insufficient to determine which one will be selected. In these cases, as Arthur (1994, p.13) pointed out 'there is an indeterminacy of outcome'.

Adoption of technologies that compete under diverse regimes can be appropriately modeled as a nonlinear Polya process (cf. Arthur, 1989, 1990a, 1990b; Arthur et al., 1987). In the simplest regime, when technological competition is characterized by constant and decreasing returns, the probability of a technology of being chosen depends on its current market share. As each adoption is independent of the previous one, market share should converge to a point where they equal the probability of technology adoption. Therefore, under constant and decreasing returns two technologies or products performing the same function will end up sharing the market according to each technology's intrinsic value and technical possibilities. Therefore, markets characterized by constant and decreasing returns can be called ergodic markets.

Under increasing returns to implementation, the probability of adoption depends on the numbers of adoptions holding each technology at a particular time. Markets of this kind can be called nonergodic markets. Within these kinds of markets there are those where increasing returns may drive the outcome toward a single dominant technology, with small events early on selecting the technology that takes over. This particular type of nonergodic markets can be termed tipping or indeterminate markets. This indeterminacy relates to the "selection problem", how one allocation outcome is 'selected' over time by small historical events when there are several possible long-term results.

6.5. TECHNOLOGICAL COMPETITION UNDER UNCERTAINTY AND INERTIA

In high tech markets the commercial success of emerging new technologies is both highly uncertain and inertial. As regards uncertainty, in addition to the problem of trying to discern the true potential of a new generic technology, there is also the difficulty of foreseeing the precise direction in which the said technology will evolve. Indeed, as depicted in Figure 6.2, the emergence of a new generic technology generally opens the door not just to one specific technological path, but rather to a whole variety of possible trajectories in product design and process technology.

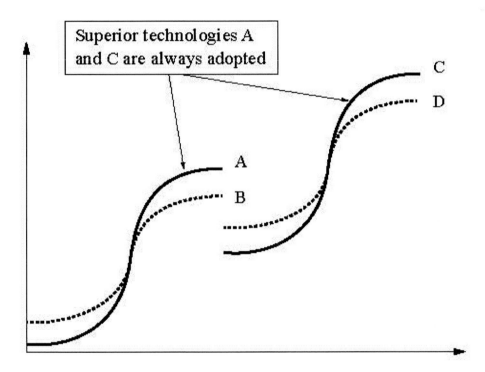

Figure 6.2. Uncertain and Inertial Technological Trajectory: superior technologies A and C are always adopted.

On the other hand, the inertial forces unleashed by commercial success are a lot more powerful than those that the classical models of diffusion suggest. Abernathy and Utterback (1978), Abernathy and Clark (1985) and Teece (1986) among others, have rightly underlined that in addition to the rigidities which may affect individual workers or machines and individual intermediaries or users, there are *systemic rigidities* of a much greater scope and importance. Every successful generic technology has a complex web of complementary technologies woven around its core. Once such an integrated and expensive, in terms of purchasing and usage, technological system is in place, its momentum becomes enormous. Consequently, once a specific new technology becomes part of a dominant system, it will become increasingly more difficult to dislodge, even by worthy alternatives. This is depicted in Figure 6.2 where technology B (the inferior one) is foreclosed by the entrenchment of technology A (the superior one), which will only be displaced by the much superior technology C.

Uncertainty and inertia can combine to cause decisive first-mover advantages, which may grant unassailable market dominance to an early technological trajectory. Yet, these authors (i.e. Abernathy and Utterback, 1978; Abernathy and Clark, 1985; Teece, 1986) do not go far enough in recognizing that in the real world, optimal technological cycles, trajectories and discontinuities, such as options A and C in Figure 6.2, are not unalterable realities. They largely ignore and or minimize the self-reinforcing (and not simply inertial) nature of commercial success and the consequent unpredictability of technological evolution in general and of 'dominant designs' in particular. With this, they also overlook that a technology's success is tributary to the competitive decisions (often arbitrary and myopic) of the major players in an industry, as they are to any set of exogenous technical parameters.

Abernathy and Utterback (1978) did not believe in the research lab as an optimal selector of new technologies and they did question the optimality of selection by the market, but only to a small degree. The early articles written together by Abernathy and Utterback are thoroughly ergodic markets-oriented. Nowhere in them is it hinted that *a dominant design* might not be optimal or that its lasting power might not be inevitable. Later on, Abernathy and Clark (1985) made a strong case for contingency in the maturity and decline of technologies and industries. They thus rejected in no uncertain terms the deterministic view of technological life cycles. Paradoxically, however, their emphasis on historical contingency did not extend to the emergent phase of a new generic technology. They continued to suggest or imply that within a given generic technology, a specific "dominant design" will be chosen strictly on the basis of its relative merit. As for Utterback, in his more recent writings (Utterback, 1994; Utterback and Suarez, 1993), he fully acknowledges that indeterminacy characterizes both the emergence and the decline of a generic technology.

Our observations on technological competition have shown that markets, in the presence of increasing returns to adoption, tend to become very unstable and tipping (i.e. to discriminate sharply between winners and losers) often occurs on the basis of minimal, perhaps almost random, market share differences among the various offers and regardless the relative merit and potential of a new technology. From two comparable competing technologies A and B (see Figure 6.3) in a market characterized by unbounded increased returns to adoption, only one will win the race for dominance (lock-in). But, a priori, it is hard to determine which technology will tip the market (indeterminacy). Furthermore, it is not always sure that the market will select the superior option (sub-optimality). Then, the market is not necessarily an optimal selector of optimal technologies.

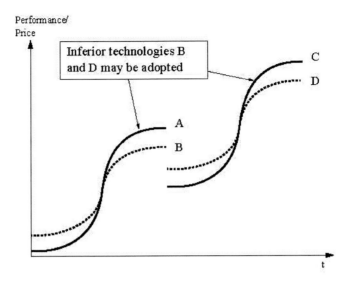

Figure 6.3. Indeterminate Technological Trajectory: Inferior Technologies B and D may be adopted.

Another aspect the work on technological competition under increasing returns has shed light on is related to the implications of market instability for the management of risk. Ergodic models tacitly assume that new technologies are cheap to develop, hard to improve, stand alone, easy to appraise, easy to use, and strongly protected through patents. This implies technologies arrive at the market fully developed before diffusion and that the process of development and the diffusion itself can be separated from each other. Ergodic models, then, introduce a very limited level of uncertainty.

In the models of indeterminate technological change, in contrast, new technologies are expensive to develop, subject to further improvements, often due to systemic nature, difficult to appraise and use and with weak patent protection. Therefore, their adoption become self-reinforcing not only for the reputation effect of market success, but also for the significant improvements that technologies accumulate during their spreading As the diffusion process confers value to technologies and not only conspicuousness, a technology that initially did not deserve being chosen may end up meriting it. Consequently, according to Foray (1993), the market becomes not only a selector of adequate technologies, but a creator of dominant, superior ones. Under these circumstances, technological sponsors do not face an information problem, but an indeterminate scenario, as Arthur (1994) has indicated. Thus the most effective way to manage totally contingent and unpredictable results in unstable environments is to invest aggressively in marketplace share as the market takes off.

6.6. STANDARDS AND INCREASING RETURNS

Early models of technology diffusion explicitly recognized the general notions of adoption externalities and self-reinforcing dynamics. The epidemic model specified that the diffusion of a new technology, much as that of a potent virus, would be a self-reinforcing process since every user of the respective technology would turn into one of its ardent promoters. What these models, however, failed to recognize was that diffusion can increase considerably the value, and not simply the reputation, of the fresh expertise. In other words, the early models were too focused on the information externalities and neglected to take into account another source of selfreinforcing in diffusion, namely, increasing returns to adoption.

In recent years, technological competition and the emergence of a scientific monopoly over a whole market has been the privileged topic of the literature on standards (David and Greenstein, 1990). This literature has identified three processes by which technological standardization can be attained through government regulation through mandated standards, voluntary agreements through formal or standardization committees, and market competition. The first two processes, often called de jure standardization, usually result in a standard with public-good characteristics. Standards selected through the market de facto standards, on the other hand, are usually owned by a firm, which can therefore exclude other firms from its use. Every standardization process has its own theoretical interest at heart, but here we will focus exclusively on de facto standardization, which is identified with the economic literature on technological competition under increasing returns.

6.7. NETWORK EXTERNALITIES

At the basis of what we know about technological competition is the literature on network externalities (Katz and Shapiro, 1992, 1994; Economides, 1996) in which market size relates to increasing returns, and benefits grow with the size of competing networks; just as scale economies, learning, or reputation effects, and positive network externalities are a self-reinforcing diffusion dynamic. Network effects, however, differ from the other self-reinforcing mechanisms in several important respects. First, while the benefits of scale economies, learning and (some) reputation effects can only be reaped at the time of purchasing the product in question, most of the benefits accruing from network externalities can be enjoyed well past the point of purchase and throughout the entire life cycle of the product. Second, network effects are considerably forward looking and less bounded and therefore more powerful than scale and learning effects. In fact, because they cast a shadow into the future, network effects can combine with reputation effects to create extremely powerful and lasting self-reinforcing dynamics in market success.

Since most of the benefits accruing from network externalities can be enjoyed throughout the full life cycle of a product, new users faced with a multiplicity of competing technical options will have to make their choices not simply in function of what the majority of post purchasers have already chosen, but also in function of what the majority of interface users are likely to choose. Interestingly, while very pessimistic user expectations about an overall emerging market can be self-dampening, optimistic expectations about the success of a specific technical format in a battle of standards could easily become self-fulfilling. The greater the number of people who think that a given technical option is likely to become dominant, the more new users will side with it and the more likely and pronounced the dominance will in fact become. Third, while scale economies and learning can only be a source of increasing returns to adoption and while users' learning costs (or switching costs) can exclusively be a source of inertia, both reputation effects and network externalities, in contrast, can act as both strong inertial and increasing returns to adoption.

6.8. INCREASING RETURNS IN INDUSTRIAL COMPETITION

The analysis so far has gradually recognized the central role of increasing returns mechanisms in generating and sustaining dominant firms and technologies. Clearly, while scale economies, the resource-based loop, the Schumpeterian (i.e. innovation- based) loop, reputation, and the different categories of learning help to explain some of the most basic occurrences of dominant firms and slanted industrial structures, only increasing returns to adoption, a notion intrinsically connected to Schumpeterian economics, can explain most of the instances of technological dominance which we see in contemporary high-technology markets. Thus the integration of all these increasing returns mechanisms, as Figure 6.1 shows, results in a quite complete explanation of industrial competition. Such an explanation combines the self-reinforcing loops based upon resources and innovations (loops A and B), scale economies, learning, and reputation (loops C) with the loops based upon increasing returns to adoption. These loops are of two kinds. A set of further loops, composed of a mesh of scale economies, learning, reputation effects, infrastructure effects, and network effects, links increasing competitive advantages with increasing returns to market share. A last set of loops indicates that, if increasing returns to adoption are present and considerable, market share becomes a strategic asset well worth investing on in an aggressive manner through vigorous production capacity expansion, price reductions, infrastructure development, and alliances with manufacturers of complementary technologies, products, and services.

As a model of increasing returns mechanism in industrial dynamics, the one described here seems to be rather comprehensive. It can explain the polarized outcomes that are common in most industrial sectors and describe business competition as a dynamic and cumulative process. A final, but not less interesting, feature of this model of industrial competition is that it is general, in the sense that it is capable of describing simultaneously the three levels of industrial competition. It elucidates how technological adoption, the number and growth of firms, and industrial structure combine and cause each other. In other words, the general model of industrial competition gives a picture of how industrial competition is a process in which technological competition affects the size of the firms competition in a given industry and how the growth of the firms, in turn, influences the structure of that industry. That is why technological adoption goes between conduct and performance in the chain of causality that leads from the size of the firms to industrial structure.

6.9. INCREASING RETURNS, STRUCTURAL CHANGE AND DEVELOPMENT PATHS: AN EXAMPLE

The seminal article formalising the 'big push' theory of industrialization is that of Murphy et al., (1989). In their model, firms choose between a constant returns and an increasing returns of technology based on their expectations of demand. However, these choices spill over into aggregate demand creating a strategic interaction among sectors in their technology adoption decisions. Thus, under certain conditions, there exist two equilibria: with all firms choosing the constant returns or all choosing the increasing returns technology. Clearly, in the latter equilibrium, all households are better off.

While the Murphy, Shleifer and Vishny model (Murphy et al., 1989) shows how increasing returns, and a wage effect, aggregate to strategic complementarity among sectors, it does not lend itself readily to the debate concerning the degree of balance in industrialization policy. First, the static content leaves open the question of whether the intervention should take the form of anything more than indicative planning. Second, the most commonly discussed policy instrument in the industrialization debate is the subsidization of investments. However, in the Murphy, Shleifer and Vishny example, use of this instrument biases one toward a more unbalanced policy. To see this, observe that it is the role of the government to facilitate a move to the industrialising equilibrium. This means that the government must subsidize a sufficient amount of investment to make it profitable for all sectors to adopt the modern technology. Given the binary choice set, there then exists some minimum critical mass of sectors that must be targeted to achieve a successful transition.

A greater range of successful industrialization policies might be more plausible, however, if firms had the choice of a wider variety of technology to choose from. One might suppose that targeting a large number of sectors to modernize a little and targeting a small number of sectors for more radical modernization might both generate a big push. Thus, to consider the balanced approach properly, a greater technological choice space is required. What would be the choice variables available to the government provided it would be able to pick up what is likely to be increasing returns industries in the future? First, in each period, the government can choose the set of firms that it targets for structural change. Second, for each targeted firm, the government can choose a target level for 'increasing returns industry' modernization in the period. Along this vein, the government could choose to target the same number of firms in each period but induce those firms to modernize gradually over time. Or in contrast, the government chooses a single level of modernization to occur across all firms and all periods. It then targets a mass of firms each period for entry and modernisation. This means that industrialization policy is solely characterized by the critical mass of sectors targeted, and the target level of modernization. Given a parameterized development path, the most significant parameter represents the strength of increasing returns in the technology adopted by industrial sectors which generates a rationale for 'big push' intervention (Gans, 1994).

To evaluate how economic characteristics how the strengths of complementarities and increasing returns should affect a government's policy choices and industrial policies, is also a key area of interest. Big Push theories of industrialization could lead to 'development traps', if sequential industrialization would add more diminishing returns than increasing returns industries, which could be a result of government's coordination failure. When a development trap is purely the result of coordination failure, then to escape from the trap would require the government to synchronize the expectations of individual agents with targeted investment in industrialization activities. If a government were to announce that firms should modernize to a certain degree, even if this were believed perfectly by individuals and firms, each firm might still have an incentive to wait before investing. In that case, the optimistic expectations by the government would not be realized and the policy would be ineffective. Irreversibility and the time lag of production mean that history rather than expectations matter (Krugman, 1991). The previous level of industrialization determines what path the economy will take in the future. This is why it is difficult to characterize the industrializing paths of the economy (Sauer et al., 2003; Trindade, 2005).

6.10. INDUSTRIALIZATION POLICIES AND DEVELOPMENT

In the context of a big push development strategy the government faces a tradeoff between the number of sectors it targets and the degree to which it wishes them to modernize, that is, it chooses the critical of sectors that must be targeted at any point in time in order to generate an escape from a development trap and to achieve increasing returns. Let us take a simple case where the industrialization policy takes the form of a 'big bang', that is intervention occurs for one period only granting that the resources exist in that period to allow for such a policy. This means that the industrialization policy is solely characterized by the critical mass of sectors targeted, s^*, and the target level of modernization, f. Suppose naturally that individual transition costs are non-decreasing in f, the optimal critical mass in terms of f can be described by the path:

$$s^*(f,\phi) = (f+1)^{\theta(1-\sigma)} [((1-\delta)(\sigma-1)/L\,\bar{\lambda})^{(1-\sigma)/(\sigma-1-\sigma)} - s_I)] + s_I . \qquad (6.1)$$

Substituting this into the objective function with cost c $(f,1; s_I, \phi)$, the 'big bang' industrialization policy problem becomes:

$$\min_f (f+1)^{\theta(1-\sigma)} [((1-\delta)(\sigma-1)/L\,\bar{\lambda})^{(1-\sigma)/(\sigma-1-\sigma)} - s_I)] \, c\,(f,1; s_I, \phi) \qquad (6.2)$$

where use is made of the symmetry of the cost functions and the fact that $s*-s_I$ firms are targeted, ϕ could represent any given exogenous parameter, i.e. σ, θ, δ, α, or $L\,\bar{\lambda}$, a given parameter linked to L.

In designing an optimal industrialization policy it shows that a cost minimizing policy in the industry transition entails setting certain development model (exogeneous) parameters such as labor productivity improvements (θ), upstream firms discount future earnings (δ), and the fixed size of the labor force ($L\,\bar{\lambda}$), the number of basic industrial sector varieties (s_I), the product linkages between intermediate input producers (σ), and the use of the intermediate input composite (α); the latter two showing a certain degree of interaction referring to as the returns to specialization (Romer, 1987), as in Chapter 3.

Discussing these parameters qualitatively in terms of comparative statics would indicate industrial change. Raising any of these parameters θ, δ, $L\,\bar{\lambda}$, and s_I increases the marginal returns to upstream firms in both their entry and modernization decisions. Raising θ means that sunk costs are translated into labor improvements more effectively. Similarly, since the costs of modernization and entry are carried today and most of the returns occur in the future, the more likely they are to undertake those actions.

A large market, a higher $L\,\bar{\lambda}$, also raises the marginal return to entry and modernization. Finally, more industrial varieties mean that the past level of industrialization is greater, thereby, reducing the marginal costs of inducing firms to adopt more modern technologies. Given this, the responsiveness of firms to inducements by the government is enhanced when any of these parameters is raised. Therefore, the higher are these parameters, the fewer firms need to be targeted to facilitate an escape (from a development trap).Of these parameters θ has probably received the most discussion. In many ways, this parameter represents the strength of increasing returns in the technology adopted by upstream producers. This is because higher levels of θ imply that, when they choose to modernize, upstream firms will choose technologies involving greater sunk (or fixed) costs. Therefore, while one requires some degree of increasing returns or economies of scale in production to generate a rationale for a 'big bang' intervention, the stronger are those increasing returns supports a more unbalanced industrialization policy.

This relates back to arguments made previously on balanced vs. unbalanced growth. Of the three other parameters, only the discount rate δ seems to have been given a potential role in the past debate on industrialization policy. Matsuyama (1992) interprets the discount rate as a measure of the effectiveness of entrepreneurship in coordinating investment, with a low discount rate indicating the existence of greater entrepreneurial resources. If so, then the above result seems to imply that with a relative scarcity of entrepreneurial talent a more balanced approach should be followed. The comparative statics results for α and σ require more restrictions because each of these has two effects. On the one hand, lowering σ and increasing α raises the strength of strategic complementarities among upstream sectors. This tends to favor a more balanced growth approach. On the other hand, α and σ each affect the marginal returns to entry and modernization of firms. The second effect reinforces the first and leads to a more balanced strategy, which is, lowering σ and lifting α so as to increase the marginal returns to entry and modernization.

A lower σ also implies stronger technical complementarities. This effect is sometimes referred to as the returns to specialization (Romer, 1987). The consequence is that a lower σ raises the marginal returns to employing a greater variety of inputs in production. The higher is σ the weaker are the linkages among intermediate input sectors. Conversely, stronger linkages between sectors raise the marginal return to targeting an additional sector for change supporting the arguments of the balanced growth strategy. Looking at α, it is a measure of the appropriability of the returns from supply an additional intermediate input. As Romer (1994) discusses, the larger is α, the greater is the surplus gained by intermediate input producers from the employment of their product in final good production. Therefore, producers of inputs targeted in an industrialization policy are more likely to react positively (in terms of adopting better technology) when the appropriable returns from the introduction of their variety is larger. This effect would tend to favor a more unbalanced approach as α increases.

Summarizing, we have outlined the role of several parameters in influencing the kind and degree of balance in industrialization policy. Factors addressed in the earlier literature such as strength of linkages, increasing returns and entrepreneurial resources all influence the composition of the 'big push'. By considering a 'big bang' policy, some results are possible. For instance, as developed at length in this chapter, strong increasing returns in conjunction with weak sector linkages tend to favor a more unbalanced approach in order to minimize costs.

6.11. INCREASING RETURNS MECHANISMS AND TECHNOLOGICAL COMPETITION

The strategic importance of increasing returns to technology adoption is unquestionable. In a strictly ergodic market technological options eventually obtain the share of the market they deserve in proportion to their value and technical possibilities. In non-ergodic situations, in a tipping market, on the other hand, the winner takes all or most and the losers (no matter how worthy and how many of them there are) loses all or much. Due to this, the introduction of factors causing tipping markets determines the outcomes of technological competition. This framework not only captures the interplay of institutional arrangements, resources and networks of firms and industries in industrial competition, but also delineates very concrete regularities, which can provide us with a simple but powerful tool to explain endogeneously, and in a dynamic way the firm's growth, industrial structure, and technological competition.

This chapter suggests a Schumpeterian model of industrial competition and growth extending through increasing returns mechanisms to neoclassical models of industrialization. In contrast to the approaches that underline a specific aspect of industrial competition and/or base their explanation on a reduced number of factors and against conventional economics that overlooks increasing returns mechanisms, this model links the increasing returns mechanisms that determine endogenously inter- firm asymmetries and the kind of industrial structure which emerges during this competition process. This framework also emphasizes the fact that the emergence of dominant firms and the evolution of industrial structure are strongly intertwined with the process of technological change and diffusion.

One of the most important contributions of the work on increasing returns is in having shown that the emergence and persistence of technological monopolies is not an exogenous datum, largely determined by scientific and technical parameters, but is strongly influenced by vibrant market forces stemming from self-reinforcing mechanisms. In the presence of strong, global and long lasting increasing returns, the actions and omissions of the main actors in the industry in question affect considerably the final result of technological competition. To the extent to which these actors are capable of fully perceiving and exploiting strong increasing returns in emerging markets, they can ensure the entrenchment of their technology as the industrial standard by investing in those strategies that bring about market share. Once entrenched, and to the extent they are capable to exploit inertial forces, established firms can ensure the persistence of their technologies well beyond the time warranted by their relative technical value.

This chapter also shows that technological monopoly should be attributed to increasing returns in general, but it is network externalities in particular what has caused some important markets to be dominated by a technological monopoly. In fact, at the level of technological competition, the only thing the other sources of increasing returns to adoption do is to exacerbate the implications of network effects, but they do not turn, isolated from network effects, a market tipping. The most obvious and direct reason for technological monopoly is that the components of a given network are compatible and constantly interconnected. The telephone and the fax are examples of networks where physical interconnection and compatibility have led to technological monopoly.

Winner-takes-all markets are associated with cases where there is often intense competition in innovative activity but the future market is such that competition in it is, over a reasonable timeframe, not sustainable. Thus firms compete to attain a position of dominance. Perhaps the most famous example of a winner-takes-all market is that for operating systems for desktop PCs. It is instructive to recognize that this market benefits from massive economies of scale in production protected by intellectual property rights (very low marginal cost of supply compared with very large fixed costs of initial product development) and substantial economies of scale in consumption (due in large part to the network effects associated with the relationships between the operating system market and the related applications software markets).

Identification of such markets is important because it affects the focus of competitive concerns. Most obviously, if there are strong grounds to believe that a future marketplace is a winner-takes-all market, it is perhaps not appropriate for a competition authority to block a merger or agreement between firms on the basis that this will create a dominant position or lessen competition in this future market. By definition, the nature of the market is such that its existence guarantees that a firm will be dominant in it, at least in the medium term. This illustrates an important point relevant to wider issues in competition policy: it is typically better to have a situation where a firm is dominant in a relevant market than for that market not to exist at all. Instead, any intervention must be based on the premise that the merger (i.e. agreement) lessens or distorts competition on some other, perhaps related market or in competition in the innovative activity associated with the winner-takes-all market. Similarly in dominance cases, if we anticipate that a market is subject to winner-takes-all properties, then it is difficult to establish a case that a firm has abused its dominant position in monopolizing this market; the market is naturally prone to monopolization. Rather, analysis of an alleged abuse of dominance associated with this market should focus on how a dominant position in a related market (perhaps an access market) could be used to distort competition in the innovative activity associated with the winner-takes-all market, or how a dominant position in the winner-takes-all market could be abused to maintain that position, in effect used to distort competition in the innovative activity associated with the future generation of that market.

In this chapter we also advanced our understanding of the technical and institutional factors which are likely to affect the nature of technological competition. In doing so, we add to the dimensions of strength and duration, the dimension of scope of increasing returns. The distinction between strength, duration and scope is useful to realize that, contrary to popular and academic literature, a market for virtual network technologies with content dimensions not necessarily will end up with a technological monopoly. With this distinction in mind and against those who think that strong indirect network externalities always act as tipping mechanisms, we can also show that strong indirect network externalities are compatible with fairly ergodic market dynamics, if the scope of such externalities happens to be rather narrow.

By taking the telecommunications or the media industry, for example, we can show that strong network externalities are necessary but not sufficient conditions to produce technological monopoly. Short usage life of content and technology incomparability are technical and necessary conditions for technological monopoly in software intensive virtual network technologies to happen. But these technical aspects of virtual network technologies are not a sufficient condition to produce technological monopolies. In Chapter 4 we showed that network externalities require not only to have high levels of strength, but also to be global in scope. Under certain institutional conditions strong indirect network externalities may be rather localized, which leads to very ergodic market results. Under these conditions markets are shared by the competing technologies according to their intrinsic value.

Technical and institutional factors causing different levels of strength duration and scope of increasing returns to adoption are relevant to determine whether a market is tipping or ergodic. This has some implications. A first inference is that not all network technology is equally systemic. If there are strong network externalities but with a local scope, the systemic nature of a network becomes rather limited. In this case the systemic nature of the given network would be rather local compared with the actual network, which is global in nature.

Strength, duration, and scope of increasing returns are also useful to determine in a more detailed way the nature of cooperation. When network externalities are strong and global, content-intensive virtual network technologies become rather systemic. In these circumstances, the main sponsors of the competing technologies may produce some components of the system, but the rest of it may be out of their reach. For instance, a PC producer may be incapable to produce software or microprocessors, and microprocessor producers may not be able to produce software or hardware. Consequently, technological competition in markets characterized by strong and global increasing returns is more in connection with complex networks of firms than with conventional industrial array of firms producing homogeneous products. In contrast, in markets with weak and local network externalities, competition takes place mainly between firms than between networks of firms. This is so, because in this kind of markets products are not systemic.

REFERENCES

Abernathy, W.J. and J.M. Utterback (1978), 'Patterns of Innovation in Technology', Technology Review 10, 40-47.

Abernathy. W. J. and K. B. Clark (1985). 'Innovation: Mapping the Wind of Creative Destruction', Research Policy 14, 3-22.

Aghion, E. and E. Howitt (1998), Endogeneous Growth Theory, Cambridge, Ma., MIT Press

Arrow, K. (1962), 'The Economic Implications of Learning by Doing', *Review of Economic Studies* 29, 155-173.

Arthur, W. B. (1989), 'Competing Technologies, Increasing Returns and Lock-in by Historical Events', *The Economic Journal.* 99, 116-131.

Arthur, W. B.(1990a), 'Positive Feedbacks in the Economy', Scientific American, February 22, 92-99.

Arthur, W. B. (1990b) 'Silicon Valley Location Cluster. When Do Increasing Returns Imply Monopoly' ,*Mathematical Social Science* 19, 235-51.

Arthur. W. B. (1994), Increasing Returns and Path Dependence in the Economy, Ann Arbor, The Univ. of Michigan Press

Arthur W. B., Ermoliev, Yu. M. and Yu. M. Kaniovski (1987), 'Path-dependent Processes and the Emergence of Macro-structure', *European Journal of Operational Research*. 30, 294-303.

Arthur, W. B. and D. A. Lane (1993), 'Information Contagion', *Structural Change and Economic Dynamics* 4, 81-104.

Chandler, A. D.(1990), Scale and Scope: Dynamics of Industrial Capitalism. Cambridge, The Belknap Press of Harvard University Press

Cohen, W. M. and R. C. Levin. (1989). 'Empirical Studies of Innovation and Market Structure', in Richard Schmalensee and Robert D. Willig. eds., Handbook of Industrial Organization. Amsterdam, North-Holland

David, P. and S. Greenstein (1990), 'The Economics of Compatibility Standards: an Introduction to Recent Research', *Economics of Innovation and New Technology* 1, 3-41.

Economides. N.(1996), 'The Economics of Networks'. International Journal of Industrial *Organization* 25, 1-18

Feller, W.(1957), An Introduction to Probability Theory and its Applications, Vol. I, New York, John Wiley and Sons

Foray, D. (1993),'Standardisation et Concurrence: Des Relations Ambivalentes', Rev. d'Economie Industrielle 63, 30-45

Francois, P. and H.L. Lloyd-Ellis (2002), 'Animal Spirits through Creative Destructions', mimeo, Economics Dept., Queen's Univ. Kingston, Ont., May

Freeman, C. (2003) ,'A Schumpeterian Renaissance ? ', Science and Technology Policy Research Unit, Univ. of Sussex, Brighton, SEWPS 102, July

Gans, J.(1998), 'Industrialization with a Menu of Technologies: Appropriate Technologies and the 'Big Push' ', *Structural Change and Economic Dynamics* 9, 333-348

Gottinger, H.W. (2003), Economies of Network Industries , London ,Routledge

Henderson, B.D. (1975), 'The Market Share Paradox', in Y. Brozen, ed. The Competitive Economy, Morristown, General Learning Press, 286-287

Hirsch, W.Z. (1956), 'Firm Progress Ratios', Econometrica 24, 136-143

Katz, M. and C. Shapiro (1992), 'Product Introduction with Network Externalities', The *Journal of Industrial Economics* 40, 55-84

Katz, M. and C. Shapiro (1994), 'System Competition and Network Effects', *Journal of Economic Perspectives* 8, 93-115

Krugman,P.R. (1991), 'History versus Expectations', *Quarterly Journal of Economics* 106(2), 651-667

Matsuyama,K. (1991),'Increasing Returns, Industrialization and Indeterminacy of Equilibrium', *Quarterly Journal of Economics* 106(2), 617-650

Matsuyama,K. (1992), 'The Market Size, Entrepreneurship, and the Big Push,'*Journal of the Japanese and International Economie*s 6, 347-364

Murphy, K.M., Shleifer, A. and R.W. Vishny (1989), 'Industrialization and the Big Push", *Journal of Political Economy* 97, pp.1003-1026

Nelson, R. and S. G.Winter (1982), *An Evolutionary Theory of Economic Change*, Cambridge, Harvard Univ. Press

Nelson, R.(1986), Evolutionary Modeling of Economic Change, in Stiglitz, J. and G. F. Matthewson, eds., New Developments in the Analysis of Market Structure, Cambridge, MIT Press

North,D.C.(2005), Understanding the Process of Economic Change, Princeton, Princeton Univ. Press

Penrose, E. (1995), The Theory of the Growth of the Firm, Oxford, Oxford Univ. Press (pb)

Porter, M. E. (1980), Competitive Strategy, New York, Free Press

Romer,P.M.(1987), 'Growth Based on Increasing Returns due to Specialization', American Economic Review 77 (2), 56-62

Romer, P.M.(1994), 'New Goods, Old Theory, and the Welfare Costs of Trade Restrictions,' *Journal of Development Economics* 43, 5-38

Rosenberg, N. (1982), Inside the Black Box: Technology and Economics, Cambridge, Cambridge Univ. Press

Sauer,C., Gawande, K. and G. Li (2003),'Big Push Industrialization: Some Empirical Evidence for East Asia and Eastern Europe,', Economic Bulletin 15(9), 1-7 (http://www.economicsbulletin.com/2003/volume15/EB−03O40005A.pdf)

Schumpeter. J.A.. (1942), Capitalism. Socialism. and Democracy, New York, Harper

Shapiro, C. and H. R. Varian (1999), Information Rules, Boston: Harvard Business School

Teece,D.(1986),'Profiting from Technology Innovations', Research Policy 15(6), 285-305

Trindade,V.(2005) 'The big push, industrialization and international trade: The role of exports', *Journal of Development Economics* 78, 22-48

Utterback,J.M.(1994), Mastering the Dynamics of Innovation, Boston, Harvard Business School Press

Utterback, J.M. and Suarez,F.F. (1993), *Innovation, Competition and Industry Structure*, Research Policy 22, 1-21

Chapter 7

GROWTH AND INSTITUTIONS

Mattheus F. A. Goosen

7.1. INTRODUCTION

One of the most significant areas of research in economics as well as a major theme of this book is in trying to comprehend the factors that contribute to economic growth and political change, and how this affects the economic rise and decline of nations. There are a variety of institutional arrangements or determinants which influence the economic development process across countries (Abrams and Lewis, 1995; Loomis, 2009; Schlueter, 2007; Greif, 2006; Dixit, 2008; Gottinger, 2009). These include political structure, political stability and relative size of government, civil liberties, property rights, and economic incentives. This knowledge is important, for example, to spur technological innovation in industries and countries, thus giving them a competitive edge (see Chaps. 1-2). Abrams and Lewis (1995), as a case in point, analyzed the growth rates for ninety nations from 1968 to 1987. They found that political order as well as economic incentives and personal freedoms were significant determinants of growth. David Landes (1998) in his book on "The Wealth and Poverty of Nations" argues that the history of the past 500 years should be Eurocentric. It is primarily the story of how expansionist Europeans and their ex colonies have grown very rich at the expense, to some degree, of the rest of the world. In fairness, Landes also argues that the history of the world from 500 to 1500 should be primarily Islamocentric.

In this chapter we will argue that consensual political orders result in more flexible institutions that provide better incentives for economic growth through a market-oriented competitive environment. Corruption is also an outcome of a country's institutions and will normally but not always have a negative effect on economic growth. Furthermore, economic freedom also shows up in the form of industrial competition, or racing, among nations by creating value added products through rivalry as reflected in an increase of gross domestic product. This is discussed in detail in Chapters 1 and 9. In addition, the field of economic governance has shown that diverse economies have used various institutions, at various times, to carry out these functions. We will join the debate on whether political institutions cause economic growth, or whether, alternatively, growth and human capital accumulation lead to institutional improvement. Positive factors on growth, for instance, include consensual political systems that are flexible, a competitive environment with fiscal incentives that allows for continuous improvement in efficiency, industrial competition that allows for economic choices (as discussed in more detail in Chap. 3), and a well developed educational system to help provide competent human capital for formal institutions such as courts. Negative institutional factors affecting economic growth are corruption due to fiscal and political decentralization resulting in stagnation due to reduced economic choices, and autocrats or dictators that make poor policy choices.

Democracies, with their higher levels of personal freedoms, grew more quickly than non-democratic regimes. However, they also showed that lower income countries grew more rapidly than those with higher income. In a comparable study reported by Barro (1998) for a similar time period and number of countries, it was shown that the economic growth rate was improved by higher initial schooling and life expectancy, lower fertility, lower government consumption, better maintenance of the rule of law, lower inflation and improved trade. In contrast to Abrams and Lewis (1995) study, Barro (1998) found that political freedom had only a weak effect on growth, but this effect was non-linear. For example, at low levels of political rights, an expansion of these rights stimulated economic growth. However, once a moderate amount of democracy had been attained, then a further increase reduced growth. In contrast, there was a strong positive effect of the standard of living on a country's inclination for democracy.

Amongst the successful studies on institutions as economic growth determinants are the theories of Douglass North's 'cultural heritage' hypothesis, and Mancur Olson's 'country-specific economic policy' hypothesis (Schlueter, 2007; North 1994, 2005a, 2005b; Olson 1996, 2000). While North (1994) defines informal and formal institutions as humanly-formulated restrictions that govern the opportunities for economic growth, Olson (2000) uses the term more in the sense of formal institutions. Olson goes even further by outlining that the structure of institutions are not just constraints of market activities, as with North, but that they can also act as incentives for trade (Schlueter, 2007). Both scholars claim the universality of their approaches in explaining real world economic history and share the notion of the role of the state in providing well-defined individual property rights, low transaction cost levels, and well-developed national capital markets to achieve economic growth potential. On the other hand, their propositions differ substantially in the foundation of economic policy and its ability to adjust over time. Furthermore, Schlueter (2007) was able to demonstrate that an economic growth pattern for small and remote countries, such as New Zealand and Argentina, cannot be solely explained either by North's nor Olson's theory. A combination of both theories and additional amendments were needed to account more precisely for the actual economic histories of the two countries. In a related study, Thorbecke and Wan (1999) reported, on Taiwan's development experience. They scrutinized the role of government in the successful transition to a more market oriented economy and looked at the transferability of this understanding to emerging states. It was noted that Taiwan's development experience is poorly understood by economists in developing countries.

During his academic career North evolved from a traditional fiscal theorist into a historical economist (i.e. the latter combines economic theory and economic history) (Vandenberg, 2002; Rutherford, 2001). As part of this evolution, North also borrowed readily from other intellectuals such as Simon (1998), Olson (2000) and Coase (1992). In contrast, it has been noted that Olson stayed with the same idea or concept throughout his career;

attributing economic growth to opportunistic behavior of individuals and groups (McLean, 2000; Schlueter, 2007). North (2005b) remarks that economic markets tend to become inertial or complacent over time in the absence of a stimulus such as innovative institutional transformation. This is the same idea that democracies become less efficient at adapting to changing circumstances over time due to emergence of special interest groups (e.g. lobbyists) (Baumgartner and Leach, 1998; Loomis, 2009).

Chapters 1-3 showed that a critical driving force for economic growth among states is a built-in and historically observable rivalry in stature, influence and economic performance that drives countries to get ahead or not to fall too far behind. Numerous kinds of races were examined including frontier races among leaders and would-be leaders, as occurs, for example, with different leagues in major sports events, where there are catch-up races among the different teams. Chapter 4 developed a model to analyze the patterns of catching up, falling behind and getting ahead that was identified with technological racing (i.e. industrial competition) among nations or regional economic entities.

The field of economic governance studies and compares institutions and processes that support economic activity using empirical and case studies as well as theoretical models (Williamson, 2005). Dixit (2008) remarks that different governance institutions are optimal for different societies, for different kinds of economic activity, and at different times. As economic activity increases, formal institutions usually become better than informal ones, but the latter provide a useful function under the shadow of formal ones, even in the most advanced economies. Diverse economies have used various institutions to carry out these functions at different times with varying amounts of success.

Cecchetti, et al. (2010) notes that the monetary calamity that erupted in mid-2008 led to a sudden increase of public debt in many advanced economies. Governments were required to re-capitalize banks, to take over a large part of the debts of failing financial institutions, and to introduce large stimulus programs to revive demand. The projections of public debt ratios lead Cecchetti et al. to conclude that the path pursued by fiscal authorities in a number of industrial states is unsustainable. Radical actions are needed to limit the rapid growth of current and future liabilities of governments and reduce their adverse consequences for long-term growth and fiscal stability.

Glaeser et al (2004) revisited the discussion over whether political institutions cause economic growth, or whether, alternatively, growth and human capital accumulation lead to institutional improvement. They found that most indicators of institutional quality used to establish the proposition that institutions cause growth, as outlined for example in North's and Olson's theories (North 1994, Olson 2000) were constructed to be conceptually unsuitable for that purpose. Results suggested that human capital is a more basic source of growth than are the institutions, poor countries get out of poverty through good policies, often pursued by dictators, and subsequently improve their political institutions. As an example, in a recent interview Paul Kagame, the man who ended Rwanda's genocide in which 10% of the country's population was killed in just 100 days, was quoted as saying that as the country's President, he does not want foreign aid. He wants investment and free trade. "We believe in free enterprise, free market and competition…So we have to make sure there is a conducive environment for people to be creative and innovative," he told the interviewer (Jolis, 2010). In September 2009, the World Bank named Rwanda its "top reformer of business regulation," as the country soared to 67th place from 143rd the year before for ease of doing business." Many African leaders, however, have been criticized for hanging on to power well beyond their term limits. Whether Mr. Kagame will be one of the exceptions to this trend remains to be seen.

This chapter examines institutional structures, including autocracy and democracy, as economic growth determinants. Economic governance, industrial racing as well as the effects of corruption are also discussed and related to both developing as well as developed nations, including Asian countries. In addition, the debate on whether political institutions cause economic growth, or whether, alternatively, growth and human capital accumulation lead to institutional improvement is assessed. The long term goal is to better comprehend the factors that contribute to economic expansion and political transformation, and how this affects the growth of states.

7.2. Cultural-Dependent Learning and Economic Emergence of Countries

Gradually over time, a country's belief system develops and helps to shape institutions, both informal and formal; this is what we term culture. These are the guidelines, regulations or sets of laws by which individuals have to operate. Douglas North's work primarily deals with understanding the interaction between a country's cultural heritage and economic growth (North, 1994; Schlueter, 2007). In particular, his theory states that countries with thriving economies owe their success to cultural differences in comparison to states with non successful economies. North (2005a, 2005b) notes that institutions are central in creating property rights (like real estate ownership), the rule of law, and competition. This provides stability or order which is essential for ensuring economic growth. His model of order-maintaining systems has two poles or sets of political order with an autocratic regime (i.e. authoritarian political order) on one end and a democracy (i.e. consensual political order) on the other (Table 7.1) (North 2005b).

Table 7.1. Key characteristics of countries that are able to adapt to external changes quickly and correctly due to their ability to obtain a consensus as a result of their flexible culture (adapted from North, 2005b; Schlueter, 2007)

- Employ common belief system to set up self-enforcing limits for politicians
- State should have an effective constitution that assigns citizen rights and places limits on government decision making
- Well defined property and personal rights
- State officials must adhere to obligations and rights

Anarchy can come about as a result of far-reaching changes in the rules. Disorder in a country and thus chaos in an economic system, can result, for example, from the death of an autocratic or dictatorial ruler, or from an economic calamity. The later, for example, weakens the underlying consensus in a democracy.

North (1994) uses the success of Britain and its former colonies and the failure of Spain and its colonial settlements as a prime example to support his cultural heritage theory (Schlueter, 2007). In the case of the British model, due to their common cultural backgrounds former colonial countries (e.g. USA, Canada, Australia, and India) share almost identical informal and formal institutions (i.e. consensual political order). These states have institutional backgrounds that provide incentives through a market-oriented competitive environment. Their institutions have evolved into consent-oriented democracies that are adaptable to changes, which assure the rule of law as well as property rights.

On the other hand, the failure of Spain and its former colonies (e.g. Latin America) has been attributed to its economic institutions and political structure (North 1994). These countries shared a common cultural heritage of autocratic and centralized institutions that were inflexible to changes. This failed to establish essential elements for modern economic growth. We can go on to speculate that while this argument for a failed economic state held for the last 400 years, in more recent times Spain itself has managed to reinvent itself by moving from an autocratic and inefficient dictatorship, with the demise of General Franco, to a consensual democracy with a vibrant economy. Perez-Diaz (1993) described the emergence of democratic Spain, and similar to North (1994) emphasizes the importance of culture in shaping collective identities, and these in turn frame interests.

Overhead or transaction costs are also critical in shaping the structure of institutions. Autocratic Britain being isolated on an island did not have to rely on a large standing army and thus avoided large overhead costs (North, 1994; Schlueter, 2007). The government started to provide property and civil rights in return for more revenue. This evolved into a democracy by the establishment of a parliament that served and represented the whole country. A key example from the medieval period is the Magna Carta, an English legal charter which was http://en.wikipedia.org/wiki/Charter originally issued in 1215 (Holt, 1992). Magna Carta required the King of England to proclaim certain rights pertaining to the country's citizens, respect legal procedures, and accept that his privileges would be bound by the law. Autocratic Spain on the other hand being on the European mainland had to contend with large overhead costs in order to maintain a substantial standing army for protection from aggressive neighbors. The financing for the army was provided primarily by the gold supplied from its North and South American colonies during the 16th century. Spain's autocratic system was reinforced when this source of funds dried up, resulting in disorder. The country's preference for a centralized monarchy, for example, undermined competition and the rule of law by granting monopoly rights for additional revenue and by property confiscation as a means of domestic taxation. North (1994) goes on to argue that Latin America inherited all these features of disorder from Spain: an autocratic and centralized system, lack of self government, as well as a lack of competition, and well specified property rights. As a result these regions could not experience economic growth during the previous centuries due to the inheritance of the wrong institutions (North, 1994; Schlueter, 2007).

Adaptability to changes is key cultural factor that influences economic growth. North (2005b) notes that during periods of economic and/or political turmoil, some societies are able to re-establish order faster than others because of their distinctive belief system. These adaptive efficient countries have flexible institutional matrixes (i.e. belief systems) that are able to achieve a consensus relatively quickly to any changes in political and economic scenarios, whether internal or external. He goes on to provide several key attributes of such countries including establishing citizen and property rights, and making sure that state officials adhere to these rights (Table 7.1). States with an authoritarian political order have informal institutions which are unable to adapt quickly and/or successfully to economic changes since there is no consensus within the society (North, 1994). This results in disorder which is detrimental to economic growth.

7.3. INCENTIVES AND ECONOMIC GROWTH

Unlike North (1994), Olson (1996) rules out cultural heritage as a primary source of successful economic growth; Olson (2000) emphasizes proper incentives as the main source for thriving economic expansion. Particularly he notes that official institutions and the fiscal policies of the ensuing political organizations determine economic achievement. For example, if the proper formal institutions are in place, then individual property rights are secure since contracts can be enforced (e.g. no illegal confiscation of property by autocratic governments). In addition, by limiting rent-seeking behavior and providing currency stability, transaction costs (i.e. overheads) are reduced. This helps economic growth, and is similar to North's (1994) reduced overhead concept as a key factor for successful economies.

In contrast to North's (1994) two tier order maintaining system (i.e. authoritarian and consensual/democratic political orders), Olson (2000) proposed a three-level hierarchy political framework for describing economic growth: anarchies (roving bandits), autocracies (stationary bandits or dictatorships) and democracies (majorities or consensual). All three systems share common characteristics that their main tools are taxation and profit-maximizing individuals. The overall effectiveness for economic growth is dependent on the type of order-maintaining system (Table 7.2).

Table 7.2 Olson's Order Maintaining Political Systems and Economic Outcomes (adapted from Schlueter, 2007)

	Anarchies	Autocracies	Democracies
Is there order in the country?	No	Yes, but without the consent of the governed	Yes, with the consent of the governed
How is the power distributed?	Arbitrary	Monopoly of the autocratic regime	Monopoly of a majority
Formal policies and regulations are specified by	There are none	The head of state	The majority of the voting public
Is there rule of law?	No	Yes, but only enforced in the interest of the head of state	Yes and enforced in the interest of the majority
Concern of the head of state in the people?	Slight	Yes; encompassing	Yes; encompassing
Compliance achieved?	No conformity	Yes, by coercive force of the ruler	Yes, by checks and balances as well as oercive force
Individual property and civil rights secured?	No	No	Yes
Level of Taxation?	Highest	Medium	Lowest
Public goods/services available?	No	Yes, but only provided as long as head of state makes profit	Yes
Level of investment?	Low	Medium	High
Incentives for economic growth?	Low	Medium	High

The lowest order is found with anarchies which also have the lowest economic growth. While both autocracies and democracies have order in the country, only the later has property and civil rights secured for its citizens. This provides a greater incentive for economic growth. Consensual (i.e. democratic) systems also have the lowest taxation rates and highest investment rates, in Olson's model, thus giving greater incentives for economic growth.

Unlike North's cultural heritage theory (North 1994), Olson (2000) rules out a link between culture and type of government; According to Olson (2000), democracy can be easily accepted if mental models (i.e. country specific experience) of the people were shaped by negative incidents such as war (i.e. harmful feedback loops). This would explain the emergence of Spain over the past 30 years from an economically weak autocratic state; into an energetic democracy with an equally vibrant economy (Perez-Diaz, 1993; Solsten and Meditz, 1988). The negative feedback loops were provided by Spain's devastating civil war in the 1930's, followed by 40 years of repressive dictatorship and poor economic growth. With the death of General Franco in the mid 1970's the country easily accepted democracy.

For the spontaneous emergence of a democracy, Olson (2000) explains that several conditions must be met: there must be a balance of powers so that no special interest group prevails (i.e. no autocratic ruler or mini-autocracies are created), and the state should be geographically protected from aggressive neighbors. This process of the unplanned appearance of a democratic state, which he terms an accident of history, applies to Britain as an island nation and its evolution from a feudal state, with its mini-autocracies, into a parliamentary (i.e. consensual) system. The physical isolation also allowed for low overheads, since no large standing army was required for protection from aggressive neighboring regimes. This resulted in rapid economic expansion as shown by the industrial revolution in the 18th and 19th centuries. This same argument could also be applied to the island nation of Taiwan (Thorbecke and Wan, 1999) by its transition over the past 50 years from an autocracy to a democracy with its more market oriented economy. It can be summarized that the open-minded self concern of the people in a state can lead to a democracy, no matter what culture exists.

Olson (2000) argues that democracy in countries such as Britain and the US emerged accidentally as a coincidence in history. The economic development in Britain during the industrial revolution of the 18th and 19th centuries as well as the more recent US trade and industry phenomenon, resulted from an independent judiciary, checks and balances in the legal systems so that no single group/person could emerge as a dictator/autocrat, a secure common law, and a bill of rights which made contracts enforceable and secured individual property rights. These factors working together allowed for economic incentives and rapid financial growth in a flexible and secure environment. A key factor in the evolution of consensual political orders (i.e. democracies) is the formation of formal institutions that have power-sharing arrangements and that secure property and contract rights. Olson (2000) goes on to explain that the US was successful because it effectively transferred formal institutions from Britain. The feedback loop mechanism in these consensual organizations also allowed for social stability since people felt that they were part of the process and thus supported the institutions.

On the detrimental side, for long established democracies there is an increase in overhead costs as well as corruption and loss of competition through lobbying (Clemens, 1997; Loomis, 2009). Over time there is the emergence of special interest groups, such as in the industrial sectors, which persuade the rational but poorly informed politicians and electorate to support their very narrow aims. In the US for example, the fact that there are more special interest lobbyists than elected politicians is a major concern (Baumgartner and Leach, 1998). As a result democracies become less efficient at adapting to changing circumstances over time. In the case of autocratic Spain during the last two centuries, poor market policies such as creation of trade monopolies, created the motivation to get around existing laws and to engage in corruption and unofficial economic (i.e. black) markets. The failure is thus due to the wrongly set financial incentives of a state and a lack of well-defined property rights. Poorly defined and poorly enforced property rights, for example, can lead to unlawful confiscation by autocratic rulers of an individual's real estate holdings and bank accounts.

This results in instability in society as well as a loss in economic incentives (Vandenberg, 2002; Rutherford, 2001).

While North's (1994) interactive learning process views transaction costs as being the result of a country's cultural history, Olson (2000) holds the view that overheads are the result of coincidence (i.e. an accident of history); the latter being depend on conventional official governance structures (Table 7.3).

Table 7.3 The Main Differences between the Cultural-Dependent and Country-Specific Theories as Economic Growth Determinants

	North's Cultural Dependent Learning Theory	Olson's Country-Specific Economic Policy Theory
Cultural tradition important?	Yes	No
Key determinants for economic development	Formal and informal state institutions	Formal institutions
Political spectrum and hierarchy	Consensual political order Authoritarian political order	Democracy Autocracy Anarchy
Establishment of democracy	Due to path-dependent intellectual heritage; culturally inherited belief system is key determinant	Accident of history; as long as correct country-specific institutions and economic policies are in place then there will be successful political and economic outcomes, irrespective of cultural heritage
Corruption	Granting monopoly rights for additional revenue; property confiscation (authoritarian political order)	In democracies, lobbying/special interest groups causes corruption For autocracies. formation of trade monopolies, created motivation to get around existing laws and to engage in corruption and unofficial economic (i.e. black) markets
Main weakness of model/theory	Does not address effect of multinational organizations/ companies	Does not address effect of multinational organizations/ companies
Incentives	Institutions provide incentives through a market-oriented competitive environment	Opportunistic behavior of individuals and groups
Overhead/transaction costs	Interactive learning process allows for the lowering of overhead costs through communication and sharing of a consensual belief system	Lowest for a democracy
Individual property rights established?	Yes, both individual and group property rights ensured by the state. Collective or group learning key factor in development of rights.	Yes, individual property rights are central concept; individuals are profit seeking, opportunistic, even in group actions

Although both theories put the government or state at the center of their institutional models for defining and enforcing property rights, they fail to address multinational corporations and non-governmental organizations and their influence on economic development and outcomes (McLean, 2000; Fiani, 2004; Chowdhury et. al, 2005). However, by assigning the primary responsibility to the government, differences between religions is subdued, such as between Catholicism in the Spanish model and Protestantism in the British model. It has been noted that the power of religion, if any, in economic change, is still not well understood (Greasley and Oxley, 2000).

7.4. ECONOMIC GROWTH OF ASIAN COUNTRIES

The economic progress and catch-up of Asian states such as Japan, Taiwan and South Korea, as well as China and India, countries with the highest populations on the planet, has been extraordinary (Chaps. 3 and 8; Wan and Wan Jr, 2004; Thorbecke and Wan, 1999). This has facilitated their incorporation into the world economy and has nurtured globalization.

Table 7.4. Historical Change in Per Capita GDP, in terms of 1990 international Geary-Khamis dollars, of Five Countries (adapted from Maddison, 2006 and 2007)

Year	1700	1820	1870	1900	1920	1940	1960	1980	1995	2003
UK	1250	1706	3190	4492	4548	6856	8857	12931	17495	21310
USA		1257	2445	4091	5552	7010	11328	18577	24484	29037
Japan		669	737	1180	1696	2874	3986	13428	19849	21218
S. Korea		600	604	-	1009	1442	1105	4114	11818	14673
China			530	545	-	-	673	1067	2653	4803

Chapter 1 argues that economic growth essentially embodies a technology race or industrial competition between nations. The swift growth of several Asian economies, in comparison to the UK and the US, is shown in Table 7.4, where changes in GDP per capita are compared.

All five countries went through different stages of industrialization within a period of 300 years. Mokyr (1990) in The Lever of Riches argues that technological creativity and subsequent growth was a contributing factor in the rise of the West. According to Mokyr two main factors were involved in the unbelievable surge in European technological creativity; money-oriented common sense that encouraged Europeans' attempts to control the environment, and the divided character of European political structure that spurred competition (i.e. industrial racing; see section 7.6 and Chap. 2) since many countries feared to fall behind their neighbors. He defined two types of technological changes; gradual improvements termed microinvention, as occurred in agriculture and naval technology, and groundbreaking discoveries termed macroinvention, as with developments of Gutenberg's printing press and James Watt's steam engine. Although Mokyr compares Sung China and Europe briefly and acknowledges the superiority of Chinese technology in the fifteenth century, he does not differentiate clearly between macro and microinventions, although he implies that the latter was more important. Surprisingly, the Chinese ignored important macroinventions such as Su Sung's water clock, which led to stagnation in technological progress.

Over the past century, Asian states such as South Korea and Japan have gone through periods ranging from, autocracy to democracy; or using North's theory, authoritarian political order to consensual political order (North, 1994). South Korea, for example, endured a 20 year period of disorder and anarchy starting from the 1930's to the mid 1950's (i.e. Japanese invasion, Second World War and Korean War). Once stability and order were re-established the country adopted a consensual political order (i.e. democracy) which aided its economic recovery as shown by the rapid increase of the GDP by a factor of 13 over a 40 year period (i.e. from GDP of 1,105 in 1960 to 14,673 in 2003). This transformation into a democracy can be best explained by Olson's negative feedback loop. According to Olson (2000), democracy can be easily accepted if mental models (i.e. country specific experience) of the people were shaped by negative incidents such as war (i.e. harmful feedback loops).

In a related study, Rostow (1983) looked at the advent of industrialization, for several Asian countries in comparison to the US and the UK. In the case of South Korea, for example, there was a transit period, termed take-off time, during which the GDP per capita grew to US $2000; this occurred around 1970 (Table 7.4). Assuming that the take-off time is the period during which an economy transits its GDP per capita from $1000 to $2000, he compared the length of that period and the number of years needed to reach $5000 of GDP per capita. Chapters 1-3 looked at this transition time in terms of multiple kinds of industrial races including frontier races among leaders and would-be leaders on a global and local scale, corresponding, for example, to different leagues as in major sports events where there are catch-up races among the different teams. Getting ahead, catching up and falling behind processes are taking place amongst industry leaders and followers, as well as stragglers within a group of countries that are in pursuit of higher levels of power, welfare and productivity. This can be linked to the theory of North (2005b) who noted that during periods of economic and/or political turmoil, some societies are able to re-establish order faster than others because of their distinctive belief system. Adaptive efficient countries, such as modern Japan and South Korea, have flexible institutional matrixes (i.e. belief systems) that are able to achieve a consensus relatively quickly to any changes in political and economic scenarios, whether internal or external. Confucianism, an ethical system developed in ancient China, which dealt with individual morality and beliefs, and the proper exercise of political power, and Shintoism, an ancient Japanese religion closely tied to nature, have also played a role in the development of the flexible belief systems in these countries (Wan and Wan, 2004).

Rapid transformations in economic growth can also be explained by Olson's negative feedback loop (Olson, 2000); periods of war and turmoil make a society more receptive to consensual political order (i.e. democracy) with its resultant stability and development of flexible institutions that aid in efficient economic growth. This applies to Japan and South Korea which transformed from autocracies into democracies during the mid 20th century. China is currently an authoritarian political order with a rapidly expanding economy. However, it has gone through a period of anarchy during the first three quarters of the 20th century (i.e. civil war, Cultural Revolution) which has also made it more receptive to the need for flexible institutions. Whether the Chinese economy can continue along its present path or will slow down to growth rates similar to other economies after the take-off phases, depends on the growth of the capital stock, technological change, government policy for such economic resources and institutional changes to put the economy on a sustained growth path.

In East Asia, such a sustained growth as shown by Japan after the World War II has also been accomplished by Singapore, Hong Kong, and Taiwan. The recent economic growth of these Asian economies has been accompanied by great social transformation of each country such as urbanization, and growing enrollment in general and higher education. These improvements in economic growth can be explained by the formation of institutions that are responsive to changes in both the internal and external environments. The success of these countries was accomplished by new social, industrial, and financial policies (i.e. flexible institutional structures) that were well-suited to domestic and international environments of each country and, at the same time, by the strong, sometimes almost coercive interventions in the market (Song,1990).

Chapter 3 notes that the economies of South-East Asia (i.e. Singapore, Thailand, Malaysia and Indonesia) have adopted different institutional structures from Japan and South Korea, by opening their markets to foreign direct investment (The Economist, 1995). In addition, China is now in the situation of looking on a sustained growth for advanced industrialization. In an attempt to assist in this process, the government has begun an effort to introduce more flexible institutional structures. However, it is important to remember that the institutional structure of East Asian nations is subject to some weakness as well as strength, such as the lost decades of Japan, from 1989 to today, the financial crisis affecting Korea in 1997 and beyond, as well as the persistent cronyism in China and Korea.

7.5. ECONOMIC GOVERNANCE, PERFORMANCE AND EVOLUTION OF INSTITUTIONS

Formal and informal institutions evolve under different conditions in order to best support economic growth in a country by protecting property rights, enforcing contracts and organizing collective action which provides the appropriate infrastructure of rules, regulations and information that are needed for workable arrangements among individual and corporate economic players (Dixit, 2008; Williamson, 2005). Landes (1998), for instance, in his *"Wealth and Poverty of Nations"* has combined quantitative economic history with institutional analysis to produce a captivating historical overview of economic growth. What Landes does is to assess the mutual relationship between technology and society to analyze examples of states that succeeded as well as failed. DeLong (1998) notes that several lessons from this book include: try to ensure that a state's government is a regime that enables innovation and production, rather than a government that maintains power by a redistribution of wealth from its enemies to its friends; recognize that the task of a less-productive economy is to imitate rather than innovate; and be familiar with that as things change we need to change with them.

Diverse economies have used various institutions to carry out functions at different times with varying amounts of success, as shown by the industrial policies and catch-up competition between different Asian states. The field of economic governance studies and compares these institutions and processes that support economic activity using empirical and case studies as well as theoretical models (Williamson, 2005). In contrast, corporate governance analyses the internal management of a corporation and the rules and procedures by which a corporation deals with its stakeholders.

Corporate and economic governance are often connected since the problems faced by an internal organization (e. g. information and commitment costs) are often similar to property and contract transaction costs (Coase, 1937). This section will deal primarily with economic governance. The concept of economic governance covers many areas including institutions and organizational behavior, economic development and growth, industrial organization, law and economics, political economy and comparative economic systems. In order to get a better

Table 7.5 Various Dimensions of the Concept of Economic Governance (adapted from Dixit, 2008)

Dimension	Categories
Purpose of the institution	Protection of property rights against theft by other individuals and usurpation by the state itself or its agents
	Enforcement of voluntary contracts among individuals
	Provision of physical and regulatory infrastructure to facilitate economic activity and functioning of protection and enforcement categories
Nature of the institution	Formal state institutions that enact and enforce laws, including legislature, police, judiciary, and regulatory agencies
	Private institutions, such as arbitration forums, that function under the state law
	For-profit private institutions that provide information and enforcement, such as organized crime and security agencies
	Group enforcement through social networks and norms

grasp of the concept he has organized it along different dimensions and categories covering the purpose as well as the nature of the institution (Table 7.5).

The latter, for instance, were subdivided by Dixit (2008) into four categories; formal state institutions that enact and enforce laws, including legislature, police, judiciary and regulatory agencies; private institutions, such as arbitration forums, that function under the state law; for-profit private institutions that provide information and enforcement, such as organized crime and security agencies; and group enforcement through social networks and norms.

As an example of the evolution of an early institutional structure, Greif et al. (1994) reported on how groups of traders in medieval Europe took collective action to counter a ruler's incentives to violate the member's property rights. Another key instance from this period is the Magna Carta, also called Magna Carta Libertatum (the Great Charter of Freedoms), an English legal charter which was http://en.wikipedia.org/wiki/Charter originally issued in 1215 (Holt, 1992). Magna Carta required King John of England to proclaim certain rights pertaining to the country's citizens, respect legal procedures, and accept that his powers would be bound by the law. It supported what became the writ of habeas corpus, allowing appeal against unlawful imprisonment. Magna Carta was the most significant early influence on the governance process that led to the rule of constitutional law today, including the United States Constitution. It was the first document forced onto an autocratic ruler by a group of his subjects (i.e. the barons) in an attempt to limit his powers by law and protect their property rights.

The sequence of economic and political reforms matters, with Giavazzi and Tabellini (2005) arguing that states that implement economic reforms first and then democratize do much better in most dimensions than those that follow the opposite route. A recent example of this is the transformation of the old Soviet Union into Russia and the evolution of modern

China. The latter with its more flexible industrial policies and management system implementing economic reform first, has had a greater impact on the world economy.

Much debate remains about the exact measures of the excellence of an institution, and how these affect economic results. Furthermore, democracy and authoritarianism come in many different varieties. Barro (1999) for example finds that there is an optimum level in the relationship between economic growth and degree of democratic freedom; more democracy raises growth when political freedoms are weak, but depresses growth when a moderate amount of freedom is already established. Persson (2005) found that the exact type of democracy matters for developing policy and economic outcomes; parliamentary, proportional and permanent democracies appeared to encourage more growth promoting structural policies, whereas presidential and temporary democracies do not. The exact reason for this is not well understood even after reviewing the literature on lawmaking organizations (Keefer, 2004).

In a report for the World Bank, Kaufman et al. (2005) constructed six measures of institutional quality (Table 7.6).

Table 7.6 Measures of Institutional Quality (adapted from Kaufman et al, 2005 and Dixit, 2008)

Type of Quality	What is measured?
Voice and accountability	Political, human and civil rights
Political instability and violence	Likelihood of violent threats to, or changes in, government, including terrorism
Government effectiveness	Competence of bureaucracy and quality of public service delivery
Regulatory burden	Incidence of market unfriendly policies
Rule of law	Quality of contract enforcement, police, and courts as well as likelihood of crime and violence
Control of corruption	Exercise of public power for private gain, including petty and grand corruption and state capture

Three of these, rule of law, control of corruption, and political instability and violence, deal with protection of property rights and enforcement of contracts while the first one, voice and accountability relates to governance since good communication can reduce problems between citizens and agencies of the state.

Governance is also affected by government effectiveness and regulatory burdens. It can be argued, however, that the method of construction of these six measures of institutional quality relies on subjective perception, and is thus subject to error.

The protection of property rights supplied by the state is often supplemented by private security agencies; the latter works cooperatively with the police. In addition, information gathering constitutes a major source of advantage for private agencies/ systems over formal law (Dixit, 2008). Enforcement of a contract in a court of law, for example, requires proof of misconduct by one of the parties. Information gathering can be done more effectively by private agencies. The most notable item about commercial contract disputes is that private alternatives, such as arbitration by industrial experts, are almost always tried first. Only as a last resort will one of the parties file a suit in a formal court of law (Williamson, 1995). The advantages of expert arbitration are often recognized by formal legal systems with the courts standing ready to enforce the decisions of expert industry arbitrators.

Formal governance at the international level works through institutions such as the World Trade Organization. The procedures of their sovereign country members are subject to self-enforcement and are thus similar to social networks (Bagwell and Staiger, 2003). Arbitration of international contract disputes works in a similar way (Mattli, 2001). While such arbitrators lack direct power to enforce their decisions, they are normally backed by treaties that ensure enforcement by national courts.

Organized crime also plays a role in governance (Gambetta, 1993; Bandiera, 2003). If a state, for example, is unwilling to protect certain kinds of property or enforce certain kinds of contracts, such as illegal activities, then private institutions, such as organized crime, can emerge to perform these functions for a profit. Gambetta (1993) argues that the Mafia emerged in 19th century Sicily in order to fill a vacuum left by a lack of state protection. Landowners started hiring guards from former feudal lords, as well as bandits, to protect their property. Eventually the Mafia's role expanded to provide contract enforcement in illegal markets. In a similar fashion the Japanese Yakusa evolved just after the end of the Second World War, and the Russian mafia after the fall of the Soviet Union; in both cases to fill a vacuum left by a temporary weak state (Dower, 1999; Varese, 2001).

The information function of organized crime, such as the Mafia, is comparable to that of credit ranking agencies and Better Business Bureaus (Dixit, 2004); keeping track of previous contract violations, informing a customer of the history of a potential business partner, and providing punishment if a customer's trading partner violates their contract. In the case of a Mafia enforcer, anyone who cheats a customer of the Mafioso is subject to the possibility of physical violence. With a Better Business Bureau, if a company misbehaves, after having joined the organization, then it is subject to a poor rating or blacklisting. As economic activity increases, formal institutions usually become better than informal ones, but the latter provide a useful function under the shadow of formal ones, even in the most advanced economies.

7.6. CORRUPTION AND GROWTH

Several years ago, Svensson (2005) as part of a study on the effects of government regulations and corruption on economic growth interviewed the chief executive officer (CEO) of a successful Thai manufacturing company. During the interview the CEO exclaimed: "I hope to be reborn as a custom official." Svensson noted that when a well-paid CEO wishes for a job with low official pay in the government sector, corruption is almost surely a problem. The funds allegedly embezzled by the former presidents of Indonesia and Philippines, Mohamed Suharto and Ferdinand Marcos, as an example, are estimated to be $10 billion and $35 billion, respectively (Transparency International, 2004; Svensson, 2005). The former President of Zaire, Mobutu Sese Seko, looted the treasury of some $5 billion, an amount equal to the country's entire external debt at the time he was removed from office in 1997. An internal IMF report found that nearly $1 billion of oil revenues, or $77 per capita, vanished from the Angolan state treasury in 2001 alone (Pearce, 2002). This amount was about three times the value of the humanitarian aid received by Angola in the same year, in a country where three-quarters of the population survives on less than $1 a day and where one in three children dies before the age of five. As a final example, the effect of the earthquake in Turkey that took thousands of lives in 2004 would have been much less severe, according to a government report, if contractors had not been able to pay bribes to build homes with substandard materials (Kinzer, 1999). The World Bank Institute estimates that total global bribes in a year are about $1 trillion, about 3 percent of world GDP (Rose-Ackerman, 2004).

A common definition of public corruption is the misuse of public office for private gain. Corruption defined this way would include, for example, the sale of government property by government officials, kickbacks in public procurement, as well as bribery and embezzlement of government funds. The most disturbing forms of bribery include the diversion of money for public programs and the harm caused by firms and persons that pay bribes to avoid health and safety regulations.

Corruption is an outcome of a country's institutions. For example corruption shows up when people pay bribes to avoid penalties for harmful conduct such as theft or risky waste disposal. On the other hand, corruption can also arise due to poor policies or inefficient institutions resulting in bribes being paid to the regulators by individuals seeking to get around the rules (Djankov et al., 2003). Unlike taxes, bribes bring no funds to government treasuries and they also involve higher transaction costs than taxes due to the secrecy surrounding their payments (Shleifer and Vishny, 1993). Even in a democracy bribing is similar in some ways to lobbying in the form of campaign contributions (Harstad and Svensson, 2004).

Assessing corruption across states is not easy due to the secretive nature of bribery and the range of forms it takes. Several types of corruption measures have been reported. The International Country Risk Guide (ICRG) (Mauro 1995) produced by private risk assessment firms, measures the likelihood that high government officials will demand bribes and the extent to which illegal payment are expected throughout government departments. The Corruption Perception Index (CPI) is based on a number of average ratings from different sources (Transparency International 2010). This is produced by Transparency International and is the most widely distributed.

A complementary measure derived by Kaufman et al. (2003) is Control of Corruption (CC) which is drawn from a larger set of data sources and includes a broader definition of corruption.

Lastly, the International Crime Victim Surveys (ICVS) was developed by the United Nations Office on Drugs and Crime, and focuses on individuals rather than companies (United Nations Office on Drugs and Crime, 2010). Countries that have the worst rankings for corruption are listed in Table 7.7. Note that not all states are ranked and that country coverage differs. All measures are scaled such that an elevated value indicates higher corruption. All of the countries with the highest levels of corruption are developing states with primarily low income levels and closed economies (Sachs and Warner 1995).

As we saw in the section on governance, institutions develop in response to a country's income level and needs (Dixit, 2008; Lipset, 1960). For example, education and human capital is needed for the efficient operation of formal institutions such as courts. Government abuses such as bribery are more likely to go unnoticed and unchallenged when the electorate is uneducated (e.g. illiterate). Education is also more likely to lead to a free press rather than a government controlled press, with the former increasing the chances of reporting public sector misbehavior, such as corruption (Besley and Burgess, 2002). Empirical evidence suggests that richer countries have lower corruption. This is consistent with the theories of corruption that argue that institutional quality is shaped by economic factors. Svensson (2005) reports that corruption is closely related to GDP per capita and to human capital; the higher the GDP and level of education the lower the probability of dishonesty. Increased salaries of

Table 7.7. The most Corrupt Countries. The bottom 10 percent most corrupt countries from each data set. A higher score within each category indicates higher corruption (adapted from Svensson, 2005)

Country	CC	Country	CPI	Country	ICRG	Country	IGVS
Equatorial Guinea	1.9	Bangladesh	8.7	Zimbabwe	5.8	Albania	0.75
Haiti	1.7	Nigeria	8.6	China	5	Uganda	0.36
Iraq	1.4	Haiti	8.5	Gabon	5	Mozambique	0.31
Congo. Dem. Rep.	1.4	Myanmar	8.4	Indonesia	5	Nigeria	0.30
Myanmar	1.4	Paraguay	8.4	Iraq	5	Lithuania	0.24
Afghanistan	1.4	Angola	8.2	Lebanon	5		
Nigeria	1.4	Azerbaijan	8.2	Myanmar	5		
Laos	1.3	Cameroon	8.2	Niger	5		
Paraguay	1.2	Georgia	8.2	Nigeria	5		
Turkmenistan	1.2	Tajikistan	8.2	Russia	5		
Somalia	1.2	Indonesia	8.2	Sudan	5		
Korea, North	1.2	Kenya	8.1	Somalia	5		
Zimbabwe	1.2	Cote d'Ivoire	7.9	Congo Dem Rep	5		
Indonesia	1.2	Kyrgyzstan	7.9	Serbia Montenegro	5		
Angola	1.1	Libya	7.9	Haiti	4.8		
Bangladesh	1.1	Papua New Guinea	7.9	Papua New Guinea	4.8		
Cameroon	1.1						
Niger	1.1						
Sudan	1.1						
Azerbaijan	1.1						
Tajikistan	1.1						
Sample size	195		133		140		44

Notes:
CC (Control of Corruption) index takes values between -2.5 to 2.5.
CPI (Corruption Perception Index) takes values between 0 to 10.
ICRG (International Country Risk Guide) corruption indicator takes values between 0 to 6.
ICSV (International Crime Victims Survey) incidence of individual bribes.

civil servants combined with deregulation, for example, were primarily responsible for the emergence of an honest and competent public administration in Sweden in the last century (Lindbeck, 1975). The same can be said for modern day Singapore.

A positive relationship has also been observed between corruption and market regulation (De Soto, 1989). What can account for this? Government regulations that raise barriers give public officials the power to demand and collect bribes (De Soto, 1989). Thus deregulation may reduce corruption by reducing the extent to which public officials have the power to extract bribes. In addition, the primary social losses of corruption come from propping up of inefficient companies (Murphy et al, 1993). However, it is still very difficult to quantify corruption. While, the micro evidence (i.e. within a country) and case studies say that corruption is bad for growth, the macro evidence (i.e. cross country) is inconclusive (Mauro, 1995; Reinikka and Svensson, 2005).

Svensson (2005) argues that there are several areas where further study is needed. Experimentation and evaluation of new tools are required to enhance accountability in research on corruption. Secondly, the differential effect of corruption is also an area that requires more examination. For example, China and Brazil have both undergone recent decentralization and are perceived to be equally corrupt. China which is fiscally decentralized (i.e. local governments have primary control over spending) but politically centralized (i.e. central government has control over regulations) has shown strong economic growth, in spite of the corruption. In comparison, Brazil is both fiscally and politically decentralized and has shown very poor economic growth and extreme corruption (Mazzara, 2006). Mazzara argues that market preserving federalism accounts for a component of China's economic success and part of Brazil's continuing fight with corruption. China's fiscal decentralization but lack of political and administrative decentralization has permitted the formation of local competition that discourages corruption and encourages economic growth. In contrast, Brazil's political decentralization has left the central administration powerless when it comes to enforcing economic policies that guarantee constancy and competition. In a related study using a panel of 60 countries, Swaleheen and Stansel (2007) concluded that countries with low economic freedom where individuals have limited economic choices, corruption reduces economic growth. However in countries with high economic freedom, corruption was found to increase economic growth by providing a way around government controls.

7.7. PUBLIC DEBT AND ECONOMIC GROWTH

Next to problems of corruption there is the concern about public debt which after accumulation could overwhelm a country's wealth (Patton, 2010). It is intriguing how to properly relate economic expansion to the growth and level of public debt, a timely subject which may be a future constraining factor; see, for instance what has happened to Dubai, Greece, Japan, UK, and possibly very soon the United States. Cecchetti, et al. (2010) noted that the monetary calamity that erupted in mid-2008 led to a sudden increase of public debt in many advanced economies. Governments were required to re-capitalize banks, to take over a large part of the debts of failing financial institutions, and to introduce large incentive programs to revive demand. In addition, a swiftly maturing populace presents a number of countries with the prospect of enormous future costs that are not entirely recognized in existing budget projections.

Japan has been living with a public debt ratio of over 150% without any adverse effect on its cost. So it is possible that investors will continue to put strong faith in industrial countries' ability to repay, and that worries about excessive public debts are exaggerated. As a matter of macroeconomic theory, so long as the debt/income ratio is constant, an economy could live with any level of debt. Cecchetti, et al (2010) take a longer and less kindly view of current developments, arguing that the aftermath of the financial crisis has brought the simmering fiscal troubles in industrial economies to the boiling point. The projections of public debt ratios lead Cecchetti et al. to conclude that the path pursued by fiscal authorities in a number of industrial states is unsustainable. Radical actions are needed to limit the rapid growth of current and future liabilities of governments and reduce their unfavorable consequences for long-term growth and fiscal stability.

The politics of public debt vary by country. In some, due to unpleasant experiences, there is a culture of thriftiness. In others, however, extravagant official spending is commonplace. As an example of the latter, Michael Pento (2009) reported that the Persian Gulf emirate of Dubai is seeking to defer debt payment on nearly $90 billion in liabilities from its state-run companies. Like many other over-leveraged enterprises and some countries across the globe, the government of Dubai made a massive gamble on real estate that has turned out poorly. Even economic giants like Japan and the United States need to take heed, with the latter also suffering economically from the near failure of large real estate companies like Freddie Mac and Fannie Mae.

The examples produced over the last few years should send a stark warning to the U.S. as well as the European Union that they cannot continue to operate at current levels of monetary and fiscal extravagance. The ramifications of taking on too much debt are that unless the party in question can be bailed out, the de-leveraging process usually leads to default and insolvency. It makes no difference whether it is a business, like AIG, or a country. Either way, the entity in question must always be able to service its debt, either by generating revenue or by taxation. If the venture or state becomes too extended, it becomes dangerously dependent on continuous economic growth or on continually low interest rates. Taking these warnings to heart, Saudi Arabia's government, for instance, has used the budget surplus of recent years to reduce public debt from SR660bn (i.e. $176 bn USD) in 2002, representing 82% of GDP, to SR237bn ($63 bn USD) in 2008, which represents 13.5% of gross domestic product. High oil prices led to record budget and external current account surpluses in 2008, despite the public expansionary fiscal policy and surge in imports. Part of the surplus has been used to repay domestic debt, which fell by 5% to 13.5% of GDP (AMEinfo.com, 2009).

Reinhart and Rogoff (2010) in a recent paper argued that higher debt may stunt economic growth (Wall Street Journal, 2010). They reported that countries with a gross public debt exceeding 90% of their annual economic output tended to grow a lot more slowly. In particular for developed states above the 90% debt threshold the average annual growth rate was about 2% lower that for states with a public debt of less than 30% of their GDP. This is of particular importance to countries such as the U. S. where growth in government debt, for example, stood at 85% of GDP in 2009 and is expected to surpass 100% within 5 years. However, while they found that the threshold for public debt was similar in advanced and emerging economies, emerging markets faced a lower threshold for external debt, which is usually denominated in a foreign currency; When external debt reached 60% of GDP for emerging states, then annual growth declined by about 2%.

In their book Public Debt and Economic Growth, Greiner and Fincke (2009, pp 71-82) observed that an increase in community liability must be accompanied by an increase in the primary surplus of the government to guarantee sustainability of public debt. They presented an endogenous growth model and assumed that the primary surplus rises as public debt increases so that sustainability of public debt is given. Greiner and Fincke analyzed how different debt strategies affect stability and the long-run growth rate. It was demonstrated that the economy is always stable under a balanced public budget while when the government runs permanent deficits it is stable only if the primary surplus reacts sufficiently strongly to higher public debt. Furthermore, Greiner (2008) also ran their endogenous growth model with human capital, where human capital formation is the result of public education. The government finances expenditures in the schooling sector by the tax revenue and by public deficit. A sensitivity analysis of the dynamics of the model was presented and it turns out that the parameter determining the reaction of the primary surplus to changes in public debt is decisive as concerns the stability of the model. For more information on the importance of human capital formation see Section 7.9 where Glaeser et al (2004) revisited the discussion over whether political institutions cause economic growth, or whether, alternatively, growth and human capital accumulation lead to institutional improvement.

Two main problems states in the European Union with respect to economic growth and the public debt crisis are Greece and Spain (Wharton University, 2010). The economic outlook is bleak for Spain. The weak points of Spain's economy are its high unemployment rate and its low productivity, which are interconnected. In 2007, Spain's unemployment rate was 8.3%. By the end of November, the rate reached 19.4%. That compares with an average rate of 10% among the 16 euro zone countries. The recession is forcing Spain to lessen its dependence on foreign investment from levels that approached a maximum of 10% of GDP prior to the crisis to only 3.6% during the third quarter of 2009. The government introduced the Law of the Sustainable Economy, which took effect in mid 2010. Its main goal is to build an economic model based on energy efficiency and new technologies. Educational reform (i.e. human capital formation) is also part of this new approach.

7.8. ECONOMIC GROWTH, INDUSTRIAL RACING AND CATCH-UP

As described in Chapters 1 and 4, industrial competition among nations or regional economic entities has been an essential driving force for economic growth. Rivalry pushes a state's standing, prestige, power and economic performance thus allowing a country or a region to get ahead of their competition. Institutions can support this competitive process by encouraging entrepreneurship, fostering education and training, and by making it easier for companies to set up new businesses. Chapter 2 argues that economic growth essentially embodies a science and technology race between industrialized nations. This economic or industrial contest creates value added products through competition as reflected in an increased GDP. Prime examples of this catch-up process are the countries in the Arabian Gulf (e.g. Saudi Arabia, Kuwait, UAE, Oman, Qatar and Bahrain). Increased revenues from oil resources over the past few decades are being used, for instance, to set up new educational institutions. In Saudi Arabia the number of universities has more than doubled, increased from 10 to 24 over a period of 5 years (NAJD Online Academy, 2010). In addition the government has implemented a Science and Technology Strategic Plan called Vision 2020 to help diversify the economy (Al-Suwaiyel, 2008). To assist in this development, entrepreneurship is being encouraged through workshops, and programs such as Badir (Al Hargan, 2009). Badir is an initiative of Saudi Arabia's National Research Institute - King Abdulaziz City for Science and Technology (KACST). The initiative aims to assist people in the commercialization of technology research and opportunities through supporting the growth of emerging technology-based businesses in the Kingdom. It remains to be seen if the country can improve its efficiency sufficiently to make a success of this program.

There is also an increase in the participation of women in the Arabian Gulf region's governmental institutions even up to the cabinet level. In Oman, for example, the head of state and government is the hereditary Sultan who appoints a cabinet called the Diwans to assist him. In the early 1990s, the Sultan instituted an elected advisory council, the Majlis ash-Shura, though few Omanis were eligible to vote. Universal suffrage for those over 21 was instituted in 2003 and over 190,000 people (74% of those registered) voted to elect the 84 seats (Ministry of Information, 2009). Two women were elected to seats. The country in 2010 also had three women ministers (i.e. Minister of Higher Education, Minister of Social Development and Minister of Tourism). While there are no legal political parties nor, at present, any active opposition movement, as more and more young Omanis become educated, it seems likely that the traditional, tribal-based political system will have to be adjusted. Many of the Arabian Gulf countries are going through a similar catch-up process in human capacity building and institutional structures development. Glaeser et al (2004) argues that much evidence points to the dominance of human capital for both industrial growth and democratization. Their results were consistent with a perspective on institutions outlined by Djankov et al. (2003); the greater the human and social capital of a community, the more attractive are its institutional opportunities.

The collective nature of science and technology development is at the root of industrialization and economic progress. Institutions can assist in this technology race by helping to identify the most promising skill options, and by promoting entrepreneurship (Baumol, 1993). This can be done, for instance, through government sponsored strategic workshops for the private and public sectors. Chapters 2 and 3 investigated multiple kinds of races including frontier races among leaders and would-be leaders on a global, regional and local scale. Abramovitz (1986) explained the central idea of the catch-up hypothesis as trailing countries adopting a backlog of unexploited technology. While a leader is restricted in increasing its productivity by the advance of new technology, trailing countries, such as China, India and the Arabian Gulf states, have the potential to make a larger leap as they are provided with the privilege of exploiting the backlog in addition to newly developed technology. Formal institutions can assist in exploiting this potential by instigating technological entrepreneurship programs through government incentives, as well as by fostering education. Years of education can be used as a replacement for technical competence. This concept is most closely associated with the work of Lipset (1960), Przeworski (2004a and 2004b), and Barro (1999) who believed that educated people are more likely to resolve their differences through negotiation and thus provide greater stability which in turn is the key to economic growth.

Chapter 4 describes the development of a model to analyze the patterns of catching up, falling behind and getting ahead in technological racing (i.e. industrial competition) among nations or regional economic entities. The impact of social institutions arises by allowing the potential technology gap to be modified by them. It allows for more complex growth dynamics. The model achieved the goal of merging the neoclassical system with slow technology diffusion and institutional variations. Model predictions and empirical observations indicated that new technology adoption rates vary between countries. This variance could be mostly due to the social capabilities of those countries that demonstrate various competence levels of adoption promoted by bureaucratic efficiency, including a low level of corruption, and democratic rights (Economist, 2005). A good example is Latin

America which carries relatively high adoption rates but overall the region has failed to take advantage of its potential because of poor political and social institutions.

In terms of catch-up times, Chapter 4 demonstrates that unless Europe, East Asia and even the Arabian Gulf, reduce their inefficiency levels, they must rely on higher accumulation rates to continue to catch-up with countries such as the United States. Institutional frameworks are important in achieving this improved efficiency. The bureaucratic efficiency index and the index of political and civil rights, for instance, are the main explanations for a nation's different level of productivity. Any policy that allows follower nations to better adopt foreign technology should increase their growth rate. Since the difference in technology adoption appears to be related to a nation's institutional efficiency, observations suggest that governments are well-advised to pursue policies that increase the efficiency of markets.

In summary, institutions can complement, support and advance the technological race process by enhancing the opportunities for technological entrepreneurship, by fostering education and training, particularly of women in developing economies such as the Arabian Gulf and South East Asia, and by business deregulation in order to improve efficiency.

7.9. THE DEBATE OVER WHETHER OR NOT POLITICAL INSTITUTIONS CAUSE ECONOMIC GROWTH

Glaeser et al (2004) revisited the discussion over whether political institutions cause economic growth, or whether, alternatively, growth and human capital accumulation lead to institutional improvement. They found that most indicators of institutional quality used to establish the proposition that institutions cause growth, as outlined for example in North's and Olson's theories (North 1994, Olson 2000) were constructed to be conceptually unsuitable for that purpose. Results suggested that human capital is a more basic source of growth than are the institutions; poor countries get out of poverty through good policies, often pursued by dictators, and subsequently improve their political institutions.

Economic research has identified two broad approaches to confronting the challenges in establishing a self-governing state. The first approach, which is supported by North (1994) and Olson (2000), emphasizes the need to start with democracy and other checks on government as the mechanisms for securing property rights. With such political institutions in place, investment in human and physical capital, and therefore economic growth, are expected to follow. The second approach supported by Glaeser et al. (2004) emphasizes the need for human and physical capital accumulation to start the process. It holds that even pro-market dictators can secure property rights as a matter of policy choice, not of political constraints. From the vantage point of poor countries, it sees democracy as the consequence of increased education and wealth, not as their cause.

The importance of constraining government has been stressed by many economists starting with Montesquieu (1748) and Smith (1776), and up to recent times by Hayek (1960), as well by the new institutional economists (North and Thomas, 1973). Montesquieu (1748), for example, spent nearly twenty years researching and writing L'esprit des lois (The Spirit of the Laws), covering a wide range of topics in politics, the law, sociology, and anthropology and providing several thousand citations. In this political treatise Montesquieu supports constitutionalism and the separation of powers, the abolition of slavery, the preservation of civil liberties and the rule of law, and the idea that political and legal institutions should reflect the social and geographical character of each particular region.

Friedrich August von Hayek was an Austrian-born economist and philosopher known for his defense of classical liberalism and free-market against socialist and collectivist thought. He is considered by some to be one of the most important economists and political philosophers of the twentieth century (Feser, 2007). Hayek was one of the leading academic critics of collectivism in the 20th century. Hayek argued that all forms of collectivism (even those theoretically based on voluntary cooperation) could only be maintained by a central authority of some kind. In his popular book, The Road to Serfdom (1944) and in subsequent works, Hayek argued that socialism requires central economic planning and that such planning in turn leads towards totalitarianism (Hayek, 1960). Recent work, including Hall and Jones (1999), DeLong and Shleifer (1993), Acemoglu et al., (2001, 2002), Easterly and Levine (2003), and Rodrik et al., (2002), has reached close to an intellectual consensus that the political institutions of limited government cause economic growth. The reverse idea, namely that growth in income and human capital causes institutional improvement, is most closely associated with the work of Lipset (1960) who believed that educated people are more likely to resolve their differences through negotiation and voting than through violent disputes. Education is needed for courts to operate and to empower citizens to engage with government institutions.

Countries differ in their stocks of human and social capital, which can be acquired through policies pursued even by dictators. Institutional outcomes depend to a large extent on these endowments (Djankov et al. 2003). This is supported by the experiences of South Korea, Taiwan, and China, which grew rapidly under one-party dictatorships, the first two eventually turning to democracy. Empirically, Lipset's hypothesis, that growth leads to better political institutions, has received considerable support in the work of Przeworski (2004a, 2004b) and his associates (Alvarez et al. 2000) and Barro (1999). The two views of economic and political development share some important similarities. They both emphasize the need for secure property rights to support investment in human and physical capital, and they both see such security as a public policy choice. However, the institutional view sees the pro-investment policies as a consequence of political constraints on government, whereas the development view sees these policies in poor countries largely as choices of their leaders.

Glaeser et al's (2004) view was shaped by the experiences of North and South Korea. Prior to the Korean War, the two countries were one state with similar histories (note that they were occupied by Japan from 1910 to 1945). They were also both exceptionally poor in 1950. Between the end of the Korean War and 1980, both countries were autocracies (i.e. dictatorships). South Korean dictators chose capitalism and secure property rights, and the country grew rapidly, reaching a per capita income level of US $1589 in 1980. The North Korean dictators, in contrast, chose socialism, and the country only reached the level of income of US $768 in 1980. South Korea obviously had better institutions as measured by constraints on the executive, these institutions were the outcome of economic growth after 1950 rather than its cause. Glaeser et al (2004) goes on to argue that it would be wrong to attribute South Korea's growth to these institutions rather than the choices made by its dictators.

Assessing the underlying connection between institutions and economic growth has proved particularly complex. The research approaches as outlined by North (1994), Olson (2000), Hall and Jones (1999), DeLong and Shleifer (1993), and Acemoglu et al., (2001,

2002) do not clearly show that political institutions rather than human capital have a causal effect on economic growth. Certainly, Glaeser et al (2004) goes on to argue that much evidence points to the dominance of human capital for both growth and democratization. Their results were consistent with a perspective on institutions outlined by Djankov et al. (2003); the greater the human and social capital of a community, the more attractive are its institutional opportunities. Institutions are highly persistent because history, including colonial history, shapes social choices. Furthermore institutional outcomes also get better as a society grows richer, because institutional opportunities improve. Importantly, in that framework, institutions have only a second order effect on economic performance. The first order effect comes from human and social capital, which shape both institutional and productive capacities of a society.

The results of the paper by Glaeser et al (2004) do not show that institutions do not matter. That proposition is contradicted by a great deal of available empirical evidence that has been provided by North (1994), Olson (2000), Hall and Jones (1999), DeLong and Shleifer (1993), and Acemoglu et al., (2001, 2002). Rather, Glaeser et al's (2004) results suggest that the current measurement strategies have conceptual flaws, and that researchers would do better focusing on actual laws, rules, and compliance procedures that could be manipulated by a policy maker to assess what works.

A key factor for poor countries is the policy choices made by autocrats. Democratization and constraints on government do not need to come first. The economic success of East Asia in the post war era and of China most recently, for example, has been a consequence of good economic policy decisions by autocrats, not of institutions constraining them. The Chinese example illustrates this point convincingly: Deng was one of the best dictators for economic growth while Mao was one of the worst. While Mulligan et al., (2004) present compelling evidence that democracies are significantly more compassionate than dictatorships in such policy areas as freedom of the press, torture, death penalty, and regulation of religion, Glaeser et al's (2004) evidence suggests that the Lipset (1960), Przeworski (2004a and b), and Barro (1999) view of the world is more accurate: countries that emerge from poverty accumulate human and physical capital under dictatorships, and then, once they become richer, are increasingly likely to improve their institutions.

CONCLUDING REMARKS

There is a consensus that consensual political orders result in more flexible institutions that provide better incentives for economic growth through a market-oriented competitive environment. However, even in a democracy corruption is a cause for concern such as through lobbying by special interest groups. The recent economic emergency of Asian countries such as Japan and South Korea is a good example of the effects of negative incidents such as war on the evolution of institutions. Once stability and order were re-established both countries adopted a consensual political order which aided their economic recovery.

Corruption is also an outcome of a country's institutions and will normally but not always have a negative effect on economic growth. While, the micro evidence (i.e. within a country) and case studies say that corruption is bad for growth, the macro evidence (i.e. cross country) is inconclusive. The China Brazil example shows that fiscally decentralized but politically centralized institutions can support strong economic growth, in spite of corruption. The key here is that in countries with high economic freedom, corruption appeared to increase economic growth by providing a way around government controls.

Economic freedom also shows up in the form of industrial competition, or racing, among nations by creating value added products through rivalry as reflected in an increase gross domestic product. The field of economic governance has shown that diverse economies have used various institutions, at various times, to carry out these functions. The discussion continues over whether political institutions cause economic growth, or whether, alternatively, growth and human capital accumulation lead to institutional improvement. A balanced approach is needed in this debate.

The fiscal calamity that started in 2008 has led to a sudden increase in public debt in many advanced economies. Governments were required to re-capitalize banks, take over a large part of the debts of failing financial institutions, and introduce large stimulus programs. Nations with a gross public debt exceeding 90% of their annual economic output tend to grow a lot more slowly. The projections of public debt ratios lead many experts to conclude that the path pursued by fiscal authorities in a number of industrial states is unsustainable. Far-reaching actions are required to limit the fast growth of current and future liabilities of governments and reduce their unfavorable consequences for long-term growth and fiscal stability.

If we were to try and weigh institutional factors in as far as they tend to affect economic growth. Positive factors on growth include consensual political systems that are flexible, a competitive environment with fiscal incentives that allows for continuous improvement in efficiency, industrial competition that allows for economic choices, and a well developed educational system to help provide competent human capital for formal institutions such as courts. Negative institutional factors affecting economic growth are corruption due to fiscal and political decentralization resulting in stagnation due to reduced economic choices, autocrats or dictators that make poor policy choices, and high public debt in relation to a state's annual economic output. In closing, the relationship between institutions and economic performance is complicated. However, there is now convincing evidence that countries that have an open, technologically competitive and creative environment tend to perform better economically.

REFERENCES

Abramovitz, M. (1986), 'Catching Up, Forging Ahead, and Falling Behind', *Journal of Economic History* 66, 385-406

Acemoglu, D., Johnson, S., and Robinson, J. A. (2001), 'The Colonial Origins of Comparative Development: An Empirical Investigation,' *American Economic Review* 91(5): 1369-401.

Acemoglu, D., Johnson, S., and Robinson, J. A. (2002), 'Reversal of Fortune: Geography and Development in the Making of the Modern World Income Distribution,' *Quarterly Journal of Economics* 117(4), 1231-1294.

Abrams, B. A. and Lewis K. A. (1995), 'Cultural and Institutional Determinants of Economic Growth : a Cross-section Analysis', Public Choice 83, 273-289.

Al-Hargan, A. (2009), Developing Technology Incubation Models for the Arabic World, *International Technology Incubation Forum* 2009, Riyadh, Saudi Arabia

Al-Suwaiyel, M. I. (2008), Kingdom of Saudi Arabia: Toward a Knowledge-Based Economy, 2008 Global Competitiveness Forum, 20-22 January, Riyadh.

Alvarez, M., Cheibub, J. A., Limongi, F. and Przeworski, A. (2000), Democracy and Development: Political Institutions and Material Well-Being in the World, 1950-1990. Cambridge: Cambridge University Press.

AMEinfo.com. 2009. Saudi Arabia: Public debt reduced to SR237bn (Accessed 29 July 2010) (http://www.ameinfo.com/212221.html)

Bagwell, K. and Staiger, R. (2003), The Economics of the World Trading System. Cambridge, Ma, MIT Press.

Barro, R. J. (1999), 'Determinants of Democracy,' *Journal of Political Economy* 107(6-2): 158-183.

Barro, R. J., (1998), 'Determinants of Economic Growth: A Cross-Country Empirical Study', Cambridge,Ma., The MIT Press

Baumgartner, F. R. and B.L.Leech (1998), Basic Interests: The Importance of Groups in Politics and in Political Science, Princeton, NJ: Princeton University Press, 64–82.

Bandiera, O. (2003), Land Reform, the Market for Protection and the Origins of the Sicilian Mafia: Theory and Evidence, Journal of Law, Economics and Organization 19, 218-244.

Baumol,W,J.(1993), Entrepreneurship, Management and the Structure of Payoff, Cambridge,Ma., MIT Press

Besley, T. and Burgess, R. (2002), 'The Political Economy of Government Responsiveness: Theory and Evidence from India.' *Quarterly Journal of Economics*, 117 (4), 1415-1451.

Cecchetti, S. G., Mohanty, M. S. and F. Zampolli (2010), The Future of Public Debt: Prospects and Implications, Bank for International Settlements 2010 (online) 1-22 http://www.bis.org/

Coase, R. H. (1992), 'The Institutional Structure of Production', *American Economic Review*, 82 (4), 713-719

Coase, R. (1937), 'The Nature of the Firm', Economica, 4 (16), 386-406

Chowdhury, M. J. A., Ghosh, D., and R.E.Wright, (2005), 'The Impact of Micro-Credit on Poverty: Evidence from Bangladesh', Progress in Development Studies 5, 298-309.

Clemens, E. S. (1997), The People's Lobby: Organizational Innovation and the Rise of Interest-Group Politics in the United States, 1890–1925. University Of Chicago Press

Delong, J. B. (1998). Review of David Landes The Wealth and Poverty of Nations: Why Some Are So Rich and Some Are So Poor? New York, W. W. Norton and Co., (http://j-bradford-delong.net)

DeLong, J. B. and Shleifer, A. 1993. 'Princes and Merchants: City Growth before the Industrial Revolution.' *Journal of Law and Economics* 36(2): 671-702

De Soto, H. (1989), The Other Path, New York, Harper and Row

De Soto, H. (2000), Mystery of Capital: Why Capitalism Triumphs in the West and Fails Everywhere Else. New York, Basic Books

Dixit, A. (2004), Lawlessness and Economics: Alternative Modes of Governance. Princeton, N. J., Princeton University Press

Dixit, A. (2008) 'Economic Governance', Conference on Endogenous Market Structures and Industrial Policy, 5 June, Aula Magna, Milano

Djankov, S., Glaeser, E., La Porta, R., Lopez-de-Silanes, F., and Shleifer, A. (2003). 'The New Comparative Economics', *Journal of Comparative Economics*, 31 (4), 595-619.

Dower, J. (1999), Embracing Defeat: Japan in the Wake of World War II. New York: W.W. Norton.

Djankov, S., La Porta, R., Lopez-de-Silanes, F., and A. Shleifer (2003), 'The New Comparative Economics, *Journal of Comparative Economics* 31(4), 595-619.

Easterly, W. and Levine, R. (2003), 'Tropics, Germs, and Crops: How Endowments influence Economic Development', *Journal of Monetary Economics* 50(1): 3-39.

Economist, The (1995). 'Asia's Competing Capitalisms', 336 (June 24th Leader). 13.

Economist, The (2005). 'The Tiger in Front: A Survey of India and China'., March 5, 3-16

Feser, E. (ed), (2007) The Cambridge Companion to Hayek, Cambridge University Press,

Fiani, R. (2004) 'An Evaluation of the Role of the State and Property Rights in Douglas North's.' *Journal of Economic Issues*, 38(4), 1003-1020.

Gambetta, D. (1993). The Sicilian Mafia: The Business of Private Protection. Cambridge, MA: Harvard University press.

Giavazzi, F. and Tabellini, G. (2005). Economic and Political Liberalization. *Journal of Monetary Economics*. 57, 1297-330.

Glaeser, E. L., La Porta, R., Lopez-de-Silanes, F., and Shleifer, A., (2004). 'Do Institutions Cause Growth?' *Journal of Economic Growth*, v9 (3, Sep), 271-303.

Gottinger, H. (2009), Strategic Economics of Network Industries, New York, Nova Science Publishers, Inc.

Greiner, A., and Fincke, B. (2009), Public Debt and Economic Growth (Dynamic Modeling and Econometrics in Economics and Finance) Berlin, Springer

Greiner, A. (2008),' Human capital formation, public debt and economic growth' „*Journal of Macroeconomics* ,30 (1),415-427

Greasley, D. and Oxley, L. (2000), 'Outside the Club: New Zealand's Economic Growth 1870-1993'. *International Review of Applied Economics*, 14(2), 173-192

Greif, A. (2006): Institutions and the Path to the Modern Economy: Lessons from Medieval Trade, Cambridge, Cambridge University Press.

Hall, R. E. and C.I. Jones (1999), 'Why Do Some Countries Produce so Much More Output per Worker than Others?" *Quarterly Journal of Economics*, 114(1), 83-116.

Harstad, B. and Svensson, J. (2004), 'Bribes, Lobbying and Development.' mimeo, IIES, Stockholm University.

Hayek, F. A. von (1994), The Road to Serfdom, 50th anniversary edition, University of Chicago Press, 1994

Hayek, F.A. von (1960) ,The Constitution of Liberty. Routledge, London (pbk.)

Holt, J. C. (1992), Magna Carta., Cambridge, Cambridge University Press.

Jolis, A. (2010), 'A Supply-Sider in East Africa.', Wall Street Journal, 24 April

Kaufman, D., Kraay, A. and M.Mastruzzi, (2003), Governance Matters III: Governance Indicators 1996-2002. World Bank Policy Research Working Paper No. 3106, Washington DC.

Kaufman, D., Kraay, A. and M.Mastruzzi (2005), 'Governance Matters IV: Updated Governance Indicators 1996-2004', Washington DC, World Bank research paper. Online.

Available at http://www.worldbank.org/wbi/governance/pubs/govmatters4.html accessed 8 February 2010.

Keefer, P. (2004), 'What Does Political Economy Tell Us About Economic Development – and Vice Versa? Annual Review of Political Science. 7, 247-272.

Kinzer, S. (1999). 'The Turkish Quake's Secret Accomplice: Corruption.' New York Times, 29 August, sec. 4, p. 3.

Landes, D. S. (1998). The Wealth and Poverty of Nations: Why Some Are So Rich and Some Are So Poor? New York, W. W. Norton and Co.

Lindbeck, A. (1975), Swedish Economic Policy, London, MacMillan Press

Lipset, S. M. (1960), Political Man: The Social Basis of Modern Politics, New York, Doubleday

Loomis, C. M. (2009), 'The Politics of Uncertainty: Lobbyists and Propaganda in Early Twentieth-Century America,' Journal of Policy History 21(2), in Project MUSE

Mattli, W. (2001), 'Private Justice in Global Economy: From Litigation to Arbitration', *International Organization* 55, 919-47.

Mauro, P. (1995), 'Corruption and Growth', *Quarterly Journal of Economics*, 110, 681-712.

Mazzara, A. (2006), 'Political Corruption and Economic Growth: Explaining the East Asian Growth Paradox.' Carlton College, Political Science, comprehensive exercise.

McLean, I. (2000), 'Review Article: The Divided Legacy of Mancur Olson'. *British Journal of Political Science*, 30(4), 651-668.

Ministry of Information, 2009. Government/ The Council of Oman (Accessed 29 July 2010) (http://www.omanet.om/english/government/overview.asp?cat=gov)

Mokyr, J. (1990), The Lever of Riches: Technological Creativity and Economic Progress. Oxford, Oxford University Press.

Montesquieu, C. (1748), The Spirit of the Laws. Paris

Mulligan, C., Gil, R., and Sala-i-Martin, X. (2004), 'Do Democracies Have Different Public Policies than Nondemocracies?' *Journal of Economic Perspectives* 18(1), 51-74

Murphy, K., Shleifer, A. and Vishny, R. (1993), 'Why is Rent-seeking so Costly to Growth?' American Economic Review, 83 (2) 409-414.

NAJD Online Academy, 2010. Saudi Arabia/ Education. (Accessed 29 July 2010) (http://www.alnujaidi.com/sa_education.htm)

North, D. C. (1981), Structure and Change in Economic History. New York: Norton and Co.

North, D. C. (1990), Institutions, Institutional Change, and Economic Performance, Cambridge, Cambridge University Press

North, D. C. (1994), 'Economic Performance Through Time', *The American Economic Review*, 84(3), 359-368

North, D. C. (2005a), 'Institutions and the Process of Economic Change'. Management International, 9(3), 1-83

North, D. C. (2005b), 'Understanding the Process of Economic Change'. Princeton: Princeton University Press

North, D. C., and Thomas, R. P. (1973), The Rise of the Western World: A New Economic History. Cambridge: Cambridge University Press

Olson, M., (1982), The Rise and Decline of Nations: Economic Growth, Stagflation, and Social Rigidities, New Haven, Yale University Press

Olson, M. (1996), 'Big Bills Left on the Sidewalk: Why Some Nations are Rich and Others Poor', *Journal of Economic Perspectives,* 10(2), 3-24.

Olson, M. (2000), Power and Prosperity: Outgrowing Communist and Capitalist Dictatorships, New York, Basic Books.

Patton, L. (2010), European Companies Say High Public Debt Could Hold Back Economic Debt, Hurt Business Loans. Business Week, 15 March,

Pearce, J. (2002), 'IMF: Angola's Missing Millions', BBC News, 18 October, Available at: (http://news.bbc.co.uk/2/hi/africa/2338669.stm).

Pento, M. (2009), Dubai May Be Least Of World's Debt Problems. Forbes.com http://www.forbes.com/2009/12/01/michael-pento-commentary-personal-finance-record-debt.html (accessed 11 June 2010)

Perez-Diaz, V. M. (1993), "The Return of Civil Society: The Emergence of Democratic Spain". Cambridge, Harvard University Press.

Persson, T. (2005), Forms of Democracy, Policy, and Economic Development. Working Paper No. 11171. Cambridge, MA: NBER

Przeworski, A. (2004a), 'The Last Instance: Are Institutions the Primary Cause of Economic Development?' Mimeo, New York University

Przerworski, A. (2004b), 'Geography vs Institutions Revisited: Were Fortunes Reversed?' Mimeo, New York University.

Reinganum, J. (1989), The Timing of Innovation, in: Handbook of Industrial Organization, Vol. I, Schmalensee,R. and R. Willig (eds.), North Holland, Amsterdam, Chapt. 14

Reinhart,C. M. and Rogoff, K. S. (2010), Growth in a Time of Debt, *American Economic Review Papers and Proceedings*. January

Reinikka, R. and Svensson, J. (2005), 'Fighting Corruption to Improve Schooling: Evidence from a Newspaper Campaign in Uganda', *Journal of European Economic Association*. 3 (2-3), 259-267.

Rodrik, D., Subramanian, A., and Trebbi, F. (2002), 'Institutions Rule: The Primacy of Institutions over Geography and Integration in Economic Development.' NBER Working Paper 9305, National Bureau of Economic Research (October).

Rose-Ackerman, S. (2004), Corruption and Government: Causes, Consequences, and Strategies for Reform. Cambridge, Cambridge University Press, Chapter 6.

Rostow, W. W. (1983), 'Korea and the Fourth Industrial Revolution, 1960-2000,' Paper presented at the Federation of Korean Industries.

Rutherford, M. (2001), 'Institutional Economics: Then and Now', *Journal of Economic Perspectives*, 15 (3), 173-194.

Sachs, J. D. and Warner, A. M. (1995), 'Economic Reform and the Process and the Process of Global Integration.' Brookings Paper on Economic Activity. 1, 1-118.

Schlueter, A. (2007), 'Institutions as Economic Growth Determinants: A Comparative Study of New Zealand and Argentina', Masters Dissertation, AUT (**Error! Hyperlink reference not valid.**).

Schumpeter, J. (1947), Capitalism, Socialism and Democracy, New York: Harper, Second Edition

Shleifer, A. and Vishny, R. (1993), 'Corruption', *Quarterly Journal of Economics*, 108 (3), 599-617

Simon, H. (1998), 'Bounded Rationality. In: J. Eatwell, M. Milgate and P. Newman (Eds.) The New Palgrave: A Dictionary of Economics, London: McMillan, Vol. 1, pp. 266-268

Smith, A. (1976), An Inquiry into the Nature and Causes of the Wealth of Nations, edited by Edwin Canaan. Chicago, Illinois: University of Chicago Press

Solsten, E., and Meditz, S. W. (Eds) (1988), 'Spain: A Country Study'. GPO for the US Library of Congress

Song, B. N. (1990), The Rise of the Korean Economy. Hong Kong: Oxford University Press

Svensson, J. (2005), 'Eight Questions about Corruption', *J. of Economic Perspectives*, 19 (3), 19-42

Swaleheen, M. and Stansel, D. (2007), 'Economic Freedom, Corruption, and Growth', *Cato Journal,* Vol 27 (3), 343-358

Thorbecke, E. and Wan H. A. (Eds) (1999), 'Taiwan's Development Experience: Lessons on Roles of Government and Market', Springer Netherlands, pp 456 (ISBN: 0792385136).

Tirole, J. (1988), The Theory of Industrial Organization, MIT Press, Cambridge, Mass.

Transparency International (2004), Global Corruption Report 2004. London: Pluto Press.

Transparency International/corruption/ perception index. 2010 (Accessed 29 July 2010) (http://www.transparency.org/surveys/index.html#cpi)

United Nations Office on Drugs and Crime 2010 Crime Victims Surveys (http://www.unodc.org/unodc/en/data-and-analysis/Crime-Victims-Survey.html) (Accessed 29 July 2010)

USDJ, (1973), Civil Action No. 98-civ.7076, Complaint against Visa and MasterCard, (http://www.usdoj.gov/atr/cases/f1900/1973.htm)

Wall Street Journal, The (2010), Reinhart and Rogoff: Higher Debt May Stunt Economic Growth. 4 January

Vandenberg, P. (2000), 'North's Institutionalism and the Prospect of Combining Theoretical Approaches', Cambridge Journal of Economics, 26 (2), 217-235.

Varese, F. (2001), The Russian Mafia: Private Protection in a New Market Economy. Oxford: Oxford University Press

Wan Jr, H. Y. (2004), Economic Development in a Global Environment: East Asian Evidences. Dordrecht, Netherlands, Kluwer

Wharton University (2010), Spain in 2010: Will Unemployment Prolong the Economic Crisis? http://www.wharton.universia.net/index.cfm?fa=printArticleandID=1830andlanguage=english (accessed 11 June 2010)

Williamson, O. (1995), The Mechanism of Governance. New York: Oxford University Press.

Williamson, O. (2005), The Economics of Governance. American Economic Review 95, 1-18

PART II: JAPANESE ECONOMIC GROWTH AND INDUSTRIAL POLICY

Makoto Takashima
O-Hara Graduate School of Business, Tokyo, Japan
Email: m_takashima@o-hara.ac.jp

Chapter 8

ASIAN ECONOMIES TO TAKE OFF

Makoto Takashima

8.1. INTRODUCTION

The World Bank Report on the development of East Asian economies (World Bank, 1993) has stimulated interest by economists and policy makers in rapid economic expansion by economies in this region with Japan as a leader in economic performance. Despite a monetary crisis that struck some economies by the end of the 1990s the supernormal growth rates of Asian 'tiger' economies has continued to attract great attention. Furthermore, the fiscal progress of China and India, countries with the highest populations in the world, has been remarkable, facilitating their integration into the world economy and fostering globalization (Wan, 2004).

Rapid growth of the economies of the three main East Asian states (i.e. Japan, China and South Korea) in comparison to the UK and the US is shown in Table 8.1, where changes in GDP per capita are compared among these countries which went through stages of industrialization within a period of 300 years. The First Industrial Revolution occurred in the UK toward the end of the eighteenth century and the Second Industrial Revolution was generated in the USA (and Germany) approximately 100 years later. Following on these countries' industrialization on the basis of invention and innovation, "late industrialization" took place among Asian countries such as Japan, South Korea and China (Amsden, 1989). Here the path of economic growth can be considered in view of an approximate take-off date for their industrialization. For South Korea, Rostow (1983) has indicated that their economy entered a take-off stage and completed it for a subsequent sustained growth until 1968. With his suggestion as applied to per capita GDP of that country in Table 8.1, the advent of industrialization in South Korea is to have occurred when the economy reached around US $2,000 of GDP per capita.

Assuming that the take-off time is the period during which an economy transits its GDP per capita from $1,000 to $2,000, we compare the length of that period and the number of years needed to reach $5,000 of GDP per capita after they entered the industrialization

Table 8.1. Historical Change in Per Capita GDP of Five Countries

	1700	1820	1870	1900	1920	1940	1960	1980	1995	2003
UK	1250	1706	3190	4492	4548	6856	8857	12931	17495	21310
USA		1257	2445	4091	5552	7010	11328	18577	24484	29037
Japan		669	737	1180	1696	2874	3986	13428	19849	21218
S. Korea		600	604	-	1009	1442	1105	4114	11818	14673*
China			530	545	-	-	673	1067	2653	4803

*Figure of the year 2001 from Maddison (2006). (Sources) For figures from 1700 through 1995: Maddison (2006), pp.436-443, 465-467,558-562. For figures of 2003: Maddison (2007), p.382. (Note) Figures are represented in terms of 1990 international Geary-Khamis dollars. Some of figures would look more impressive for Asian economies after WW2 if they were converted into PPP units.

following the take-off stage. The UK finished its take-off period in 1845 as it formally started its industrialization. After that, the UK spent about 70 years until it brought its per capita GDP to $5000. As for Japan, the development policy was initiated by the Meiji Government in 1868 when its GDP per capita was estimated at about $700. Japan entered the take-off stage around 1890 and is considered to have finished the preparation period for industrialization toward the end of the 1930s. Thus, Japan shows that it has spent about 40 years for the take-off period severely interrupted by World War II and its aftermath. After the War, it resumed the level of $2,000 of per capita GDP in 1950 and reached $5,000 in 1963, taking 13 years. On the other hand, South Korea is actually considered to enter its take-off period after the War, but it needed only 15 years for its finish in 1970 when the GDP per capita reached around $2,000. Attaining $5,000 in 1983, the Korean economy took 13 years following the finish of the take-off period.

Subsequent to entering industrialization following the take-off period, those economies generally spent a shorter period until they attain the next advanced state, as they finished the take-off stage later in their history. Whilst the UK needed 40 years from 1927 to 1967 and the US spent 36 years from 1906 to 1942, to double their per capita GDP from $5,000, Japan took no more than 8 years until the economy reached $10,000 in 1971 from $5,000 in 1963 and South Korea took 10 years from 1983 to 1993. This could be explained from the differences in the source of productivity progress. Economic growth of late industrializing countries on the basis of foreign technology or learning by doing generates higher productivity and the higher productivity generates higher growth. In contrast, countries on the basis of invention and innovation do give rise to higher productivity and elevated expansion. But the higher growth does not always generate new technical discoveries so that such states may fail to continue rapid economic expansion (Amsden, 1989, p.153).

China reached $2,000 of GDP per capita in 1992 and might be considered to have finished its take-off stage at that time according to the standard applied to the other four economies. Whether the Chinese economy can continue along its present path or whether it will slow down to growth rates similar to other industrialized economies after take-off phases depends on the increase of the capital stock, technological change, government policy, and institutional changes (see also Chaps. 3, 4 and 7). The importance of institutional transformation for economic growth has been advocated so far by economic historians or institutional economists such as North and Thomas (1973) and Greif (2006). This would also heavily rely on true elements of the capitalistic process such as an educated venturing class of entrepreneurs that emerges from private institutions and that largely drives the animal spirit to achieve and excel, nurtured by a benevolent state.

In East Asia, such a sustained growth as shown by Japan after World War II has been accomplished by Singapore and Hong Kong, earlier than South Korea, and a little later by Taiwan. Furthermore, accelerated economic growth has also spread to other Asian economies called newly industrialized economies (NIEs); Malaysia, Thailand, Indonesia, and two countries having a large population, China and India. The latter two are considered to have finished their take-off stage around 1990 and 2000, respectively. The recent economic growth of these Asian economies has been accompanied by great social transformation in each country such as urbanization, and growing enrollment in general and higher education.

As a matter of course, it is a common feature of the literature in development economics that special emphasis is placed on changes in productivity of production processes and a technological factor in international trade. Traditional theories in international trade, however, pay little attention to a role which technology plays in changes of trade patterns. Therefore, many of their works have been done to accommodate a technological factor in trade theories in order to shed light on the "Asian Miracle".

Originally, the introduction of the technological effects in the traditional Ricardian comparative advantage theory was argued by Dornbusch et al. (1977) and the role of technology was discussed by Jones (1970) in the conventional Heckscher-Ohlin's factor-proportions theory. In contrast to those standard static trade theories, Posner (1961) and Vernon (1966) presented a dynamic version explaining changes in trade patterns through a life cycle of goods. They stated that a commodity is initially invented and produced only in developed rich countries. Part of the product is then exported to developing countries, being followed by the mature stage when it can be produced by them with transferred technology and their advantage of lower labor costs, whilst the country which initially produced and exported it turns into an importer.

Each of these trade theories was separately contrived with special emphasis on an important but particular economic aspect in production and trade by each of the celebrated economists and has been extended so as to accommodate the effects of technological changes generally in a neoclassical framework by the followers to explain the patterns of trade flows. It seems, however, that the factor-proportions theory, to say the least of it, in the static models and the dynamic product-cycle theory could be incorporated into a single trade theory by explicitly introducing a technological factor in a theoretical framework: technical changes in production process of a commodity in the transition of industrial stages will alter the optimal factor-proportions for production, and the patterns of trade flows will undergo changes accordingly through a life cycle of a product. In this context, special attention should be paid to policy efforts by the emerging economies to introduce new goods and technologies when we consider the sources of the "Asian miracle" and analyze real features of that sustained economic growth.

The first achievement, to the best of our knowledge, of formulating the product-cycle model in a mathematical framework was made by Krugman (1979), who developed a simple general-equilibrium model to analyze North-South trade, attempting to explicitly introduce innovation in the North and eventual transferring that technology to the South in that model so as to determine the pattern of world trade and its changes over time. According to Krugman's model of the product cycle, the trade balance of a developed country which initially introduced a new good changes from a surplus to a deficit in terms of that commodity after a certain lapse of time and the balance gradually tends to zero as the technology gap reduces between the developed and developing countries.

Empirical findings, however, indicate that the real behavior of trade patterns may differ from the results given by the theoretical investigations. Gognon and Rose (1995), for instance, empirically examined with the use of disaggregated four-digit SITC level data of trade commodities, whether or not most international trade flows change dynamically as the product cycle theory states. Their investigation shows mainly "an extremely high degree of persistence" in patterns of international trade flows in terms of individual goods. As a matter of fact, there are some robust evidences that patterns of trade have changed significantly in these years in Asian countries like South Korea, Taiwan and China, and this can be explained by changes in factor endowments exerted by rapid industrialization. In this discussion, too, emphasis should be laid on the need that the traditional static Heckscher-Ohlin's trade theory of factor-proportions is linked to the dynamic technological theory of product cycle.

Another direction of research on the "Asian miracle" and the North-South trade is the development of new growth theories by, for example, Lucas (1988, 1993), Matsuyama (1991), Romer (1986), Stokey (1988, 1991a, 1991b), and Grossman and Helpman (1991). They explicitly take into consideration increasing returns to scale, accumulation of technological knowledge, or innovative and R&D activities in their theories. A characteristic common to this line of study is to construct a model by paying attention to the significance of human capital or to accumulation of technological knowledge by learning-by-doing. They assume these factors to be an important source of high growth rate of per capita income in Asian countries by causing increasing returns to scale in developing economies.

This chapter attempts to contribute to an understanding of the way and under which conditions sustained growth could become possible in Asian economies (and rising economies in general) and to know the reasons why some can create such a "miracle" and why others are unable to do so. Although it explicitly takes into consideration technological factors as well as governmental policy aspects in order to analyze the problems of Asian economic growth in line with the actual environment of the economies, the model represents only the fundamental aspects of expansion structure in a simple mathematical framework. Thus, it does not design to develop a full theory to integrate the standard static trade theories and the dynamic technological ones, which would require considerable further work, but aims to be of some help in theoretically understanding the situation of the "Asian miracle" and in having insight into the future growth path of each economy in this region.

In the next section (i.e. 8.2) we extend discussion about the analysis and controversy on the 'Asian miracle'. Krugman has expressed his thoughts about this phenomenon and the future possibilities of the Asian economies (Krugman, 1994a, 1994b). We briefly discuss his view also in reference to Lucas's paper 'Making a Miracle' (Lucas, 1993). Our own view is proposed which leads to a model for growth of the Asian economies. Section 8.3 then presents a simple growth model placing emphasis on accumulation of technological knowledge and industrial policy efforts associated with it. This is designed for explanation of Asian developing economies and for their paths of sustained growth. In Section 8.4, we look into the empirics of sustained growth; the possibilities of taking a sustained growth path are discussed in view of structural and industrial policies for Asian economies. Section 8.5 draws conclusions for the 'Asian Miracle'.

8.2. DISCUSSIONS ON THE ASIAN MIRACLE

The remarkable high and sustained growth of Japan until 1990, Hong Kong, Singapore, Taiwan, South Korea, and some other Asian economies during the last few decades has been controversially perceived as the 'Asian Miracle'. This has led to attempts to find out the sources of this growth and analyze reasons for it (Wan, 2004, p. 221). Some of these theoretical attempts are mentioned in the previous section; proposing new growth theory by explicitly assuming production functions with increasing returns to scale, innovative activities, or technology transfer mechanisms.

The underlying growth path could be positively assessed because it results in the rapid rise in per capita GDP with a comparatively high equalization of income distribution. This was the general tone of the argument in the growth literature on the Asian economies, for instance, the World Bank (1993). They argued that success was achieved due to social, industrial, and financial policies making conditions well-suited to the domestic and international environments of each country and, at the same time, by the strong, sometimes almost coercive interventions in the market and industry (Song, 1990, p.58). Amidst this general argument, Krugman expressed a different view to the Asian economic growth in his article titled 'The Myth of Asia's Miracle' arguing that "Popular enthusiasm about Asia's boom deserves to have some cold water thrown on it. Rapid Asian growth is less of a model for the West than many writers claim, and the future prospects for that growth are more limited than almost anyone now images" (Krugman, 1994b, p. 64). Krugman sees surprising similarities between the Asian economies of recent years and that of the Soviet Union some decades ago. Furthermore, Kim and Lau (1994) and Young (1992, 1994,1995) conducted empirical research on the newly industrialized East Asian economies and showed that there was little evidence of improvements in efficiency. Referring to their work, Krugman (1994b) said that the rapid growth of Asian economies seemed to be driven in large part by an astonishing mobilization of resources of labor and capital and was not achieved by gains in efficiency, thus "Asian economic growth, incredibly, ceases to be a mystery".

Krugman's views should be closely scrutinized on the basis of actual sources of development. In particular, he simply denies the sustainability of economic growth of developing Asian countries only by referring to the superficial resemblance of growth and decline of the past Soviet economy. He disregards not only the basic differences in their social and cultural systems but also in the actual performance of lasting technological progress nurtured by the nations' common quest for education, industrial enterprise achievement and international technological competitiveness. He does not provide proofs for these conjectures. They are questionable, under the neoclassical as well as endogenous growth theory. In particular, one can show that a country that is close to a leader can successfully leapfrog the leader (in a fairly non protectionist world trade regime) if the follower embraces increasing returns industries and achieves technological superiority in those industries that add to the highest value in GDP per head (after all, this is really what counts).

If Toyota were Japan, and GM the US, it shows that it could also work on an aggregate basis, the industrial variety being enlarged (see Chapters 1, 2 and 4). Although Krugman refers to the remarkable upgrading of educational standards of the work force in Asian countries, especially in Singapore, he regards them as a mere increase in labor input and appears to take the rise in labor quality relying on higher educational standards as only temporary at best. As regards this view too, in benchmarking primary, secondary and advanced vocational education and training in East Asian countries, many studies over the years have clearly shown them to be far superior to the US, except for high level university education and research. There may be deficiencies in how R&D is organized and a lack of science/technology entrepreneurship that makes a difference but these things have also been changing.

This argument puts aside the issue that advance in labor quality due to accumulation of knowledge other than school education will substantially contribute to technical advance in production and that the general upgrading of educational standards of labor force through expanded schooling in the nation will provide the economy with a sound basis for the acquisition of best-practice technology and management know-how causing efficiency growth. In relation to this, Lucas constructs a theoretical model explicitly incorporating the role of the growth of human capital into an aggregate production function in order to explain, or to narrow the theoretical possibilities of the problem of the growth miracles of East Asia (Lucas, 1993). After the discussions of this model with special attention to the on-the-job accumulation of human capital (i.e. learning by doing), he concludes that the main engine of growth is the accumulation of human capital (i.e. knowledge) and physical capital accumulation plays no more than a subsidiary role. In particular, learning on the job on a sustained basis seems to be by far the most central for the rapid and sustained rise in the living standard of a nation.

This chapter constructs a simple deterministic model to understand the rapid growth and its possible conditions with regards to Asian economies, placing emphasis on two important ingredients: accumulation of knowledge and governmental policy efforts. Krugman (1994b) has not fully investigated the role of the accumulation of knowledge and Lucas (1993) has not explicitly considered a process for its accumulation. The latter ingredient, which is related to governmental policy, has been ignored in the discussions of both scholars, at least in their explicit theoretical frameworks. The analysis of growth paths follows the scheme of the model. Subsequently, some policy implications for the promise of sustained growth for the developing economies are derived from the theoretical proposition in reference to the observation of the realities of the Asian economies.

8.3. THEORETICAL MODEL AND GROWTH PATHS

Let us first present a simple growth model best designed to characterize the main characteristics of the development path for Asian economies: high rates of physical capital accumulation, growing emphasis on accumulation of technological knowledge, and the role of policy impacts by the governments to realize accumulation for rapid economic growth. Our model is characterized by "late industrialization" on the basis of learning-by-doing and government policy efforts as indicated in Section 8.1 in relation with Table 8.1. It could be extended to analyze optimal growth paths for a certain period of time like a Turnpike model by introducing some objective function at a certain time point. We focus here on analysis of the behavior of the economic growth path under the policy efforts followed by late-industrializing economies of Asian states starting from a delayed economic situation.

In order to derive the growth path of per capita income of an economy, consider an ordinary Cobb-Douglas type production relation with per capita income at t, $y(t)$, represented by using the stock of physical capital per worker (i.e. capital-labor ratios), $k(t)$, and the accumulation of knowledge, $A(t)$, at that time, in the following form:

$$y(t) = k(t)^\alpha A(t), \quad 0 < \alpha < 1 \tag{8.1}$$

Here, α is a distribution rate for capital and varies from country to country according to the development stage and other economic and social conditions.

One of the essential efforts for emerging economies to make a take-off towards long-run growth paths is admittedly the accumulation of knowledge in its broadest sense. This knowledge includes general education for people as a fundamental condition necessary for a rise in the quality of human capital and more specific vocational knowledge such as engineering and management techniques used in actual production activity. The acquisition of this knowledge is conducted through a variety of channels, but in case of developing nations aiming at rapid catching-up with advanced industrial countries, it is usually observed that governmental policies play an overwhelmingly important role. For upgrading of educational standards for the general public, it is inevitable to implement sophisticated social policies including establishment of a comprehensive national educational system. For the acquisition of new technology, industrial policies by government have a dominant influence over the behavior of individual firms through subsidizing imports of capital goods embodying new technology, encouraging technology transfer in the form of foreign licenses and training, liberalizing capital movement to introduce direct foreign investment, as well as financially supporting R&D activity in firms of their country.

Although governmental policy interventions aiming at the accumulation of knowledge would take different forms depending on actual economic, social and political circumstances of each state and might change forms according to the situation, the efforts in the aggregate will be measured by government expenses devoted to all what is related to the acquisition of knowledge. What we have to take note of here is that the effect of policy efforts is considered to be dependent on the amount per capita or the amount as a ratio of GDP rather than the total. (Consider the relation of the total amount of government budget for R&D in observing comparative effects between Singapore and China).

Another thing to be considered in the process of knowledge accumulation is the influence of a technological gap between the developing and the developed countries on the rates of acquisition by the former. It is assumed that if a nation stops making an effort to add new technology to its stock, then that level measured by a yardstick of the contemporaneous level of the world best-practiced technology decreases at a rate, ρ. This is caused by the birth of new technical knowledge in the advanced countries on one hand, and by the continuous decline of older knowledge. Consider one typical example of technological transition from the punched card data processing system to the system of electronic computers which emerged in the computer industry in the 1960s. Owing to this technological progress, the programming technique of back panel wiring in PCDP was reduced to complete obsolescence.

From the above consideration, the process of accumulation of knowledge is represented in the following equation:

$$\frac{dA(t)}{dt} = u(t)y(t) - \rho A(t) \tag{8.2}$$

where $u(t)$ refers to a fraction of national income devoted to the acquisition of knowledge.

The process of change in physical capital per worker, $k(t)$, can be constructed on the basis of the macroeconomic relation of gross physical investment being equal to national savings. That is, the net investment to physical capital at time t is written as:

$$\frac{dk(t)}{dt} = s(1 - u(t))y(t) - \lambda k(t) \tag{8.3}$$

Here, s and λ denote national savings ratio and rate of depreciation, respectively, which are both assumed positive constants being smaller than 1. In the first term of the right side, $(1-u(t))y(t)$ is per capita disposable income net of tax for the acquisition of knowledge and thus the savings ratio has to be understood accordingly. The savings ratio is also adjusted so as to consider workers' ratio of the population.

The obsolescence rate of the stock of technical knowledge in the developing economies, ρ, is considered to correspond to the rate of technical progress of the world best-practiced technology. From Equations 8.1 and 8.3, we can derive the amount of policy efforts necessary for the developing economies not to widen the present technological gap any more and to keep pace with the progressing level of world technology by using $dA(t)/dt = 0$:

$$u(t) = \frac{\rho}{k(t)^{\alpha}} \tag{8.4}$$

This shows that the rising economies having a smaller capital-labour ratio have to continue the policy efforts in order to keep pace with the technological standards of advanced economies. The greater the pace, the more efforts are required, naturally. In the same way, we can obtain the relation of the stock of knowledge, $A(t)$, to the capital-labor ratio, $k(t)$, when $k(t)$ remains constant, $dk(t)/dt = 0$, in the equation:

$$A(t) = \frac{\lambda k(t)^{1-\alpha}}{s(1-u(t))} \tag{8.5}$$

The above model has similar expressions to what Shell presented in his study of the relationship between inventive activity and economic growth (Shell, 1966), which was highly suggestive to our study. The similarity of models takes place from a common nature intrinsic to the accumulation activity of knowledge. Special attention is paid in our analysis, however, to the policy efforts by the governments of emerging economies to make progress through transfer of technology from the advanced countries and to the initial conditions at the end of a take-off towards sustained growth in relation to these efforts with the use of this model.

Hereafter, as the first step of the study, the policy efforts are assumed to be continued with a certain level by the governments, thus:

$$u(t) = \bar{u} \tag{8.6}$$

Then, the values of $A(t)$ and $k(t)$ corresponding to $dA(t)/dt = 0$ and $dk(t)/dt = 0$ are determined to be A_* and k_*, respectively, irrelevant to time:

$$A_* = \frac{\lambda k_*^{1-\alpha}}{s(1-\bar{u})} \tag{8.7}$$

$$k_* = \left(\frac{\rho}{\bar{u}}\right)^{1/\alpha} \tag{8.8}$$

As a starting point of the analysis, with the level of the policy efforts being taken to be a time-invariant constant, we set out to derive the growth equations for $A(t)$ and $k(t)$ to know the behavior of these trajectories according to the initial conditions of the developing economies. Then the possibilities of the actual take-off towards their sustained growth will be examined by changing the levels of policy effort in connection with the present (initial) situations. First, Equations 8.2 and 8.3 are transformed into a linear system:

$$\frac{dv(t)}{dt} = \lambda w(t) - \ln(k_*) \tag{8.9}$$

$$\frac{dw(t)}{dt} = \alpha \rho v(t) - \lambda(1-\alpha)w(t) - [\ln(A_*) - (1-\alpha)\ln(k_*)] \tag{8.10}$$

where $v(t) = (1/\alpha\rho)\ln(A(t))$ and $w(t) = (1/\lambda)\ln(k(t))$. Then, this linear differential equation system is solved for $A(t)$ and $k(t)$. Thus, the solution is given in the following form:

$$A(t) = \exp\{\alpha\rho[(g_1 + h_1 e^{-\varphi_1 t_0})e^{\varphi_1 t} + (g_2 + h_2 e^{-\varphi_2 t_0})e^{\varphi_2 t} - h_1 - h_2]\} \tag{8.11}$$

$$k(t) = \exp\{\varphi_1(g_1 + h_1 e^{-\varphi_1 t_0})e^{\varphi_1 t} + \varphi_2(g_2 + h_2 e^{-\varphi_2 t_0})e^{\varphi_2 t} - \varphi_1 h_1 - \varphi_2 h_2\} \tag{8.12}$$

where constant and coefficient terms g_1, g_2, h_1, and h_2 are represented as:

$$g_1 = \left[\frac{\varphi_2 \ln(A_0) - \alpha\rho \ln(k_0)}{\alpha\rho(\varphi_2 - \varphi_1)}\right] e^{-\varphi_1 t_0} \tag{8.13}$$

$$g_2 = -\left[\frac{\varphi_1 \ln(A_0) - \alpha\rho \ln(k_0)}{\alpha\rho(\varphi_2 - \varphi_1)}\right] e^{-\varphi_2 t_0} \tag{8.14}$$

$$h_1 = \frac{\lambda}{\varphi_1 \sqrt{D}} \left\{ \ln(A_*) - \left(\frac{\varphi_2}{\lambda} + 1 - \alpha\right) \ln(k_*) \right\} \tag{8.15}$$

$$h_2 = \frac{\lambda}{\varphi_2 \sqrt{D}} \left\{ -\ln(A_*) + \left(\frac{\varphi_1}{\lambda} + 1 - \alpha\right) \ln(k_*) \right\}. \tag{8.16}$$

φ_1 and φ_2 are roots of the characteristic equation formed from the homogeneous part of the above derived linear differential equation system. These roots prove to have real values with different signs. We put them as:

$$\varphi_1 = -\mu \ (\mu > 0), \quad \varphi_2 = \omega \ (\omega > 0) \tag{8.17a}$$

In the Equations (8.13) and (8.14), A_0 and k_0 denote the initial values of $A(t)$ and $k(t)$ at $t = t_0$, respectively. These initial conditions are due to play a crucial role in the future growth paths of the economies, which will be investigated in the next section.

The time paths of $A(t)$ and $k(t)$ obtained here represent no more than the approximation to those implied by the original model postulated in Equations 8.1 to 8.3, but they preserve the fundamental nature inherent in it. Thus, Equations 8.11 and 8.12 yield the expressions for the trajectories of growth in an (A, k)-plane by a process of elimination in the following form:

$$\left| \mu \ln[A(t)] + \alpha\rho \ln[k(t)] + \alpha\rho(\mu+\omega) h_2 \right|^{\mu}$$
$$\left| \omega \ln[A(t)] - \alpha\rho \ln[k(t)] + \alpha\rho(\mu+\omega) h_1 \right|^{\omega}$$
$$= \left| \alpha\rho(\mu+\omega)(g_2 + h_2 e^{-\omega t_0}) \right|^{\mu} \cdot \left| \alpha\rho(\mu+\omega)(g_1 + h_1 e^{-\mu t_0}) \right|^{\omega} \tag{8.17b}$$

Some computational manipulations make it possible to rewrite this expression in the form:

$$\left| \left(\frac{\mu}{\alpha\rho}\right) \ln\left(\frac{A(t)}{A_*}\right) + \ln\left(\frac{k(t)}{k_*}\right) \right|^{\mu} \cdot \left| \left(\frac{\omega}{\alpha\rho}\right) \ln\left(\frac{A(t)}{A_*}\right) - \ln\left(\frac{k(t)}{k_*}\right) \right|^{\omega}$$
$$= \left| (\mu+\omega) A^{12} y_2(t_0) \right|^{\mu} \cdot \left| (\mu+\omega) A^{11} y_1(t_0) \right|^{\omega} \tag{8.18}$$

where $A^{11} y_1(t_0)$ and $A^{12} y_2(t_0)$ are obtained from the initial conditions for $A(t)$ and $k(t)$ as expressed in the following way:

$$A^{11} y_1(t_0) = \frac{1}{\mu + \omega} \cdot \left\{ \frac{\omega}{\alpha \rho} \cdot \ln\left(\frac{A_0}{A_*}\right) - \ln\left(\frac{k_0}{k_*}\right) \right\} \tag{8.19}$$

$$A^{12} y_2(t_0) = \frac{1}{\mu + \omega} \cdot \left\{ \frac{\mu}{\alpha \rho} \cdot \ln\left(\frac{A_0}{A_*}\right) + \ln\left(\frac{k_0}{k_*}\right) \right\} \tag{8.20}$$

In order to depict the trajectories of the growth paths, it is convenient to express at first the parts enclosed with the absolute value marks on the left-hand side of Equation 8.18 in the linear form. This can be done by putting:

$$x_1(t) = \left(\frac{1}{\alpha \rho}\right) \ln\left(\frac{A(t)}{A_*}\right) \quad \text{and} \quad x_2(t) = \left(\frac{1}{\lambda}\right) \ln\left(\frac{k(t)}{k_*}\right) \tag{8.21}$$

which gives:

$$\left| \mu x_1(t) + \lambda x_2(t) \right|^\mu \cdot \left| \omega x_1(t) - \lambda x_2(t) \right|^\omega$$
$$= \left| (\mu + \omega) A^{12} y_2(t_0) \right|^\mu \cdot \left| (\mu + \omega) A^{11} y_1(t_0) \right|^\omega \tag{8.22}$$

The trajectories of $x_1(t)$ and $x_2(t)$ are shown in the phase plane of Figure 8.1. In the laws of motion, attention must be paid to the properties that the growth of $x_1(t)$ or $x_2(t)$ always becomes zero when the trajectories cut across the lines:

$$x_2(t) = 0 \quad \text{and} \quad \alpha \rho x_1(t) - \lambda(1 - \alpha) x_2(t) = 0 \tag{8.23}$$

The trajectories approach an asymptotic line:

$$\omega x_1(t) - \lambda x_2(t) = 0 \tag{8.24}$$

as time goes on, one group expanding and the other dampening. The origin corresponds to the point (k_*, A_*).

After the law of motion in the phase diagram is understood, the growth trajectories of $A(t)$ and $k(t)$ are easily depicted. Since the slope of an asymptotic line extending northeastward is easily ascertained to be greater than that of the line signifying $dx_2(t)/dt = 0$ as shown in Figure 8.1, the asymptotic curve:

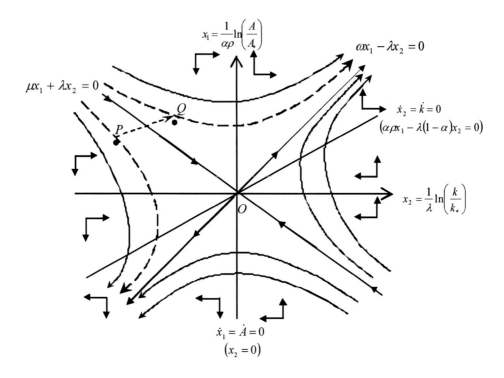

Figure 8.1. Phase Plane of Growth Trajectories.

$$\left(\frac{\omega}{\alpha\rho}\right)\ln\left(\frac{A(t)}{A_*}\right) - \ln\left(\frac{k(t)}{k_*}\right) = 0 \qquad (8.25)$$

cuts the $dk(t)/dt = 0$ curve at the point O(k_*, A_*) from below to above as it stretches to the northeast. It has already been found that the crossing point is a saddle point.

In the plane of the growth trajectories, the point O moves according to the change in the value u, policy efforts for technological progress. This means that the policy efforts might switch some growth paths which are to weaken in the future to the other paths and make them go into the trajectories having expanding properties. This possibility is exemplified in Figure 8.1 by a switch of a trajectory from P to Q. The effects of policy on the expansion paths together with the initial conditions are considered in the next section, especially with the East Asian economies in mind.

8.4. INITIAL CONDITIONS AND POLICY EFFORTS

Among the results derived from the above theoretical analysis based on a simple growth model, what seems to be of special significance from the point of view of fiscal expansion is the relationship between the initial state of an economy as the fundamental conditions for the development and the effects of policy implementation on the possibility of growth after the take-off period. As mathematical models devised by economists always do, our model presented in this paper takes into account only essential properties associated to the problems to be considered. Thus, the discussion here is not concerned with full a description about detailed aspects in the real economy, but it refers to the aspects that the model is related to. The purpose of economic model-building is to extract essential laws of behavior in relation to reality in order to better understand the actual economy and thus to make better policies.

As regards the initial conditions of an economy aimed at sustained growth for more advanced industrialization after finishing the take-off period at $t=t_0$, the model typically indicates what amounts of accumulated knowledge A and of physical capital stock per worker k are needed at that time.

Figure 8.1 shows that in order to get on the paths which will lead to sustained growth, the economy must be in the region above the line:

$$\mu x_1(t) + \lambda x_2(t) = 0 \tag{8.26}$$

in the phase plane at the initial time $t=t_0$. This region is formed by an asymptotic curve equivalent to the equation which is given as:

$$\frac{\mu}{\alpha\rho} \cdot \ln\left(\frac{A(t)}{A_*}\right) + \ln\left(\frac{k(t)}{k_*}\right) = 0 \tag{8.27}$$

in the trajectories diagram which is easily graphed out. The economies having the endowments of A and k at the initial time, $A(t_0)$ and $k(t_0)$, which are located in the region under this curve, are on the trajectories going eventually to the state at a low ebb.

This simple theoretical conclusion throws some light on the arguments concerning the growth of Asian economies. As mentioned in section 8.2. Krugman (1994b) poured cold water on the popular enthusiasm about Asian rapid economic growth, stating that Asian input-driven growth is an inherently limited process since it is not accompanied with an increase in efficiency with which inputs are used. With reference to the above conclusion seen in Figure 8.1, it seems that Krugman's view is correct: no matter how much physical capital is piled up, the economies cannot go into the trajectories eventually heading for the developed state as long as they stay in the region under the boundary curve marked by the Equation 8.27, owing to the absence of efficiency growth, that is, the low level of the accumulation of knowledge A. In that circumstance, it appears that the economies make rapid growth through high rates of mobilization of resources into production, but as the matter of fact, they may simply move to one of the upper trajectories of the same dampening nature. Then the growth is not actually sustained. In a different situation, however, where the economies have already accumulated a considerable amount of knowledge whilst the stock of physical capital is at an extremely low level, the economies could find a way to go into a sustained growth path towards the developed state. This might be possible through only a small amount of effort of accumulation of physical capital through measures like receipt of foreign aid.

Such is considered the case with Japan's economy immediately after the end of World War II, as shown in the historical data of Table 8.2. According to the standard adopted in

Table 8.1, Japan had finished its take-off stage in 1929 with GDP per capita attaining $2026. After that, the production facilities did not reach the level of the United States as a representative advanced industrial economy until around 1950 because of the devastation caused by WWII. However, no one can destroy knowledge dwelling in a nation. Japan embarked on a reconstruction of its economy after the war by employing its technological expertise associated with productive activities accumulated in peacetime (i.e. before the war) and augmented this with government financed R&D mainly in advanced strategic technologies. In the process of this reconstruction, the lack of physical capital was a vital difficulty that the government had to deal with. In order to tackle this problem, the government took a bold step called the 'Priority Production System' that directed Japan's limited resources at that time to the construction of primary production industries such as iron and steel, shipbuilding, and electric power. In so doing, Japan's economy was able to go into a trajectory of rapid and self-sustaining growth after 1950. In addition to such policy efforts, it is commonly recognized that the Korean War which occurred in the early 1950's played a definite role as an engine in sending Japan's economy to a high growth path.

Table 8.2. Japan's Catching-up with US in terms of Physical Capital per Worker

	1890	1913	1929	1938	1950	1973	1990	2003
US	4099	6913	10131	9906	15091	26259	39573	67230
Japan	194	659	1887	2012	3234	13287	34383	62905
Japan/US	0.05	0.10	0.19	0.20	0.21	0.51	0.87	0.94

(Note) Figures for physical capital per worker are values in 1990$. Physical capital is gross stock of machinery and equipment. (Source) Maddison (2007), pp.384-385.

As far as the static initial conditions are concerned, Krugman's statement on the limitedness of economic growth of the newly industrializing countries in the Pacific Rim seems to be correct on the basis of the analyses performed here. However, Krugman (1994b) disregards the fact that the continuous effort of augmenting knowledge or human skills in a nation could change the nature of an economy from 'Onetime changes' by mobilization of inputs to vitalized growth by increases in efficiency. A continuous policy effort to augment knowledge, $u(t) = \bar{u}$, moves the point $O(k_*, A_*)$ as time goes on. If this point moves towards the origin in compliance with the effort, the declining region of the economy diminishes accordingly. The behavior of the point O in response to changes in the level of u is shown in Figure 8.2. Recall that $u(t)$ denotes part of national income devoted to the acquisition of knowledge. The accumulation of information is not always implemented only by administrative measures based on governmental policies, but it could also take place in ordinary behavior of free enterprises or individuals being driven by market competition or by a desire to improve oneself. The variable $u(t)$ includes all of these activities related to the acquisition of knowledge by a nation.

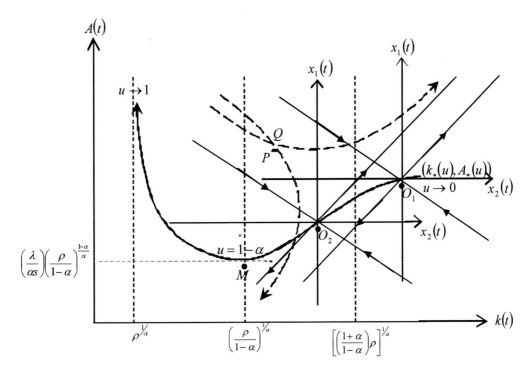

Figure 8.2. Motion of Stable (Zero Growth) Point subject to Policy Effort and Change in Growth Paths.

When the value of u is so small as to be almost zero, the initial conditions for an economy to go along the developing trajectories are highly demanding: the economy has to be equipped with a vast amount of physical capital stock along with a fairly large accumulation of knowledge at the beginning of stage of development since k_* is almost infinity and A_* takes a greater value accordingly as u nears to zero (see Equations 8.7 and 8.8). This could not be regarded as a possible situation for the economies just after the take-off stage. Even though they have a fairly high value of k_* by their policy efforts, it would be impossible for them to be equipped with a high technological state A_* at the same time. As $u(t)$ takes a larger value starting from almost zero, the conditions for growth become less demanding. This stable (zero growth) point O approaches the origin accordingly and the required accumulation of knowledge reaches the minimum value $(\lambda/\alpha s)[\rho/(1-\alpha)]^{\frac{1-\alpha}{\alpha}}$. This point M is attained by the level of the policy efforts $u = 1 - \alpha$. After that, the required levels of knowledge at the initial state increase rapidly as u approaches 1.

This is a broad outline of changes in the required initial conditions of the economies aimed at self-sustaining growth derived from the motion of the stable point $O(k_*, A_*)$ caused by changes in the level of policy efforts $u(t)$ to acquire knowledge. Then, our crucial problem is whether the Asian economies, the developments of which once have been appraised as the 'Miracle', are situated in the region having a possibility of sustained growth above the line (Equation 8.27) with their present conditions, $k(t_0)$, $A(t_0)$, and $u(t)$ just after finishing their take-off stages.

Since there are scarcely statistical evidences available especially for developing countries about a distribution rate for capital α, national savings ratio s, and other parameters related to our model, it is impossible to prove empirically whether each of the Asian economies considered to finish the take-off stage is located at present on a trajectory of sustained growth or on an eventual declining path. However, it is possible to realize the course of the policy efforts that these economies have to take under the current situation as known by sporadic evidence. Such statistics related to our model are gathered for four countries, Japan, South Korea, China, and India, and are given together with those for the United States in Table 8.3. The US data are used as a bench mark with which these economies try to catch up in their industrialization process. In Section 8.1, we assumed that the state of attaining almost \$2,000 (in 1990 US\$) is the finish of a take-off period for industrialization in Asian economies. Under this standard, South Korea and China are considered to have passed their take-off stage around 1970 and 1992, respectively, whilst Japan had finished the preparation period before WWII, in the 1930s. According to this standard, India is now just drawing to the end of the take-off stage.

Table 8.4(A) shows the historical change of GDP per capita of these four Asian countries as the ratio to that of the US. Based on these empirical figures, South Korea, China, and India are considered to have reached the end of their take-off stage with 0.130, 0.080, and 0.074, respectively, in the assumed year of finishing the take-off for each country. Looking into the statistics concerned with the initial conditions after the take-off period and the present situation given in Table 8.4 (A), (B) and (C), we can say that South Korea has already taken on a sustained growth path moving above the critical line of Equation 8.27 in the phase plane. This can be almost safely said especially due to the fact that recently South Korea has rapidly been catching up with the US level of national R&D activities as shown in Table 8.4(C). This situation should make it certain that this country enters the sustained growth region as indicated by the motion of the stable point in Figure 8.2.

On the other hand, China is supposed to be situated in a border region between declining and rising paths. Since detailed statistics on the Chinese economy are not available in order to locate its present position indicated by Equation 8.21, we cannot say for certain where China is situated in the phase plane of growth trajectories. However, the above analysis shows that an economy with a smaller fixed capital stock has to sacrifice a greater ratio of GDP for efforts on the growth of knowledge and technological advance of the nation. From this point of view, China's effort for technological advance shown in Table 8.4(C) is not yet said to be sufficient for its economy to take a sustained growth path leading to more advanced industrialization. This is because the Chinese economy is not considered to have already had a sufficient stock of fixed capital to compensate for that level of effort and the present retarded technological level supposed from evidence in Table 8.4 (D). As regards India, the same thing can be said more strongly with additional evidence on the nation's education as shown in Table 8.4 (E).

Table 8.3. Actual figures and data sources for four Asian states and the United States

[United States]

	1950	1960	1970	1980	1990	2000	2003
GDP p.c.	9561	11230	15030	18577	23201	28129	29037
ΔK	-	-	17.9	18.7	17.4	19.9	17.9
U	-	-	-	2.34*	2.65	2.74	2.68
A	-	-	-	-	11060	17554	19222
Ed-I	-	-	-	-	30.1*	36.5	38.4
ED-II	11.27	-	14.58*	-	18.04**	-	-

[Japan]

	1950	1960	1970	1980	1990	2000	2003
GDPp.c.	1921	3986	9714	13428	18789	21069	21218
ΔK	-	-	36.2	32.2	32.5	25.2	22.9
U	-	-	-	2.12*	2.79	2.99	3.15
A(	-	-	-	-	9903	12954	13564
Ed-I	-	-	-	-	-	33.4	37.4
ED-II	9.11	-	12.09*	-	14.86**	-	-

[South Korea]

	1950	1960	1970	1980	1990	2000	2003
GDPp.c.	770	1105	1954	4114	8704	14343	-
ΔK	-	-	25.6	32.2	37.1	31.1	29.9
U	-	-	-	-	1.84**	2.39	2.63
A	-	-	-	-	67	579	747
Ed-I	-	-	-	-	14.4*	23.9	29.5
ED-II	3.36	-	6.82*	-	13.55**	-	-

[China]

	1950	1960	1970	1980	1990	2000	2003
GDPp.c.	439	673	783	1067	1858	3425	4803
ΔK	-	-	-	29	25.8	36.5	42.1
U	-	-	-	-	0.73**	0.9	1.13
A	-	-	-	-	12	87	177
Ed-I	-	-	-	-	-	-	-
ED-II	-	-	-	-	-	-	-

[India]

	1950	1960	1970	1980	1990	2000	2003
GDPp.c.	619	753	868	938	1309	1910	2160
ΔK	-	-	-	-	-	-	-
U	-	-	-	-	0.7	0.77	0.72
A	-	-	-	-	12	58	87
Ed-I	-	-	-	-	-	-	-
ED-II	1.35	-	2.60*	-	5.55**	-	-

(Notes) GDP p.c.= per capita GDP.
ΔK= Gross fixed capital formation as a percentage of GDP.
U=Gross domestic expenditures on R&D as a percentage of GDP.
* = Figure of 1981, **=Figure of 1991.
A=Number of patents taken at three patent offices of the world – the European Patent Office, the Japan Patent Office, and the United States Patent and Trademark Office.
Ed-I=Tertiary education attainment for age group 25-64 as a percentage of that age group. *=Figure of 1991.
Ed-II=Years of education per person aged 15-64. *=Figure of 1973, **=Figure of 1992.
(Sources) GDP p.c.= Maddison (2006), pp.562-563; (2007), p.382.
ΔK= OECD (2007), p.37.
U= OECD (2007), p.147.
A= OECD (2007), p.151.
Ed-I= OECD (2007), p.179.
Ed-II= Maddison(1995), p.77.

Table 8.4. Historical Changes of Growth Related Factors of 4 Asian Countries

(A) Per capita GDP (US level =1.000)

	1950	1960	1970	1980	1990	2000	2003
Japan	0.201	0.355	0.646	0.723	0.810	0.749	0.731
South Korea	0.081	0.098	0.130	0.221	0.375	0.510	-
China	0.046	0.060	0.052	0.057	0.080	0.122	0.165
India	0.065	0.067	0.058	0.050	0.056	0.068	0.074

(B) Gross Fixed Capital Formation as a Percentage of GDP. (US level =1.000)

	1950	1960	1970	1980	1990	2000	2003
Japan	-	-	2.022	1.722	1.868	1.266	1.279
South Korea	-	-	1.430	1.722	2.132	1.563	1.670
China	-	-	-	1.551	1.483	1.834	2.352
India	-	-	-	-	-	-	-

(C) Gross Domestic Expenditure on R&D as a Percentage of GDP. (US level =1.000)

	1950	1960	1970	1980	1990	2000	2003
Japan	-	-	-	0.906	1.053	1.091	1.175
South Korea	-	-	-	-	0.694	0.872	0.981
China	-	-	-	-	0.275	0.328	0.422
India	-	-	-	-	0.264	0.281	0.269

(D) Number of Patents taken in Europe, Japan, and US. (US level =1.000)

	1950	1960	1970	1980	1990	2000	2003
Japan	-	-	-	-	0.895	0.738	0.706
South Korea	-	-	-	-	0.006	0.033	0.039
China	-	-	-	-	0.001	0.005	0.009
India	-	-	-	-	0.001	0.003	0.005

(E) Years of Education per Person Aged 15-64. (US level =1.000)

	1950	1960	1973	1980	1992	2000	2003
Japan	0.808	-	0.829	-	0.824	-	-
South Korea	0.298	-	0.468	-	0.751	-	-
China	-	-	-	-	-	-	-
India	0.120	-	0.178	-	0.308	-	-

(Note) Actual figures and data sources are given in data in Table 8.2.

China's government recognizes how it has to cope with this problem. In its policy objectives for the economic growth, they plan to give a high priority on the advancement of science and technology and have already set out in 2006 to pull up the level of $u(t)$ in our model by implementing the Medium- and Long-term S&T Development Plan for the period 2006-2020. In this regard, Jakobson (2007) indicates the need for institutional reforms of the present bureaucratic systems so as to promote a nation's creativity and cooperation. Along with this, she points out the need to raise the quality of education (see also Chap. 7 on Growth and Institutions). This educational situation is supposed to be much the same as in India in Table 8.4. As regards institutional changes, we have already mentioned the need in relation to the historical data of Table 8.1. The phase plane of economic growth paths of Figure 8.1, along with the change of stable point in Figure 8.2, indicate that an economy usually has to be accompanied by institutional changes in order to move into the region of sustained growth trajectories. The reason is that a good level of capital stock per worker and a sufficient growth of a nation's technological knowledge by contributing a higher share of income to R&D activities could only be reached by putting the right institutions in place and increasing efficiency (see Chap. 7).

The key for sustained growth is, for example, how the Chinese economy can push not only technological level $A(t)$ but also capital stock per worker $k(t)$ up to the region:

$$\frac{\mu}{\alpha\rho} \cdot \ln\left(\frac{A(t)}{A_*}\right) + \ln\left(\frac{k(t)}{k_*}\right) > 0 \qquad (8.28)$$

in the near future. Otherwise, its economic situation might stay in the declining region below the asymptotic line (Equation 8.27), only showing "one-time changes" in that region by mobilizing resources of labor and capital which do not embody efficiency, as Krugman expressed.

Efforts on technological progress are not limited to the activities of directly acquiring knowledge through, for instance, government financed R&D or importation of foreign techniques. Technological information can be accumulated through indirect channels, too, by importing capital goods furnished with highly advanced technology needed for production under an export promotion strategy.

Our analysis shows that policy efforts for growth and institutional improvements for efficiency by a government and a nation could ease the initial conditions required to remove the economic growth path from the state in the poverty region (below the asymptotic curve given by the Equation 8.27) to that in the prosperity region (above that curve). This effect produced by policy efforts can be explained in the phase diagrams of Figure 8.1 and 8.2 by a switch from a declining path at a point P to a self-sustaining growth path at a point Q. We do not intend here to assert the advantages in economic policy of selective interventions over the traditional laisser-faire approach. We would only like to indicate that continuous policy efforts can play an important role in improving the initial conditions of economies which remain in the poverty state and which cannot find a way to get rid of it. It is taken for granted that whether an economy in the underdeveloped state can actually move to the prosperity region, not taking only an upper growth path in the same poverty region by "one-time changes", greatly depends upon the extent to which the economy can achieve efficiency growth by the accumulation of knowledge.

CONCLUDING REMARKS

In this chapter, we have tried to analyze the fundamental structure of Asian economic growth and to bring to light the basic problem to be considered for the sake of the development of those economies. We hope that this will instigate further critical thoughts ranging from a popular enthusiasm alleging the 'Asian Miracle' to the scholarly skepticism about Asian supremacy of growth by asserting a lack of efficiency in those economies.

Economic growth as an increase in per capita national income is achieved through both quantitative and qualitative advances in economic activities: quantitative advances in the economy can be accomplished by mobilization of capital and labour inputs in production processes, while qualitative advances can be brought about by efficiency growth in the economy typically through technological improvements. In the light of this consideration, we introduced a simple mathematical model to pinpoint the basic properties of growth paths in relation to the initial state of a country intending to secure sustained growth after the take-off stage for industrialization.

Growth equations derived from the model show that all growth trajectories are divided into two groups according to the initial conditions, one of which consists of trajectories having eventually expanding properties and the other being those of eventually declining properties. The phase plane accommodating all possible growth paths is separated into two parts by an equation signifying an asymptotic curve. One is the area above the curve where all eventually expanding trajectories exist and the other is the area below the curve having all those eventually declining ones. We designated the former as the 'prosperity region' and the latter as the 'poverty region'.

An economy lying in the poverty region at the initial state will be destined to remain in a situation of low standard of living if it does not make any policy efforts to accumulate knowledge. In contrast, policy efforts could send an economy to one of the expansion paths in the prosperity region. From the properties of the poverty region which enlarges or diminishes according to the changes in the level of policy efforts, growth policy unaccompanied by increases in efficiency, that is, mobilization of resources without augmentation of knowledge, might give the economy only "one-time changes" of the state which move it into one of the upper trajectories in the same poverty region. This may correspond to the case of an inherently limited input-driven growth. The change in the present situation by the policy efforts should be motivated by institutional reforms to stimulate efficiency growth especially in Asian countries.

However, much attention must be paid to the possibility that continuous efforts to augment knowledge by a nation would lead the economy to a sheer self-sustaining growth path by moving it from the poverty region to the prosperity region, or by switching the trajectories from an eventually declining path to one of eventually expanding path. As a matter of fact, Japan has accomplished this switch in growth paths through the implementation of sophisticated economic policies characterized by a series of "economic plans" which extended over two decades after WWII. South Korea, as well to a great extent, has made high and sustained growth accompanied by structural transformation through continuous policy efforts strongly led by the government in pursuit of the Japanese model.

An economy may differ with another on the kinds of policy efforts to accumulate knowledge, depending on the differences of political and economic surroundings between them. In reality, the economies of South-East Asia - Singapore, Thailand, Malaysia and Indonesia - have taken different strategies from Japan and South Korea to acquire knowledge, by opening their markets to foreign direct investment, whilst the latter countries took the defensive policy against it. China is now in the situation of looking on a sustained growth for advanced industrialization and the government has begun the effort to make itself an innovative state. The success of this effort will depend upon how the country can improve its political and social institutions in order to overcome obstacles to efficiency improvement. Such institutional reforms are needed for each of the Asian economies, even for the present Japan toward the proceeding changes in the global surroundings of its economy.

Whether Asian economies truly have made or can make a growth miracle depends to a large extent on the increases in efficiency. At the early-industrial stage when an economy is about to start its industrialization for growth, policy measures like selective interventions and coerced mobilization of resources might prove effective for structural transformation and produce a rapid growth. But the quantitative mobilization of resources inevitably reduces the economy to a state of decreasing returns. Sheer self-sustaining growth can be achieved only by a continuous growth in efficiency through accumulation of knowledge, typically speaking in the form of technological advances in the broad sense of word. This can realize increasing returns in production. However, these improvements cannot be made by government regulations and protectionism, but can be achieved only by a continuous development of creativity inspired in a nation that has a free competitive and creative environment.

REFERENCES

Amsden, A. H. (1998): Asia's Next Giant–South Korea and Late Industrialization, New York, Oxford: Oxford University Press

Dornbusch, R.S., Fisher, F. and P.A. Samuelson (1977): 'Comparative Advantage, Trade, and Payments in a Ricardian Model with a Continuum of Goods,' *American Economic Review* 67, 823-839

Greif, A.(2006), Institutions and the Path to the Modern Economy: Lessons from Medieval Trade. Cambridge: Cambridge University Press

Gognon, J. E. and A. K. Rose (1995), 'Dynamic Persistence of Industry Trade Balance: How pervasive Is the Product Cycle?' Oxford Economic Papers 47, 229-248

Grossman, G. M. and E. Helpman (1991), 'Quality Ladders and Product Cycle,' *Quarterly Journal of Economics* 106, 557-588

Jakobson, L. (Ed.) (2007), Innovation with Chinese Characteristics – High-Tech Research in China, Hampshire UK/New York USA: Palgrave Macmillan/ Finish Institute of International Affairs

Jones, R. (1970), 'The Role of Technology in the Theory of International Trade,' in The Technology Factor in International Trade , R.Vernon, ed., Oxford, Blackwell

Kim, J.-I. and L.J. Lau (1994), 'The Source of Economic Growth of the East Asian Newly Industrialized Countries', *Journal of the Japanese and International Economies* 8(3), 235-271

Krugman, Paul R. (1979), 'A Model of Innovation, Technology Transfer, and the World Distribution of Income,' *Journal of Political Economy* 87, 253-266.

Krugman, Paul R. (1994a), 'Does Third World Growth Hurt First World Prosperity?' Harvard Business Review July August, 113-121.

Krugman, Paul R. (1994b), 'The Myth of Asia's Miracle,' Foreign Affairs, 73 November/December 63-78

Lucas, R. E., Jr. (1988), 'On the Mechanics of Economic Development,' *Journal of Monetary Economics* 22, 3-42.

Lucas, R.E., Jr. (1993), 'Making a Miracle,' Econometrica 61, 251-272.

Maddison, Angus (1979), 'Per Capita Output in the Long Run', Kyklos 32, 412-429

Maddison, Angus (1995): Monitoring the World Economy 1820-1992, Paris,OECD.

Maddison, Angus (2006): The World Economy, Paris,OECD

Maddison, Angus (2007): Contours of the World Economy, 1-2030 AD, Oxford,Oxford University Press, p.382

Matsuyama, K. (1991), 'Increasing Returns, Industrialization, and Indeterminacy of Equilibrium,' Quarterly Journal of Economics 106, 617-850.

North, D. C., and R. P. Thomas (1973), The Rise of the Western World: A New Economic History. Cambridge: Cambridge University Press

Posner, M.V. (1961), 'International Trade and Technical Change,' Oxford Economic Papers 13, 323-341

Romer, P. M. (1986), 'Increasing Returns and Long Run Growth,' *Journal of Political Economy*, 94, 1002-1037

Rostow, W. W. (1983), 'Korea and the Fourth Industrial Revolution, 1960-2000,' Paper presented at the Federation of Korean Industries

Shell, Karl (1966), 'Toward a Theory of Inventive Activity and Capital Accumulation,' American Economic Review 56, 62-68

Song, B. N. (1990), The Rise of the Korean Economy. Hong Kong, Oxford University Press

Stokey, N. L. (1988), 'Learning by Doing and the Introduction of New Goods,' *Journal of Political Economy* 96, 701-717

Stokey, N.L. (1991a), 'Human Capital, Product Quality, and Growth,' *Quarterly Journal of Economics* 106, 587-616

Stokey, N.L. (1991b), 'The Volume and Composition of Trade Between Rich and Poor Countries,' The Review of Economic Studies 58, 63-80

Vernon, R. (1966), 'International Investment and International Trade in the Product Cycle,' Quarterly Journal of Economics 80, 190-207

Wan Jr., Henry Y. (2004): Economic Development in A Globalized Environment: East Asian Evidences, Kluwer Academic Publishers

World Bank, The (1993) The East Asian Miracle Economic Growth and Public Policy. Oxford: Oxford University Press

Young, A. (1992), 'A Tale of Two Cities: Factor Accumulation and Technical Change in Hong Kong and Singapore', NBER Macroeconomics Annual

Young, A. (1994), 'Lessons from the East Asian NICs: A Contrarian View', *European Economic Review* 38, 964-973

Young, A. (1995), 'The Tyranny of Numbers: Confronting the Statistical Realities of the East Asian Growth Experience', *Quarterly Journal of Economics* 110(3), 641-680

Chapter 9

DYNAMIC COOPERATIVE INDUSTRIAL POLICY

Makoto Takashima

9.1. INTRODUCTION

In economic activities, agents such as firms, governments and other organizations sometimes behave in a cooperative way for their own self interest. In subcontracting relationships between independent firms which every now and then compete with each other in several fields, there is the case where an ordering firm gives financial and technological assistance to a supplying firm in the production relations between them. This sort of cooperative relationship in Japanese industry is analyzed by Takashima (1992) in a comparative context with the case of the United Kingdom. In global competitions which have been continuously growing, it is seen at times that firms competing in the same field of products enter into collaborative arrangements in development of goods. A more recent example is the collaborative contract between two major Japanese electronics companies, Sharp and Toshiba, where the former supplies liquid crystal displays (LCD) to the latter. The cooperative production of LCD by Japanese Sony and Korean Samsung is another example of a collaborative contract made a couple of years ago between two companies which are internationally competing in electronics products including flat screen TVs.

Government policies for industry can be seen as an arena for collaborative ventures. In the activities of technological expansion which is the focus here, private firms and government have their own objectives. Firms naturally conceive their R&D planning with the objective of pursuing their own private interests, while the government's policy is for enhancement of national economic welfare through the technological strength of the industry as a whole. Under these conditions, collaborative schemes such as research consortiums are carried out with assorted funds from the government and the private sector.

We recently examined the behavior of industry and government in a national consortium scheme for industrial R&D (Takashima, 2007). That was a static consideration based on a two-stage game model comprising a phase where industry decides on the optimal strategy to contribute to the R&D consortium and a subsequent period of government decision making with regards the consortium and industry's decision making on their own R&D efforts and facilities. The analytical concept is that of extensive dynamic game theory where the key aspects are "the order in which players move, and what each player knows when making each of their decisions "(Fudenberg and Tirole, 1991, p.67).

We are basically interested in examining national policy in order to enhance national technology through industrial R&D efforts. The aim is to analyze conflict and cooperation between industry and government in pursuit of their respective objectives for a certain period of time (e.g. ten years). In order to handle this dilemma directly, we are led to pose the problem in a more substantial way than the two-stage dynamic model. That is to study the players' behavior that evolves over time in a differential game model.

The basic structure of the current model is the same as that of the former study (Takashima, 2007) but the specific structures differ owing to a difference in analytical scope. While we divided industrial R&D activities into basic research and development in the previous study, we treated the activities in total, not distinguishing them. This is because our present interest lies in addressing the time-varying behavior of firms and governments with their different concerns about the general state of technology.

Second, we consider this time the spillover effect through imitation or free introduction of technological knowledge from society to individual firms. The importance of this effect in industrial R&D was noticed and analyzed especially by Griliches (1979, 1998) and has recently been adopted in works on technological competition among firms (for example, Aghion et al, 2001; Gottinger, 2006). Along with the positive spillover effect, we introduce the negative feedback effect of the existing technological condition on the growth rate of the state. This explains the situation where both the industry and the government should suffer a gradual reduction in effective technological capability when they do not continue R&D efforts. In addition they need to make greater efforts in R&D as they have a higher level of technological state because it is more challenging for them to enhance technology even further when they have already arrived at a sufficiently high position.

Our model of R&D in an economy is a formulation of conflict and cooperation in innovative activities between firms and governments. But it remains the same as the former two-stage game model of the R&D consortium in that it is actually a non-cooperative game between them since in the actual situation they essentially decide their optimal strategies independently according to their respective objectives, even if they make some binding agreements to cooperate within the bureaucratic system. An essential difference from the previous study is that, this time, we formulate the government policy for strengthening the technological competence of the national economy by encouraging the private sector to undertake higher R&D activities and analyze their optimal strategies in this framework with the use of a differential game model.

In this analytical framework, we pursue the evolution of the technological levels of R&D performing firms and the national economy as a whole. These variables are called 'state' variables and they evolve in association with and under the influence of actual R&D efforts of the players. These labors are decided strategically according to their respective interests and thus are called 'action' or 'control' variables. In order to explain the evolution of the technological states in this 'non-cooperative' game between private sector and government, we describe the change of state variables at an instant of time by a set of ordinary differential equations formulated with the players' action variables and the state variables. Thus, our problem is analyzed as a differential game model which is 'a subclass of dynamic games' (Dockner, et al., 2000, p.1). Alternatively, we could design a differential games mechanism as in Yeung and Petrosyan (2006, Chap.4) which sets up cooperative arrangements of R&D similar to this model.

The problem as stated here involves a private-public cooperation/partnership under the umbrella of a differential games mechanism while Chap. 2 epitomizes dynamic rivalry among technology based industries to foster economic growth and accumulate wealth among nation states as referred to in Chap. 4. In section 9.2, we present a model of R&D activities by firms and government in a public policy of enhancing industrial technology. Basic hypotheses and assumptions are explained and a game structure over time between the players is formulated as an optimization problem concerning their respective payoff functions under constraints on evolution of state variables and their initial conditions.

Section 9.3 gives a solution of the differential game model with a graphical presentation for the evolution of a realized technological state of both the firms and the government along with their optimal strategies for R&D efforts. The results lead to strategic implications that we could not have in a static model analysis of a two-stage game. Furthermore, in order to reflect on the results of Section 9.3 we introduce another pay-off function for the government's objective which attaches importance to the technological level of the national economy at the end of policy execution. The results are contrasted with those of the first model. We also discuss strategic aspects derived from these different policies. This is the task of Section 9.4. Finally Section 9.5 concludes on the progress of studies on technological policy.

9.2. MODELING R&D POLICY

R&D Policy Problem and Analytical Setup

In these days of a global market economy, technological superiority is a major concern of both private firms and governments. Manufacturing firms always strive for innovations with various measures. R&D efforts with their own research facilities play a central role in technological progress. On the other hand, government agencies aim at the enhancement of technological capabilities of the national economy as a whole. For that purpose, they undertake various political strategies including financial and other administrative supports to encourage private firms' R&D activities. Research consortiums between firms and government are examples of such strategies.

The objective of R&D activities appears to be the same for both private firms and governments in that they would pursue the highest possible technological level. In actual practice, however, each of them pursues a slightly different aim depending on the situation. A firms' goal is to attain the maximum payoff possible from technological assets through productive activities using the inventions or direct trade of new knowledge. In contrast, the main interest of the government is the highest possible technological level of the economy as a whole under the restrictions of a limited national budget. Thus, both players decide their own actions over time, occasionally in conflict and at times in cooperation with each other. In such circumstances, our problem is formulated under a differential game setup between R&D performing firms and policy undertaking government where their technological states evolve over a certain length of time. The essential specifications of this problem are as follows:

i. Our primary concern in this problem is the evolution of the technological state of the national economy $x(t)$ and that of R&D performing firms $y(t)$. In terminology of a control problem, they are "state variables" representing the state of the game at each time instant t. In what follows, we sometimes refer to the R&D performing firms totally as "industry". Their action can be considered to be that of a representative firm.

ii. The evolution of the technological states is expressed by the ordinary differential equation having strategy variables of government $u(t)$ and R&D performing firms $v(t)$. State variables themselves are included as explaining variables in the equation. Strategies are referred to as "control" variables in the literature on control theory. In our problem, these variables represent the amount of government R&D budget for support of industrial R&D and the firms' expenditures for their own R&D efforts.

iii. These R&D strategies are decided optimally by both parties at each time instant according to their respective objective function. We assume that each of the players decide their amount of R&D effort so as to maximize their own total payoff from the realized technological state after deducting the R&D expenditures over the prescribed time interval. For the government, we consider another function emphasizing the terminal state of the technology of the national economy. The function of the terminal state is called 'salvage value function' or 'scrap value function' in the literature.

iv. In solving our problem, we specify the initial conditions for the state variables, i.e. the initial states of technology in both the industry and the nation as a whole. Together with this, we assume that each party rates respectively the value of state variables at the initial time instant. That is, they are considered to start the game, envisaging the highest price that they would be willing to pay for an additional small growth of each state variable of x and y.

Problem of the Private Sector

In this technological policy, government first announces a measure of progressing technological standards of the economy through the cooperative efforts between private and public sectors. A specific example of such policies is the R&D consortium where firms and government undertake some strategic research project over a certain period of time with funds supplied by both of them.

At time 0, the government announces a political scheme of strengthening R&D efforts of firms: the government supplies research funds to firms so as to increase their R&D efforts at time t by $\theta(t)$ times. This policy is undertaken through the time horizon T. The government's final objective is not to help firms to undertake R&D activities but to enhance the technological standard of the national economy as a whole under a constraint of national budget. It is true, however, that the rise in technological standard of the economy $x(t)$ brings individual firms the benefit of harnessing advanced technological knowledge free of charge for their R&D activities. Under these conditions, R&D firms in the private sector decide their optimal action, i.e. the amount of expenditures for R&D activities $v(t)$, so as to maximize their total net technological benefit, discounted over the policy period $[0, T]$. Furthermore, in choosing their control path, they take the policy path $\theta(t)$ announced by the government as given. Thus, we can formulate this problem as a differential game with a group of R&D performing firms as a follower player and the government as a leader player. Firms' objective is given as follows:

To maximize $\int_0^T e^{-rt} \{R\, y(t) - v(t)\} dt$ \hfill (9.1)

where r is a rate of discount and R is a revenue from a unit of industry's present technological asset $y(t)$. For simplicity, we use the same discount rate for both industry and government.

Along with $y(t)$ for the technological state of the firms, let $x(t)$ denote the technological state of the economy as a whole. According to the above objective function, the firms choose their optimal strategy for R&D, $v^*(t)$, under the given control variable, $\theta(t)$, and the evolution of the state variables, $x(t)$ and $y(t)$. We assume the evolutional equations for these state variables to be:

$$\dot{x}(t) = \alpha \ln[\theta(t) v(t)] - L\, x(t) \qquad (9.2)$$

and

$$\dot{y}(t) = \beta \ln[v(t)] + M\, x(t) - L\, y(t) \qquad (9.3)$$

In these equations, L is a decay rate of technology in the absence of any research effort. Firms, however, benefit from the spillover of knowledge in the economy even in undertaking no R&D activities by themselves. This effect is represented by a factor, $M\, x(t)$, in Equation 9.3. Here, M is a number which quantifies the amount of this technical spillover from the economy to individual firms. At the start of this scheme, the values of these state variables are known to both players as:

$$x(0) = x_0 \qquad (9.4a)$$
$$y(0) = y_0 \qquad (9.4b)$$

The follower's objective function in Expression 9.1 appears not to be influenced by the evolution of technological state of the economy $x(t)$. But the value is affected indirectly by $x(t)$ through the evolution of $y(t)$ as indicated by Equation 9.3. The state $x(t)$ changes under the direct influence of government policy $\theta(t)$ as expressed in Equation 9.2. Therefore, the follower's problem must be solved under the constraints of Equations 9.2 and 9.3 with the initial condition given by Equations 9.4a and 9.4b.

Problem of the Government

The game starts with the announcement of a government's policy to encourage firms to strengthen R&D activities, by making public the basic strategy $\theta(t)$. This strategy, however, is not a direct supply of R&D funds to firms but only a general scheme of the R&D supporting program for the national economy as a whole including reinforcement of national research facilities. The actual budget is to be decided according to actual behavior of the firms.

Knowing the firms' behavior, the government decides its own optimal strategy each time. This is the game problem for the government as the leader in this situation. We assume that the leader's policy objective is given in the following way:

$$\text{To maximize } \int_0^T e^{-rt}\{P\,x(t)-[\theta(t)v(t)]\}dt \tag{9.5}$$

In this function or expression, P is a benefit factor for the nation from a unit of present technological resources of the economy $x(t)$. $[\theta(t)v(t)]$ is the total R&D expenditure of the nation which consists of the expenses for the R&D activities by both parties. Since $v(t)$ is the expenditure by the firms, the government's fund for this R&D scheme $u(t)$ is expressed as:

$$u(t)=[\theta(t)-1]v(t) \tag{9.6}$$

In this leader's problem, the evolution of state variable $x(t)$ explaining the objective function depends on the follower's control variable $v(t)$ as well as the leader's own strategy $\theta(t)$. Moreover, the follower's decision for $v(t)$ itself is made based on its payoff function of Equation 9.1 which essentially relies on the evolution of the state variable $y(t)$. Therefore, the government's game problem has the same constraints as those of the R&D firms in Equations 9.2, 9.3, and 9.4a and 9.4b.

While the follower chooses its optimal strategy $v(t)$ in taking the leader's policy variable $\theta(t)$ as given, the leader decides $\theta(t)$ in relation to the strategy chosen by the follower. Thus, the problems of both parties formulated above are concurrently solved in actual practice.

9.3. SOLUTION OF THE R&D DIFFERENTIAL GAME

Solution of the Private Sector's Problem

In solving the optimal control problems with constraints for the evolution of the state variables, we use Pontryagin's maximum principle (e.g. Dockner, et al, 2000, pp. 46-52, and Seierstad and Sydsaeter, 1987, pp. 83-88). In the first place, the Hamiltonian function for the follower's problem is given by:

$$H^F(x(t), y(t), v(t), \lambda(t), \mu(t), t) = [R\, y(t) - v(t)] + \lambda(t)\{\alpha \ln[\theta(t)v(t)] - L x(t)\} + \mu(t)\{\beta \ln[v(t)] + M x(t) - L y(t)\} \quad (9.7)$$

where $\lambda(t)$ and $\mu(t)$ are costate (or adjoint) variables associated with the state variables $x(t)$ and $y(t)$, respectively. A costate variable, which is sometimes called a 'shadow price', is considered the highest hypothetical price for the corresponding state variable that the player would be willing to pay for an additional and infinitesimal quantity of that state variable at time t. In our problem, both the firms and the government are considered to evaluate the state variables at the start of this R&D scheme but the value that they imagine for each of them should naturally be different between them according to their viewpoint.

Using this Hamiltonian, we obtain the firms' optimal condition under a certain time path $\theta(t)$ given by the government. At first, the maximum condition is derived directly from the Hamiltonian function as follows:

$$\frac{\partial}{\partial v} H^F(x(t), y(t), v(t), \lambda(t), \mu(t), t) = -1 + \lambda(t)\left\{\alpha \cdot \frac{1}{v(t)}\right\} + \mu(t)\left\{\beta \cdot \frac{1}{v(t)}\right\} = 0 \quad (9.8)$$

From this, we have the equation for the evolution of the firms' R&D strategy $v(t)$ as expressed only by costate variables:

$$v(t) = \alpha\, \lambda(t) + \beta\, \mu(t) \quad (9.9)$$

Next, we have the adjoint equations for the evolution of the costate variables associated with the state variables. For the costate variable $\lambda(t)$, we have:

$$\dot{\lambda}(t) = r\, \lambda(t) - \frac{\partial H^F}{\partial x(t)} = (r+L)\lambda(t) - M\, \mu(t). \quad (9.10)$$

In the same way, the adjoint equation for $\mu(t)$ becomes:

$$\dot{\mu}(t) = r\,\mu(t) - \frac{\partial H^F}{\partial y(t)}$$
$$= (r+L)\mu(t) - R. \tag{9.11}$$

When this R&D scheme starts, we assume that the party of the R&D performing firms has the initial values:

$$\lambda(0) = \lambda_0 \tag{9.12a}$$

$$\mu(0) = \mu_0 \tag{9.12b}$$

for these associated state variables. It means that they rate the initial technological states of the national economy and their own industry as λ_0 and μ_0, respectively, when starting their activities. Thus, these values are commonly known as the transversality condition together with the initial values of state variables $x(0)$ and $y(0)$. That is, the initial values of the follower's costate variables are formulated to be 'non-controllable' by the leader's control path.

Equations 9.9, 9.10, 9.11, and 9.12a,b constitute a set of optimum conditions for the R&D performing firms as the follower of this game under the policy path $\theta(t)$ given by the government as the leader. The optimal value of the follower's strategy $v(t)$, however, is not influenced by the given policy path as seen in the system of equations. This only results from a specific form of the follower's objective function that we use in this model.

We can have the firms' optimal strategy $v(t)$ by solving the above equations. From adjoint Equations 9.10 and 9.11 together with the initial condition Equations 9.12a and b, we obtain:

$$\lambda(t) = \frac{MR}{L_r^2} + \left(\lambda_0 - \frac{MR}{L_r^2}\right)\exp(L_r t) - M\left(\mu_0 - \frac{R}{L_r}\right)t\,\exp(L_r t) \tag{9.13}$$

$$\mu(t) = \frac{R}{L_r} + \left(\mu_0 - \frac{R}{L_r}\right)\exp(L_r t) \tag{9.14}$$

where L_r denotes $L+r$. Then, the evolution of the optimal strategy of the firms can be directly obtained by applying these expressions to Equation 9.9. However, we cannot obtain the optimal path of the firms' technological state $y(t)$ within the follower's problem since its evolution depends on the leader's strategy through the evolution of the technological state of the national economy.

Solution of the Government's Problem

When starting this R&D policy, the government announced a scheme of progressing national R&D activities in conjunction with industrial efforts by showing the leader's strategy. Actual government expenditure for this scheme is expressed in Equation 9.6. According to each control path $\theta(\cdot)$ of this scheme, firms choose the optimal strategy for their R&D activities $v(t)$ as solved in the previous subsection. The government knows this industry's response to the announced scheme and decides its actual control path $\theta(t)$ as the leader's best strategy to maximize its objective function in Equation 9.5. This is the problem of the government as the leader of the R&D policy game. In solving this problem, the government knows the industry's decision given by Equation 9.9 together with their shadow prices in Equations 9.13 and 9.14.

Since maximization by the government is subject to Equations 9.2, 9.3, 9.4, 9.10, 9.11, and 9.12, we have additional state variables $\lambda(t)$ and $\mu(t)$ in relation to the follower's decision in this leader's problem in a formal way. In addition, two additional costate variables are introduced associated with $\lambda(t)$ and $\mu(t)$ in the government Hamiltonian function. In our model, however, the costate variables in the follower's problem have been solved completely as described by Equations 9.13 and 9.14, in which $\lambda(t)$ and $\mu(t)$ evolve in time, not depending on other variables.

Therefore, our leader's Hamiltonian is given in a simpler way, without additional state and the associated costate variables, as follows:

$$H^G(x(t), y(t), \theta(t), \pi(t), \rho(t), t)$$
$$= \{P x(t) - \theta(t)[\alpha \lambda(t) + \beta \mu(t)]\} + \pi(t)\{\alpha \ln\{\theta(t)[\alpha \lambda(t) + \beta \mu(t)]\} - L x(t)\}$$
$$+ \rho(t)\{\beta \ln[\alpha \lambda(t) + \beta \mu(t)] + M x(t) - L y(t)\} \quad (9.15)$$

In this function, $\pi(t)$ and $\rho(t)$ are the leader's costate variables associated with the state variables $x(t)$ and $y(t)$, respectively, and the follower's control variable is replaced by the Equation 9.9 obtained in his optimization problem. Then, the optimality conditions for the government are given by:

$$\frac{\partial}{\partial \theta(t)} H^G(x(t), y(t), \theta(t), \pi(t), \rho(t), t)$$
$$= -\{\alpha \lambda(t) + \beta \mu(t)\} + \pi(t)\left\{\alpha \cdot \frac{1}{\theta(t)}\right\} + \rho(t)\{0\} = 0 \quad (9.16)$$

$$\dot{\pi}(t) = r \pi(t) - \frac{\partial H^G}{\partial x(t)} = -P + (r + L)\pi(t) - M \rho(t) \quad (9.17)$$

and

$$\dot{\rho}(t) = r\,\rho(t) - \frac{\partial H^G}{\partial y(t)} = (r + L)\rho(t) \tag{9.18}$$

When the government starts this policy scheme, they should estimate the marginal values for the present technological state of the economy as a whole $x(t)$ and that of the R&D performing firms $y(t)$, which become the initial conditions for the evolution of the costate variables. They are given by:

$$\pi(0) = \pi_0 \tag{9.19a}$$

$$\rho(0) = \rho_0 \tag{9.19b}$$

These values are naturally different from the firms' supposition Equations (9.12a and 9.12b) assumed in the follower's problem owing to differences in the objective between them.

From the maximum condition in Equation 9.16, we obtain the best strategy of the government:

$$\theta(t) = \frac{\alpha\,\pi(t)}{\alpha\,\lambda(t) + \beta\,\mu(t)} \tag{9.20}$$

where the denominator is the expression for the best strategy of the firms as given by Equation 9.9 and the numerator corresponds to the total R&D expenditure optimally chosen by both parties:

$$\alpha\,\pi(t) = u(t) + v(t) \tag{9.21}$$

The adjoint Equations 9.17 and 9.18 together with the initial condition Equations (9.19a and b) give the evolution of the government's costate variables associated with the corresponding state variables. The simple differential Equation (9.18) yields:

$$\rho(t) = \rho_0\,e^{L_r t} \tag{9.22}$$

and substituting this for the other adjoint Equation (9.17), we obtain:

$$\pi(t) = \frac{P}{L_r} + \left(\pi_0 - \frac{P}{L_r}\right)e^{L_r t} - M\,\rho_0\,t\,e^{L_r t} \tag{9.23}$$

In solving these equations, we used the initial conditions Equations (9.19a and b) to determine the constant terms. Here, L_r denotes $r + L$ as before. Then, having the explicit solution for the leader's costate variable $\pi(t)$ and the expressions for follower's costate variables Equations 9.13 and 9.14, we can calculate the government's optimal strategy by applying them to Equation 9.20.

Optimal Strategies and Evolution of State: A Simulation

In the preceding subsections *9.3.1* and *9.3.2*, we have found that the best strategy of the firms does not depend on the government strategy, whereas the latter's best strategy depends on the former's one, and that both strategies are not influenced directly by the evolution of state variables, as shown in Equations 9.9 and 9.20. The follower's optimal control variable $v(t)$ is expressed by his costate variables $\lambda(t)$ and $\mu(t)$ and that of the leader $\theta(t)$ depends on $v(t)$ together with his costate variable $\pi(t)$. Thus, the best strategy of either party is indirectly influenced by the evolution of the technological state through its marginal utility along the optimal strategy.

These costate variables have been explicitly obtained as Equations 9.13, 9.14, and 9.23, each of which evolves along with only time t. Then, the evolution of the state variables should be obtained explicitly by solving the ordinary differential Equations 9.2 and 9.3. Avoiding intricate expression, we only show the solution by using the control variables as follows:

$$x(t) = \alpha\, e^{-Lt} \left\{ \int_0^t e^{L\tau} \ln\left[\theta(\tau)v(\tau)\right] d\tau + x_0 \right\} \tag{9.24}$$

$$y(t) = e^{-Lt} \left\{ \alpha \int_0^t \int_0^\tau e^{Ls} \ln\left[\theta(s)v(s)\right] ds\, d\tau + \beta \int_0^t e^{L\tau} \ln\left[v(\tau)\right] d\tau + x_0 t + y_0 \right\} \tag{9.25}$$

In order to examine the dynamics of our R&D scheme model, we try to make an illustrative simulation by setting specific values for the model parameters. At first, we set the initial values for the costate variables as follows:

$$\lambda_0 = 1,\ \mu_0 = 2,\ \pi_0 = 3,\ \rho_0 = 1 \tag{9.26}$$

The costate variables have an intuitive interpretation as the marginal utility to the associated player and thus λ_0 and π_0 are the hypothetical prices set on the technological state of the national economy by the R&D performing firms and by the government, respectively. μ_0 and ρ_0, on the other hand, are those set by the respective players on the firms' technological state. The shadow price for the industry's technological state imagined by the government, $\rho_0 = 1$, however, plays no role in the dynamics of this scheme, since the path of that costate variable in Equation 9.22 does not affect the evolution of the other variables at all. Other parameters are set at:

$$L = 0.1, \quad R = P = 0.3, \quad \alpha = 2, \quad \beta = 1 \tag{9.27}$$

and we assume that the technological states of the economy as a whole and of the firms at the initial time of the scheme are on the same level:

$$x_0 = y_0 = 10 \tag{9.28}$$

In what follows, we use the player's utility functions by setting the discount rate equal to 0, for simplicity's sake, without any loss of essential results. Then, we have:

$$L_r = L \tag{9.29}$$

We operate the model for a policy scheme of ten years in this situation. The runs are conducted with three cases for M a parameter quantifying the amount of technological spillover from the economy to the firms, the values of which are set equal to:

$$M = 0.01, \ 0.05, \text{ and } 0.1 \tag{9.30}$$

The time paths of the costate variables $\lambda(t), \mu(t)$ and $\pi(t)$ are directly calculated by using Equations 9.13, 9.14, and 9.23. The evolution of the optimal strategies (control variables) chosen by respective parties, $v(t)$ and $\theta(t)$, are also obtained by substituting those calculated values for costate variables in Equations 9.9 and 9.20. Then, we have the simulation results for the dynamics of the state variables, $x(t)$ and $y(t)$, by expressing their differential Equations 9.2 and 9.3 in the form of difference equations:

$$x(t) \approx \alpha \sum_{\tau=1}^{t} \ln[\theta(\tau)v(\tau)] - L \sum_{\tau=1}^{t} x(\tau) + x_0, \quad t = 1, \cdots, T \tag{9.31}$$

$$y(t) \approx \beta \sum_{\tau=1}^{t} \ln[v(\tau)] + M \sum_{\tau=1}^{t} x(\tau) - L \sum_{\tau=1}^{t} y(\tau) + y_0, \quad t = 1, \cdots, T \tag{9.32}$$

where $T = 10$.

Figure 9.1 shows the time evolution of the control variables (optimal strategies) chosen by both the players (i.e. R&D performing firms and government) and the state variables (i.e. technological states of the firms and the national economy) realized under the R&D activities undertaken by them for three different cases of spillover effect parameter M.

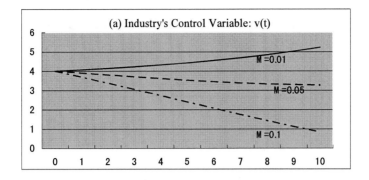
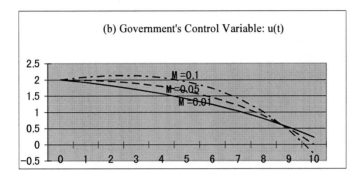
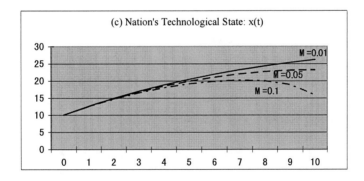
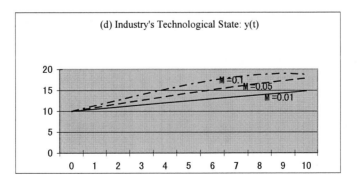

Figure 9.1. Simulation Results of Research Payoff Model.

Table 9.1. Maximum Net Benefit of R&D

	Industry	Government
M=0.01	-7.4811	3.6853
M=0.05	8.4288	9.7550
M=0.1	14.2115	15.4806

Main Results

i. When the economy has a social system where technological knowledge is diffused more freely among firms and between firms and public R&D institutions, firms' technological state progresses more over time, while the technological state of the economy as a whole advances less and the rate of progress decreases over time, the level itself beginning to fall in the later period of the scheme.

ii. As regards the R&D expenditure decided by them as the optimal strategy, firms make less R&D efforts as they are favored with a greater technological spillover. Firms depend more on the free transfer of technology instead of their own efforts.

iii. In that situation, government makes more R&D effort for most of the period. As the undertaking comes nearer to the terminal year, however, the government's expenditure for this R&D scheme rapidly decreases, and that amount becomes smaller than what the government should devote when society has a smaller spillover effect of technology.

With the above strategies, the industry and the government realize their maximum benefits after deduction of the expenditures during a period of ten years. The amounts are shown in Table 9.1. The result draws our attention to the fact that the government's net payoffs are greater than those of the firms participating in this R&D scheme in all three cases of spillover effect. This is essentially caused by the path of a nation's technological state which always evolves higher over time than that of the industry in each of three cases. The higher state of technology in the economy as a whole is the very consequence of that envisaged the policy authorities by setting a higher shadow price for the initial state of technology in the national economy than what firms set for their initial technological state. As seen in Figure 9.1, the government maintained almost the same amount of expenditures as that of the starting year for the earlier period of the scheme. This produced the relatively high evolution of the nation's state of technology over time together with the synergistic effect of the government expenditures and the firms' efforts.

9.4. SALVAGE VALUE MODEL

Government's Alternative Objective

In the preceding section, we used the same type of objective function to attain the greatest possible net payoff over the policy planning period for both parties. While the assumption is well understood as a symmetrical formulation between the two parties, the objective of the public authorities in charge of R&D policy can be considered to be the highest possible standard of technological state of the national economy at the end of the terminal point of the scheme rather than the net revenue from technological assets all through the period. However, account should be still taken of the amount of expenditures when they undertake the scheme because of the restrictive national budget.

In this section, we assume that the policy authorities of the government have the objective of making the technological standard of the economy as high as possible through financial measures to promote R&D activities of the nation. Thus, the government's objective is formulated so as to maximize:

$$F^G(\theta(\cdot)) = \int_0^T e^{-rt}\left[-\theta(t)v(t)\right]dt + e^{-rT}\left[x(T)\right] \tag{9.5'}$$

The objective function of the group of R&D firms is basically the same as given in Equation 9.1 except that we introduce a profitability parameter γ of their technological resources. It is given by:

$$F^F(v(\cdot)) = \int_0^T e^{-rt}\left\{R\left[y(t)\right]^\gamma - v(t)\right\}dt \tag{9.1'}$$

The dynamics of the state variables remain the same as Equations 9.2 and 9.3 and the actual R&D expenditure strategy by the government $u(t)$ is determined in relation to the strategy chosen by the firms $v(t)$ as shown in Equation 9.6.

When this R&D scheme is initiated, the policy authorities announce a plan of promoting the nation's R&D activities $\theta(\cdot)$ but the actual expenditure may change according to the strategies taken by firms $v(t)$. Knowing this procedure, the private sector decides its optimal strategy for each of the variable plans. This situation is the same as what we have considered so far. The evolution of the follower's optimal control variable $v(t)$ and its costate variable $\lambda(t)$ associated with the state variable $x(t)$ remain the same as given by Equations 9.9 and 9.10, respectively.

The introduction of the profitability parameter, however, changes the other follower's costate variable $\mu(t)$ into:

$$\dot{\mu}(t) = r\,\mu(t) + L\,\mu(t) - \gamma\,R\left[y(t)\right]^{\gamma-1} \tag{9.11'}$$

instead of Equation 9.11. Owing to this change, both of the follower's costate variables become controllable by the government' strategy $\theta(\cdot)$ through the evolution of the state variable $x(t)$, but the initial values for these costate variables are kept valid as stated in the condition Equation 9.12 together with the initial values for the state variables given in Equation 9.4.

In the leader's problem, we have to treat the follower's costate variables $\lambda(t)$ and $\mu(t)$ as additional state variables because their trajectories are not completely expressed by time t but depend on the evolution of the original two state variables. Thus, we have to introduce four costate variables in the leader's Hamiltonian, which is given by:

$$H^G(x(t), y(t), \lambda(t), \mu(t), \theta(t), \pi(t), \rho(t), \varphi(t), \psi(t), t)$$
$$= [-\theta(t)v(t)] + \pi(t)\{\alpha \ln[\theta(t)v(t)] - Lx(t)\}$$
$$+ \rho(t)\{\beta \ln[v(t)] + Mx(t) - Ly(t)\}$$
$$+ \varphi(t)\{(r+L)\lambda(t) - M\mu(t)\} + \psi(t)\{(r+L)\mu(t) - \gamma R[y(t)]^{\gamma-1}\} \quad (9.15')$$

The maximum condition is the same as expressed in Equation 9.20 and the adjoint equations are given by:

$$\dot{\pi}(t) = (r+L)\pi(t) - M\rho(t) \quad (9.33)$$

$$\dot{\rho}(t) = (r+L)\rho(t) + \gamma(\gamma-1)R[y(t)]^{\gamma-2}\psi(t) \quad (9.34)$$

$$\dot{\varphi}(t) = \alpha\theta(t) - \left(\frac{\alpha^2}{v(t)}\right)\pi(t) - \left(\frac{\alpha\beta}{v(t)}\right)\rho(t) - L\varphi(t) \quad (9.35)$$

$$\dot{\psi}(t) = \beta\theta(t) - \left(\frac{\alpha\beta}{v(t)}\right)\pi(t) - \left(\frac{\beta^2}{v(t)}\right)\rho(t) + M\varphi(t) - L\psi(t) \quad (9.36)$$

where the additional costate variables $\varphi(t)$ and $\psi(t)$ have no transversality condition since we assume that the follower's costate variables $\lambda(t)$ and $\mu(t)$ are non-controllable, having the initial value λ_0 and μ_0, respectively (see, Dockner et al., 2000, p.51).

Simulation Results

A simulation is carried out with the same parameters for the objective functions and the evolution of state variables as given in the previous model. The state variables and the costate variables are also assumed to have the same initial values as those in Equations 9.26, 9.27 and 9.28. As we have a new profitability parameter γ for firms' technological resources and additional costate variables $\lambda(t)$ and $\mu(t)$ for the government in our new model, we put additional conditions on them:

$$\gamma = 0.5, 1.0, 1.2 \; ; \; \lambda_0 = 1 \text{ and } \mu_0 = 1 \quad (9.37)$$

We try three runs under these different values of profitability parameter, while the spillover parameter is kept constant at the medium value $M = 0.05$. In addition, we still use the assumption $L_r = L$.

The simulation results are given in Figure 9.2. This model is concerned with two aspects that the above simulation has left unexplained. It considers that the profitability parameter γ should take a small value when the firm's technology lags behind the domestic and international standard and the value gradually becomes greater as the firm progresses more in technology. This simulation explains how firms behave in R&D activities according to their technological stage. Another aspect that we are interested in is how the planning authorities change their strategy when the government transforms the policy objective from the R&D payoff maximization to the attainment of a maximum possible technological state of the national economy at the end of the policy period.

The evolution of 'Industry's Control Variable: $v(t)$ ' in Figure 9.2 shows that firms continue to make greater efforts in R&D activities in a lagged technological state represented by a smaller profitability parameter while they go to change their strategy to reduce their R&D expenditures over time in a more advanced state. This is almost the same situation where we considered different values for the technological spillover effects M from the domestic and foreign economies to individual firms in the simulation of the previous model. The dynamics of firms' R&D efforts under the different values of M are shown in Figure 9.1(a), which almost completely corresponds to Figure 9.2(a) for the evolution of different parameters. This means that as far as the strategy during a certain period is concerned, R&D profitability has an effect on private firms' R&D expenditure decisions in the same way as R&D spillover has.

Concerning the government's strategy, however, the chosen optimal dynamics shows quite a different result in this salvage model from the result of the previous payoff model. We saw in Figure 9.1(b) that the government's R&D expenditure decreases almost every year in the R&D net payoff model. In the salvage model, in contrast, the optimal value of the government's R&D budget continuously increases throughout the planning period in all three runs with different profitability parameters as revealed in Figure 9.2(b). It is clearly shown that the strategic variable grows over time for the case of a profitability parameter $\gamma = 1.0$. This corresponds to the simulation run of the payoff model with spillover parameter $M = 0.05$ except the difference in the objective functions for the leader (i.e. government). This marked contrast in the optimal dynamics of the leader's control variable $u(t)$ between these two models is naturally caused by the transformation of the leader's objective from the payoff functions into the salvage function. The transformation yields a rising evolution of the nation's technological state $x(t)$ in the salvage model aiming at the highest possible $x(T)$ at the end of the planning period. Figure 9.2 shows that the planning authorities choose their optimal dynamics of the control variable $u(t)$ so as to compensate for the R&D efforts of the private sector and to attain their objective optimally. The state $x(t)$ in the salvage model evolves at a higher rate under the chosen strategy especially in the latter period than the state variable in the previous payoff model (Figure 9.1 (c)). The dynamics does not make any perceptible differences between three different profitability parameters as we can see in Figure 9.2 (c).

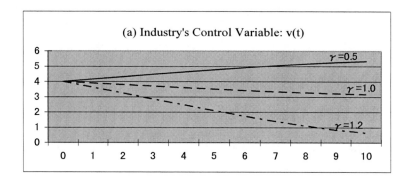

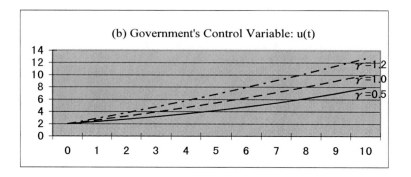

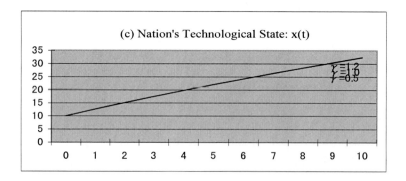

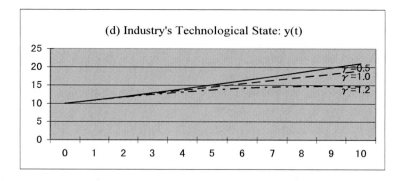

Figure 9.2. Simulation Results of Government's Salvage model.

Table 9.2. Maximum Net Benefit of R&D – Salvage model for Leader

M=0.05	Industry	Government
γ=0.5	-39.2040	20.1475
γ=1.0	8.9212	19.1534
γ=1.2	28.8884	19.0374

Table 9.2 shows the attained values of objective of each party in the model with salvage value function for the government. In comparison with the results of the previous model, we can indicate at least three effects by this change of the leader's objective. At first, the government attained a far greater objective value than the value attained in the payoff model for each case of the follower's R&D asset profitability parameter γ. The leader's greater attainment in this model can be directly noticed for the case γ=1.0 where the parameter values for M and γ are given the same as those in the payoff model.

Secondly, the attained values of the government do not change much between different cases of the profitability parameter, while the payoff values of the firms change greatly according to the different values of the parameter. This result tells us that the small change in the R&D asset profitability affects greatly the firms' payoff attainments. It is indicated by the great effects of the parameter change on the optimal strategy of R&D expenditures by the firms as shown in Figure 9.2 (a).

Another noticeable result is that the transformation of the government's objective into the maximum technological state of the economy at the end of the planning period increases a firms' payoff attainments (see comparable cases of $M = 0.05$ and $\gamma = 1.0$) as well as the government's own attainments. This is brought about by the spillover effect on the private sector from the rising technological state of the national economy. Thus, the government R&D policy to aim at the highest possible national technology is considered to have an effective synergism in technological progress between public and private sectors.

Finally, in a previous work (Takashima, 2007), we examined the behavior of firms and government in a national scheme called R&D consortium formulated as a static two-stage game model. Since the situation should change stochastically, especially in the innovative activities, we may still develop our problem to an analysis in a continuous-time stochastic framework, as was done, for example, by Marschak and Radner (1972) in the earlier literature and by Yeung and Petrosyan (2006) more recently.

CONCLUDING REMARKS

Our concern in this paper was to address the problem of dynamic R&D behavior of private firms and policy authorities with their respective goals. A private firms' objective is naturally the maximization of payoff with respect to their innovative activities, while the government aims at attaining the highest possible standard of technology for the national economy as a whole under a limited national budget. Technological knowledge, however, is characterized by its public nature that it diffuses of its own accord among organizations and is commonly used for further innovative activities. This brings a bilateral incentive of cooperation and competition (or noncooperation), a game theoretic nature, to the parties in innovative activities.

In a previous work, we examined the behavior of firms and government in a national scheme called R&D consortium by formulating it as a static two-stage game model. The present work was to extend the previous analysis to the problem formulated as a model of a continuous-time framework. The analysis based on the static model indicates that firms' attitude for the consortium changes according to their research productivity and the government attitudes and that the government tries to compensate the deficiency of the necessary R&D expenditures by the firms so as to reach optimally the national planning objective. The present analysis proves that those main findings are essentially still maintained in a dynamic framework.

The dynamic analysis provides us with further results enriching our knowledge on research policy. In order to attain the maximum payoff for a certain period of years, both parties tend to make greater efforts in R&D activities during the early years. This can be seen more evidently in the government attitude when it makes up the deficiency in the national research efforts caused by a decrease in a firm's efforts owing to their reliance on a greater spillover effect of technology. In a situation of a smaller spillover effect, the private sector makes a greater effort and then it enables the government to make a reduced amount of effort. Owing to the firms' efforts, the nation's technological state evolves higher over time in the planning period although the firms' status of technology remains lower than the condition in a greater spillover situation. When the government aims at a highest possible national state of technology at the end of the planning period, it shows a natural change in their strategy so as to increase the expenditures all through the period. The firms' strategy scarcely changes, however, in this adjustment of government objective but they enjoy the benefits of a greater technological payoff through the spillover from the growing state of national technology brought by the greater R&D expenditures of the government.

In closing, we have studied the behavior of different organizations in an area of technological development by the use of a two-stage static game theory and by an extension of the problem to a time-varying formulation. Since the situation will change stochastically, especially in innovative activities, we may still develop our problem to an analysis in a continuous-time stochastic framework.

REFERENCES

Aghion, P., Harris, C., Howitt, P. and Vickers, J. (2001) 'Competition, Imitation, and Growth with step-by-step Innovation,' *Review of Economic Studies* 68, 467-492.

Dockner, E. J., Jorgenson, S., Long, N. V., and Sorger, G. (2000) Differential Games in Economics and Management Science, Cambridge, Cambridge University Press.

Fudenberg, D. and Tirole, J. (1991). Game Theory, Cambridge, Ma., MIT Press.

Gottinger, H. (2006) Innovation, Technology and Hypercompetition, London, Routledge

Griliches, Z. (1979), 'Issues in Assessing the Contribution of Research and Development', *Bell Journal of Economics* 10, 92-116

Griliches, Z. (1998), R&D and Productivity, the Econometric Evidence, Chicago, The Univ. of Chicago Press

Marschak, J. and R. Radner (1972) ,Economic Theory of Teams, Cowles Foundation for Research in Economics at Yale University.

Seierstad, A. and K. Sydsaeter (1987), Optimal Control Theory with Economic Applications, Amsterdam, North-Holland

Takashima, M. (1992), 'The Japanese Subcontracting Relationship' in Thoburn, J. T. and M. Takashima, Industrial Subcontracting in the UK and Japan, Avebury, England, Ashgate Publishing

Takashima, M. (2007) ,'Research Consortium and Firms' Strategy: A Case of Japan's R&D Policy,' Annual Report of Ohara Graduate School of Business, No.1, Tokyo 129-146.

Yeung, D. and Petrosyan, L. (2006), Cooperative Stochastic Differential Games, New York,Springer Science+Business Media, Inc.

Chapter 10

INNOVATION SYSTEMS AND JAPANESE R&D POLICIES

Makoto Takashima

10.1. INTRODUCTION

Besides investment in research activities in fields of national interest such as military and space technologies, some governments take the initiative in promoting industrial research by providing institutional facilities and public funds. Industrial policy actions taken by the Japanese government since the 1960s have attracted the attention of other manufacturing countries. The consistent cooperation between the government and the industry in industrial R&D activities has been regarded as one of the main engines that strengthened Japan's postwar industrial competitive edge. As a matter of fact, policy interventions in respective industries have been incentivized to induce the private sector towards further development particularly during the period of Japan's economic recovery after the Second World War (WWII).

The Ministry of International Trade and Industry (MITI; now, METI, Ministry of Economy, Trade and Industry) has carried out the national strategy for advancement of industrial technologies through its subordinated institution, AIST (Agency of Industrial Technology) (see, for example, Thurow, 1992, pp. 144 –149). Presently, the national strategies for R&D of METI are generally carried out through NEDO (New Energy and Industrial Technology Comprehensive Development Organization), under which the former AIST (now, General Institute of Industrial Technology) is placed together with universities and private firms in terms of technological policy. These three sectors receive financial and other management support for all phases of their R&D activities from basic research to practical development from NEDO which is acting as the central governmental institution in charge of undertaking comprehensive national policies of technology.

The basic scheme for the technological strategies has been organized under the Law of Research Cooperatives for Mining and Industrial Technology and the Law of Research Facilitation of Key Technology, which were enacted in 1961 and 1985, respectively. Based on these legislations, the AIST successively inaugurated the Large Scale Industrial

Technology R&D Project in 1966, the Sunshine Project in 1974, the Moonlight Project in 1978, and the New Sunshine Project in 1993. In particular, the Super High Performance Electronic Computer (1966 to 1971), the Super LSI technology (1976 to 1980), and the V-th Generation Computer (1982 to 1995) were some of the development programs which were executed under the Large Scale Project. These schemes caught the attention of foreign observers, who felt that such measures were somewhat heavy-handed in the framework of a free competitive economy.

The purpose of these national R&D projects was to induce Japanese industry to help it to succeed in international competition, to assist it in establishing its own innovative technology, and not to have to rely on imported foreign technology in order to keep the national economy developing by its own efforts. In implementing these projects, AIST organized research consortia where researchers and scientists from private firms and universities and those in AIST jointly worked on specific research subjects. Research expenditures were basically financed by the government but generally firms were expected to supply as much funding and resources as possible for participating in the consortia. Mixing government and private funds was useful for reducing risk which otherwise private firms would incur. Furthermore, the consortia may have induced private firms to increase their R&D efforts by supplying them with intermediate research results which could lead to successive practical innovations for new as well as improved products and processes. For example, the total expenditure for the Super High Performance Electronic Computer development project was 10 billion yen at the current rate (about $34 million USD at the 1975 rate) for six years (AIST, 1972).

While 80 percent of R&D investments are made by industry, Japan's cooperative R&D scheme currently has been extended to cooperation among industry, academia and the government. "Fundamental Plan of Science and Technology" was developed by the government under the fundamental law of S andT established in 1995 in order to promote the nation's S&T policies. This Science and Technology Plan was implemented for three consecutive terms: the first term plan from 1996 to 2000 was carried out by using government funds of 17 trillion yen ($188 billion USD) and the second term plan with 24 trillion yen ($266 billion USD) for the next five years ending in 2005. The third term plan from 2006 to 2010 has government funds in the amount of 25 trillion yen ($277 billion USD).

These joint research schemes with government funds have generally been favorably accepted by the industry, as private firms found it difficult to finance their own R&D activities whose results were intrinsically uncertain, and the resources were generally scarce in those days. Private firms are generally considered to be risk averse, especially during periods of financial difficulty and thus the national economy tends to be short of the socially optimal standard with regard to investment in industrial R&D. In addition, when private firms tend to secretly monopolize the fruits of research activities made by their own efforts despite the availability of patenting system, the tendency prevents new ideas from diffusing widely in the business. Thus, such a Japanese policy measure as the government-financed research consortium may be a useful and an efficient strategy from the public point of view. In connection with this, Thurow (1992, p.148) noted that "Even if national strategies could be made to work theoretically, many Americans argue that they cannot work practically. Sometimes this argument is narrowed still further to state that even if national strategies are shown to work abroad, they could not work in the United States because of its brand of special-interest-group politics". In the U.S., too, a considerable magnitude of R&D is undertaken in cooperative arrangements between federal laboratories and private firms although it is not conducted as a national strategy for the industry. The issue is the way of transferring publicly funded research results to the private sector, i.e., whether they may become a private monopoly by granting patent rights to contractors (Jaffe and Lerner, 2001).

Although the advantages and usefulness of government-led research consortia have been generally advocated, the scheme has received little scrutiny so far about its validity and effectiveness. The purpose of this chapter is to explore the possible attitudes of government and private sector, based on a simple theoretical model about the actual structure of cooperation between them, and then to examine how the results explain the actual developments of the cooperative R&D schemes. This should give us some insight into whether and to what extent the scheme of research consortia can be economically practical in encouraging private R&D efforts and in strengthening the industrial technology of the state.

The fundamental features of our analytical model are as follows:

i. Industrial research consists of two phases, i.e. the first is basic research and the second practical development. Firms cannot proceed to development activities without the successful results of basic research.
ii. In order for Japanese industry to strengthen its technological competitiveness, the government realizes that it is important to deprive the private sector of the risk involved in research activities by supplying public funds to basic research.
iii. The planning authorities envisage a certain desirable standard of R&D effort for the whole nation and consider it useful to inaugurate a cooperative research scheme between government and industry, i.e. a research consortium, and to induce private firms to participate in it and to contribute their R&D resources. The government tries to fill the shortage in the total envisaged standard of expenditures, but the usage of public funds should be preferably small.
iv. Basic research is undertaken by the consortium in competition with private firms' laboratories in the industry, but the fruits from the government-led laboratories under the scheme of the consortium are basically made available to the private sector as a "public good", while those obtained by the firms' in-house labs are to be monopolized by them under the patent scheme.
v. Industrial policies are essentially indicative nature; the government cannot dictate to the private sector in any way. It neither compels private firms to increase their research activities, nor forces them to contribute to the government-led consortium. Both government and industry decide their strategies in such a way as to maximize their respective payoffs in response to the opponent's decision in the scheme.

10.2. THE MODEL

Industrial R&D Structure Accompanied by National Consortium

According to the basic scheme specified above, we construct a model as shown in Figure 10.1. Industrial research activities are divided into two distinct phases, i.e., basic research and applied or practical research (i.e. development). In reality, many companies usually take this distinction into consideration and we can often see that the former activities are conducted in

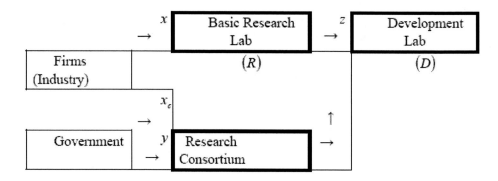

Figure 10.1. Industry-Government R&D Structure.

specially established laboratories. Research agenda related to the latter are undertaken in development laboratories which are more affiliated with production facilities. In Japan, for instance, we have experienced a period when big companies, among others, competitively established the so-called "Central Research Laboratories" for basic research in the sixties and seventies. Practical development of product or process innovation is undertaken as a result of basic research. Thus, it can be said that the product of basic research supplies the "infrastructure" for industrial innovation as a whole and therefore the technological competitiveness of an economy. Industry obtains the product of basic research through three channels, i.e., its own efforts, public activities of the country (i.e. government and university), and purchase from foreign countries. In this analysis, we do not consider the introduction of foreign technology, as we focus here on the problem of national strategies for enhancing the fruits of research by private firms within the state's borders.

Government-led research consortia are set up in order to strengthen industry's technological and economic competitiveness.

They are established for the phase of basic research and, as a general rule, the intellectual products are made available free of charge as "public goods" to industry. In this scheme, private firms can obtain the research products required for them to proceed to the second phase of research from two sources, i.e., their own basic research laboratories and government-led consortia. Therefore, the focus of analysis moves to strategic reactions in the basic research phase between government and industry. The government's expenditures may depend on how much the industry spends on basic research by themselves (i.e. in their own labs) and how much resource they are willing to contribute to the consortium. Industry may decide their strategies according to how much the government prepares to supply the consortium with public funds.

Objective Functions of Industry and Government

In our model, we treat private firms collectively as the industry and investigate its research efforts, i.e., how it chooses its research strategies in the given technological environment, in response to government research strategies. Sah and Stiglitz (1987) investigated a similar topic of firms' research efforts. However, they paid attention to the implications for industrial organizations, with the result that the number of firms in the economy has no impact on the total research effort. We focus our attention on the problem of research effort of the industry as a group of private firms responding to the government-led research scheme. Referring to Figure10.1, we state specifically that the profitability of research activities consists of the rent (i.e. patent and other intellectual revenues) from successful basic research (R) and the revenues from practical development of new product and process innovations (D), each in current value.

The government's research strategies are those explained in points ii and iii of the fundamental scheme, in the previous section. The government has the desirable standard of research activities for the nation as a whole and it decides the magnitude of public funds y to be supplied to the consortium, trying to lead the efforts to that target. We denote it by B* Under the principles of basic research iv and industrial policies v, the industry (a group of private firms) optimally decides the amount of resources for basic research, x and x_c; x is the amount of research funds invested in the firms' own basic research activities and x_c is the value of resources contributed to the consortium when they participate in that cooperative activities.

Research activities are intrinsically uncertain in producing a successful result. Thus, the result (success or failure) by spending a certain amount of expenditures v on a research project is only expressed by a probability function, $p(v)$. Then, the industries expected payoff from the research activities of the two consecutive phases is written as a quasi-linear utility function:

$$u_f(x, y; x_c) = R \cdot p(x)[1 - p(x_c + y)] + \delta \cdot D\{1 - [1 - p(x)][1 - p(x_c + y)]\}p(z) - (x + x_c + z) \tag{10.1}$$

where δ is a discount factor for the second phase of the research (i.e practical development). Variable z is the industry's efforts in the second phase and is taken as exogenous in the present analysis, as our attention is focused on the strategies for the basic research. However, for the industry's strategy, consideration of the expected revenues from the second phase becomes indispensable because they essentially depend on the probability of success in the research activities of the first phase which are undertaken by private firms' laboratories and the consortium in parallel with each other. We assume that firms can obtain the rent from the first phase of research only when they have succeeded in finishing their basic research projects by their own efforts prior to the government-led consortium.

Our model is similar to that of Grossman and Shapiro (1987) in that it considers two successive "stages" of research and that successful completion of the first stage is a prerequisite for the ultimate phase of research. However, we cannot rely on their advantageous method of translating the probabilities of success p into variables to be handled directly in equations by inversion of the function p (v) because our problem concerns the change in success probabilities of research projects in the consortium where funds are supplied by both government and participating firms.

The objective function of the government can be derived from the feature iii (i.e. planning authorities envisage a certain desirable standard of R&D effort) which states the national strategy. We specify it as:

$$u_g(y,x;x_c) = -\frac{1}{2}\left\{[B^* - (x + x_c + y)]^2 + \theta \cdot y^2\right\} \tag{10.2}$$

where θ is a policy measure to be taken by the planning authorities. It allows them to change the magnitude of government funds according to the technological situations of the industry. We take $\theta=1$ as a benchmark for the policy measure. The authorities will set it less than 1 when they think it necessary for the government to make greater efforts for basic research.

The objective of private firms is to choose their magnitude of research expenditures x and x_c so as to maximize the value of the net revenue (Equation 10.1), whereas government aims to maximize its objective function (Equation 10.2) by choosing the optimal value of public fund y for the consortium activities. Then, these functions become each player's von Neumann-Morgenstern utilities which correspond to each set of strategies taken by both the players (von Neumann, and Morgenstern, 1953, 55-60).

Probability Function of Achieving Success

We specify here a simple form of the probability function of achieving success in a research project when investing a certain amount of funds. Let p^* denote the projected goal of success probability. (Usually, it will be set $p^*=1$, but it may be less than one when some intermediate goal is aimed at for a difficult project.) We denote the probability of success attainable with supply of resources (funds) v by $p(v)$. Then, the gap between the projected goal and the probability attainable with v is $q = p^* - p(v)$. We assume that this gap could be reduced by further effort, i.e., by investing more funds, and that the reduction rate states the technological difficulty of a project, which is written to be a (>0). It takes naturally a smaller value for a more difficult project. Thus, we have:

$$-\frac{1}{q} \cdot \frac{dq}{dv} = a \tag{10.3}$$

Then, having $p(0) = 0$ as another acceptable assumption, we obtain the following probability function:

$$p(v) = p^* (1 - \exp(-av)) \tag{10.4}$$

In order for us to know the achievability of this function for success probability, it may be useful to understand it from a different viewpoint of a stochastic phenomenon. The expression $\exp(-av)$ means the probability that there occurs no success at all with the use of funds v. This is proved to be the Poisson distribution with the average av, formulating the probability that no event occurs in the interval of time v. Then, if we consider all the events of one or more successes to be a successful event, we can take $1-\exp(-av)$ to express the success probability that can be achieved with research fund v. In the following analysis, we set $p^* = 1$, for simplicity's sake, which has little influence on the essential results.

10.3. ANALYSIS

We first make clear how the industry and the government choose their amounts of research expenditures in order to maximize their own objective functions, Equations 10.1 and 10.2, respectively. Private firms have to decide on two variables, the amount of resources to be invested into their own basic research labs, x, and joining the research activities in the government-led consortium, x_c. The government has to decide on the amount of funds to be supplied for the consortium, y, under the predetermined national target, B^*.

The value of the target B^* and the scheme of government-financed consortium aiming at this goal are made public beforehand. Under the circumstance, the industry as a group of participating firms decides first to what extent it should contribute to the consortium (that is, x_c). In this sense, the industry is regarded as a Stackelberg leader in the first stage of this game. Taking this information, the government is going to decide on its research budget, but it depends upon another decision of firms, i.e., the magnitude of basic research in private firms' research labs. The firms' decision for their laboratories, however, is also influenced by the government decision for the consortium. For instance, if the government supplies such a large fund as to achieve a likely success of the consortium, they might consider it profitable to take a free ride on its research results instead of investing in their own labs. The industry and the government will choose their respective research funds x and y concurrently in the second stage of the game as in the Cournot model. Note that the firms know the behavior of this concurrent decision to be taken by both parties in the second stage when they decide the contribution to the consortium in the first stage.

Thus, this situation reduces to a sub-game perfection and the decision process constitutes a sub-game perfect (Nash) equilibrium having two stages of decisions (see, for example, Fudenberg and Tirole, 1991, 70-77; and Dockner et al., 2000, 21-27). Now x_c becomes the 'history' at the first stage and (x, y) forms the 'action profile' at the second stage. $x(x_c)$ is a strategy for the industry and $y(x_c)$ is that for the government and they are decisions contingent on the 'history' x_c. However, in the actual procedure, the optimal choice for x_c is found by working backward from the second stage. The decisions in these two stages take place in the same phase of basic research depicted in the diagram of Figure 10.1. The first and second phases in the figure mean physical time periods during which basic research and practical development research take place consecutively.

With the 'history' x_c in the first stage, we have the first-order condition with respect to x for the industry (i.e. private firms):

$$a(R+W(z))\exp[-a(x+x_c+y)]-1=0 \tag{10.5}$$

where $W(z) = \delta \cdot D \cdot p(z)$ denotes the present value of expected revenue from the practical research (development) in the second phase under the condition that the prerequisite results have been obtained by either private firms' laboratories or the consortium or the both. The first-order condition with respect to y for the government becomes:

$$[B^* - (x+x_c+y)] - \theta \cdot y = 0 \tag{10.6}$$

These equations lead to the optimal reaction functions, $r_f : Y \to X$ and $r_g : X \to Y$ for the industry and the government, as follows, respectively:

$$x(y;x_c) \in \arg\cdot\max_{x}(u_f(x,y;x_c)) = \frac{1}{a}\ln[a(R+W(z))] - x_c - y \tag{10.7}$$

$$y(x;x_c) \in \arg\cdot\max_{y}(u_g(y,x;x_c)) = \frac{1}{1+\theta}[B^* - (x+x_c)] \tag{10.8}$$

Looking at the point iii (i.e. The planning authorities envisage a certain desirable standard of R&D effort for the whole nation) described in the national research strategies, we know that the planning authorities indicate $B^* \geq x + x_c + y$. It means that they should arrange the targeted standard B^* to be greater than or equal to $\frac{1}{a}\ln[a(R+W(z))]$. Let $\alpha(x_c)$ denote $\frac{1}{1+\theta} \cdot (B^* + \theta \cdot x_c)$. Then, when $x + x_c + y$ is greater than or equal to $\alpha(x_c)$, we have the Nash equilibrium at the second stage:

$$x^N = \frac{1}{\theta} \cdot \left\{\left(\frac{1+\theta}{a}\right)\ln[a(R+W(z))] - B^*\right\} - x_c \tag{10.9}$$

$$y^N = \frac{1}{\theta} \cdot \left\{B^* - \frac{1}{a}\ln[a(R+W(z))]\right\} \tag{10.10}$$

As far as $x + x_c + y$ is greater than $\alpha(x_c)$, we have positive values for x^N and y^N at the Nash equilibrium. As the total value of basic research expenditures, $x + x_c + y$, decreases and draws near to $\alpha(x_c)$, x^N tends to come close to zero, while y^N approaches to $\frac{1}{1+\theta}(B^* - x_c)$ which is actually equal to a fixed value given by Equation 10.10. When the situation further shifts to force both the parties to be $x + x_c + y \leq \alpha(x_c)$, where there is no Nash equilibrium with a positive x any more, both the industry and the government will keep their choices, $x = 0$ and $y = \frac{1}{1+\theta}(B^* - x_c)$, respectively.

Up to here, we have some noticeable results from this model. In Equations 10.9 and 10.10, $R + W(z)$ is the expected total revenue (at constant value) of the industry under the condition that the first phase of R&D activities (basic research) has been successfully achieved in the private firms' laboratories. Denoting $\frac{1}{a}\ln(a(R + W(z)))$ as A, the optimal strategies of both the parties are determined by the relation between B^* and A. We observed above that the planning authorities should determine B^* so as not to be less than A. Hence, the optimal choice of the government at the Nash equilibrium in the second stage is basically to supply the consortium with public funds such that it fills the gap between B^* and A. At this point, we know that the government's optimal choice is determined regardless of the value x_c, i.e., the industry's contribution to the consortium. In another part of the industry, however, the optimal choice for their investment in the private firms' basic research labs depends on the extent to which they take part in the consortium activities. We also have to note that the industry always decides the magnitude of its efforts for basic research activities such that it becomes totally optimal in their own laboratories and the consortium. Thus, $x^N + x_c$ is determined, depending on the values of B^* and A.

How the industry allocates the efforts between a firm's own research labs and the joint activities in the consortium is decided by working backward to the first stage. Under the Nash equilibrium, the value of the industry's payoff function becomes:

$$u_f^N(x_c) = R \cdot \exp\left[-\frac{a}{\theta}(B^* - A)\right] \cdot \exp(-ax_c) + [W(z) - z] - \frac{1}{a} - \frac{1}{\theta}\left[(1+\theta)A - B^*\right]$$

(10.11)

Therefore, the optimal choice by the industry at the first stage reduces to $x_c = 0$. This result is the same when the situation coerces both the parties to have, $x + x_c + y \leq \alpha(x_c)$, i.e., $A \leq \alpha(x_c)$. In this case, the industry's optimal choice at the second stage becomes also $x = 0$. Thus, when the revenues from firms' research activities cannot be expected to be much, or when the government research strategy is seen to be aggressive with a high target for the national research activities, the industry's strategies for basic research is to take a complete free ride on the government financed research and to utilize the results of basic research for its practical applications.

In the normal situation, i.e., $A \geq \alpha(x_c)$, where there exists the Nash equilibrium giving nonnegative strategies given by Equations 10.9 and 10.10, the industry's interest is to decide its efforts for basic research as the total magnitude for both firms' own activities and possible contribution to the consortium, as we saw above. In this situation, the industry's optimal allocation of funds means to invest them into only its own activities and to contribute nothing to the government-led consortium. This result may be what one would suspect intuitively from the specifications of our model, because private firms can put the fruits of the consortium in use for their applied research at the second phase for free of charge, whether or not they contribute to the joint activities and no matter how much they contribute to it.

However, considering the effect that the industry's contribution has on their expected revenue at the second phase through the success of the joint activities at the consortium, the industry's refraining from the contribution is a result to be noted. Analytically, it comes from the implicit presumption that the consortium success is of the same probability density function as that of the industry. In reality, Japanese firms do not seem to have had a very positive position toward joint research at government-led institutions, particularly after they have grown to be equipped with the resources that could bring them considerable research revenues, i.e., $R + W(z)$ in our model. Although it is not that they have completely refused to join the consortium as our theoretical analysis tells, it seems that they have shown a sort of cooperative attitude to the administration. They have contributed to the government-led joint activities to the extent that they can have information about the movements of competing firms and the trends in the government's industrial policies by participating in them.

10.4. EMPIRICAL ANALYSIS

From a simple model of Japan's industrial R&D strategy, we have derived the following results:

i. The industry (i.e., the private sector) decides to increase the optimal amount of basic research activities as the total R&D revenue is expected to grow, and it conversely decreases it as the government sets a greater target for the national level of basic research.
ii. The government decides the amount of optimal funds with which it supplies the national R&D consortium, regardless of how much the industry contributes to it, and the expenditure grows as the authorities set their sights on a greater national level for the basic research activities and lessens as the industrial revenue from R&D becomes greater.
iii. As far as the industry determines its behavior only based on the expected revenue from the genuine R&D activities, its optimal amount of contribution to the national consortium reduces to zero, that is, the best strategy for the industry is to take advantage of using the research results obtained in the consortium for its development research free of charge by taking part in the national activities with the possible smallest monetary sacrifice in spite of the fact that its contribution affects its development research revenue through the effect on success probability at the consortium.

The purpose of this section is to examine empirically how this model and the derived results are applied to the actual behavior of the industry and the planning authorities with regard to R&D strategies. However, no one can ascertain the theoretical optimum of any economic reality. Here, we are trying to perceive a high possibility of each party's realized behavior being in line with its optimal strategy by investigating whether or not the conditions for this strategy are satisfied in the actual developments in Japan. In other words, we try to examine empirically how the necessary conditions have been met for the optimal strategy to be taken by both the industry and the government in terms of their basic research activities in the private firms' labs and the national R&D consortium.

The research expenditures made by industry and government during the period 1975 to 2004 are shown in Table 10.1. The Survey of Research and Development by the Japan's Statistical Bureau classifies Japan's R&D performers into four sectors, i.e., Industry (Business enterprises), Non-profit Institutions, Public Organizations (Government, Local governments, Special corporations and Independent administrative institutions) and Universities and Colleges. Research funds by Government (and Local governments) are mainly supplied to Government Research Institutes and Universities and Colleges but for our present purpose of investigating the strategies for industrial R&D, we put the activities at universities and colleges out of consideration.

The Statistics Bureau performed a survey of R&D in Japan by classifying research activities into three types: basic research, applied research and development.

We treat here the first two together as Basic research activity which is expressed as $x + x_c$ for the expenditure of industry in our consortium model discussed in the previous sections.

The expenditure of government y is for Research Institutes and the total amount taken by this sector is regarded as Basic research. The actual expenditures by both parties are as seen in the Table 10.1. If they took their optimal decision subject to our model, x_c should be zero and the figures of $x + x_c$ and y given in the table should become the values for Nash equilibrium, x^N and y^N, respectively. In the previous analysis, we found that the necessary condition for a nonnegative Nash equilibrium is $A \leq B^* \leq (1+\theta)A$, but even when this condition is satisfied, it is not always sure that the players will take their optimal strategy. As far as both the parties select nonnegative values of expenditure for its basic research and these values are assumed to constitute the reaction functions, Equations (10.7) and (10.8), the nonnegative value conditions are naturally always satisfied as is shown in the table. We assume per capita GDP as the value of policy measure taken by the authorities θ in the government's objective function, Equation 10.2. However, the decisions for research expenditure actually taken by industry and government remain to be checked regarding their optimum levels. We have some evidence for industry's decision to contribute to the R&D consortium, which is denoted by x_c in our model. The optimal strategy of the industry towards the public research consortium was found to reduce its contribution to zero as long as private firms regard the cooperative scheme as a facility to utilize the research results free of charge and do not see any other benefits in participating in it.

Table 10.1. R&D Expenditures of Industry and Government

	Industry		Government(2)	p.c.GDP(3)	R&D Revenue	Basic Target
Fiscal Year	Basic(1)	Development	Total	index	Estimates	Estimates
t	X+Xc	Z	Y	θ	R+W(z)	B*
1975	0.6909	2.0442	0.5356	0.60	3.4093	1.5483
1976	0.6945	2.1106	0.5516	0.62	3.4770	1.5863
1977	0.7241	2.2597	0.5487	0.64	3.5708	1.6236
1978	0.7618	2.3425	0.6020	0.67	3.9110	1.7656
1979	0.8738	2.6466	0.6435	0.70	4.5594	1.9654
1980	0.9674	2.8882	0.6946	0.71	5.2693	2.1541
1981	1.0907	3.2100	0.7949	0.72	6.5903	2.4617
1982	1.1917	3.4562	0.7872	0.74	7.2355	2.5632
1983	1.3426	3.8393	0.7983	0.76	8.5079	2.7442
1984	1.4876	4.1945	0.8183	0.78	10.0312	2.9449
1985	1.7177	4.7740	0.9018	0.81	13.7302	3.3487
1986	1.8423	5.0498	0.9559	0.83	16.4134	3.5910
1987	1.9701	5.3104	1.0657	0.86	20.8197	3.9576
1988	2.1595	5.7565	1.0323	0.91	24.3322	4.1342
1989	2.3853	6.2728	1.0082	0.95	29.7700	4.3514
1990	2.6344	6.8316	0.9978	1.00	37.7959	4.6300
1991	2.7543	7.0475	1.0524	1.02	45.0017	4.8852
1992	2.7205	6.8689	1.1624	1.03	48.5697	5.0748
1993	2.5617	6.5649	1.2864	1.03	46.9039	5.1690
1994	2.6052	6.4020	1.2289	1.03	46.2518	5.1007
1995	2.6959	6.7003	1.3901	1.06	59.4419	5.5588
1996	2.8048	7.1343	1.3167	1.10	61.6517	5.5748
1997	2.9008	7.5281	1.2851	1.10	65.7592	5.5991
1998	2.9583	7.8310	1.4057	1.08	78.5708	5.8758
1999	2.8264	7.9112	1.5028	1.08	75.8760	5.9506
2000	2.9543	7.9714	1.5477	1.09	90.1973	6.1837
2001	3.0423	8.5932	1.5342	1.07	97.1640	6.2199
2002	2.9663	8.7014	1.5150	1.08	88.3495	6.1181
2003	3.1126	9.1658	1.5468	1.12	105.5622	6.3846
2004	3.1422	9.2444	1.5864	1.15	113.1371	6.5450

Sources: Statistics Bureau, Ministry of Internal Affairs and Communications (MIC), Survey of Research and Development, and Indicators of Science and Technology (as for R&D statistics); Population Census and Population Estimates (as for population statistics), Economic and Social Research Institute (ESRI), Cabinet Office, Annual Estimates of National Account (as for GDP statistics).

Notes: Figures for R&D expenditures are expressed in trillion (10 times12) yen and put at real value based on year 1995 by using the R&D deflators for natural sciences and engineering.

(1) 'Basic' is the expenditures for "basic research" and "applied research" as defined in the Survey on Research and Development (SR&D).

(2) Research expenditures of 'Government' are those by "Public organizations" as defined in SR&D, which consist of "Government," "Local governments," "Special corporations and Independent administrative institutions". The statistical classification fro "Public organizations" is not the same for years of 1980 and before. Therefore, we estimated the statistics for the period of 1975 through 1980 with the use of the data for "Research Institutes" in the "Survey of Research and Development." Notice the figures for 'Government' here do not include the research funds for universities and colleges. 'Total' means the figures of expenditures for all phases of R&D activities.

(3) 'p.c.GDP' is per capita GDP which is put on a constant yen basis by using the GDP deflator (base year is 1995) and is made an index with 1990 as a benchmark year.

There is no comprehensive information specific to the research consortium activities between public research institutes and private firms. Since the cooperative research activities have been performed so far with the initiatives of the governmental institutes, we assume that the sector of nonprofit and public research institutes is the nucleus of the consortium in which private enterprises take part with a specified research objective. Looking into the survey statistics about the source of research funds for each performing sector, we know how much funds the industry ('Companies') supplies to the governmental research institutes (or 'Public Organizations). The figures for some recent years are 10,048 million yen in 1995, 20,550 million yen in 1998, and 26,918 million yen in 2003, which are 0.10 percent, 0.19 percent and 0.23 percent of the total research fund of the industry in each respective year. Notice should be taken that these are the ratios for the total expenditure of 'Industry' and not that of the 'Nonprofit and Public Research Institutes'. We do not know how much the latter sector spends on the consortium projects. Taking these figures for x_c, we know that the industry's contribution to the consortium has proved minimal. This may demonstrate that industry has chosen almost the best strategy towards the joint research scheme from the point of view of total benefits brought by its R&D activities including their development of new products and processes, as suggested in the model.

When the actual decision of the industry $x + x_c$ and that of the government y are assumed to be optimal as given by a Nash equilibrium, the industry's possible R&D revenue $R + W(z)$ and the planning authorities' national target B^* can be estimated by applying those values to the reaction functions, Equations 10.7 and 10.8 in section 10.3. These estimates are shown in the last two columns of Table 10.1. From Equation 10.10, it is known that the national target B^* is drawn up to be greater than the total expenditures for basic research at the time by θy, which indicates that the authorities induce the government to provide bigger funds for the consortium when the national economy is still in a less developed state.

As our basic model, Equation 10.1, states, the industry's possible R&D revenue relies largely on the extent of research activities in the development phase in addition to the technological level of the industry at the time. Thus, in order to have proof that the actual decisions by both parties are derived from such objective functions as described in our model, we try to see how the estimated values for $R + W(z)$ are explained by the research expenditure for development activities z and the general state of technology at the time t.

The estimated equation is:

$$\ln(RW_t) = -0.0965 + \underset{(6.3830)}{0.0531 t} + \underset{(10.2991)}{1.5258 \ln(Z_{t-1})} \qquad (10.12)$$

$$t = 1976, \cdots, 2004 \qquad \bar{R}^2 = 0.9916$$

where RW_t is a time series of estimates for the industry's potential research revenue $R+W(z)$ and Z_t is the actual data for the industry's expenditure for development research z. The variable for general technological state t actually takes time index from 2 through 30. Equation 10.12 was estimated using a classical linear regression model. Having t-values as parenthesized figures, this relation proves statistically plausible with the estimated parameters of high significance at conventional levels of acceptance. This structural analysis may give us another insight into how the industry and the government should essentially behave concerning the research consortium as envisaged in our model.

Lastly, apart from the examinations directly related to the previous model, we investigate how much private and public research efforts have contributed to the progress of Japan's R&D performance. Table 10.2 shows the actual results of R&D activities according to two kinds of statistics over a period of thirty years from 1975 to the latest 2004, i.e., number of patent applications, PAT, and technology trade (ratio of receipts to payments), TTR. We try to explain the technology trade ratio by the expenditures for basic research in the industry $(x+x_c)$, research in the governmental institutes (y), and development activities in the industry (z).

Estimations were carried out on a growth model:

$$(TTR)_t = \alpha (ASX)_{t-1}^{\beta}(ASY)_{t-1}^{\gamma} e^{\delta(ASZ)_{t-1}} \qquad (10.13)$$
$$t = 1976, \cdots\cdots, 2004$$

where the variables are defined as follows:

$(TTR)_t =$ Japan's technology trade of year t expressed by ratio of receipts to payments,

$$(ASX)_{t-1} = \sum_{t=1975}^{t-1}(X+X_c)_s + (X+X_c)_{1975} \times 10$$

$$(ASY)_{t-1} = \sum_{s=1975}^{t-1} Y_s + Y_{1975} \times 10$$

$$(ASZ)_{t-1} = \sum_{s=1975}^{t-1} Z_s + Z_{1975} \times 10$$

Table 10.2 Japan's Performance of R&D Activities

Year	Patents(1)	Trade of Tech(2)	Year	Patents	Trade of Tech
t	PAT	TTR	t	PAT	TTR
1975	135,118	0.394	1990	333,230	0.912
1976	135,762	0.470	1991	335,933	0.939
1977	135,991	0.491	1992	338,019	0.912
1978	141,517	0.635	1993	332,345	1.103
1979	150,623	0.553	1994	319,938	1.247
1980	165,730	0.666	1995	334,612	1.435
1981	191,645	0.674	1996	340,101	1.558
1982	210,922	0.654	1997	350,807	1.897
1983	227,743	0.863	1998	359,381	2.130
1984	256,205	0.986	1999	360,180	2.342
1985	274,373	0.799	2000	387,364	2.386
1986	290,202	0.860	2001	386,767	2.274
1987	311,006	0.761	2002	369,458	2.560
1988	308,908	0.789	2003	362,711	2.682
1989	317,566	0.998	2004	368,416	3.117

Sources: Japan Patent Office, Annual Report of Patent Administration (as for patent statistics); Statistics Bureau, MIC, Survey of Research and Development (as for technology trade statistics).
Notes: (1) Figures are patent applications by Japanese persons only.

The second term on the right side of the last three variables is added to take into account the accumulated research activities before the observation period. The model (Equation 10.13) is formulated so as to consider the effects of "basic" research activities by the industry $X + X_c$ and the government institutions Y on the basis for the development research activities of the industry. In formulating this model, we consider that the nation's technological strength as expressed in technological trade attributes to industrial development activities for new products and processes on the basis of scientific research and public R&D policies.

The estimated results for the model (Equation 10.13) are given in the line of Equation (10.13) of Table 10.3. These results were sought as the coefficients of a least-squares hyperplane on the basis of the next linear regression equation (Equation 10.13a) derived from the above original model (Equation 10.13):

$$\ln(TTR)_t = \ln\alpha + \beta\ln(ASX)_{t-1} + \gamma\ln(ASY)_{t-1} + \delta(ASZ)_{t-1} + u_t \qquad (10.13a)$$
$$t = 1976, \cdots, 2004$$

The parameter of accumulated basic research of industry ASX is estimated to be negative. It would be difficult to explain this theoretically but the estimated coefficient is not statistically significant. In contrast, the research by Government institutes ASY is estimated to have a positive effect on the growth of Japan's technological trade ratio and is more significant statistically. The estimated result shows that Japan's technological strength expressed by the technological trade ratio has progressed mainly through the development research activities by industry ASZ. Public activities such as research consortia have had some positive influences for active research efforts undertaken by the private sector mainly in its development research for new products and processes.

Table 10.3 Effects of Expenditures on R&D Performance

Equation	Coeff. $\ln(ASX)_{t-1}$	Coeff. $\ln(ASY)_{t-1}$	Coeff. $(ASZ)_{t-1}$	Coeff.Determ.
(10.13a)	-1.8774 (-2.6821)	2.3204 (2.7359)	0.0114 (6.2394)	0.9545
(10.13b)	-	0.0860 (0.4861)	0.0100 (5.1315)	0.9436
(10.13c)	0.0037 (0.0255)	-	0.0108 (5.3485)	0.9431

Notes: 'Coeff.' means 'Coefficient of'. Items in the uppermost row represent the estimated value of β, γ, δ in turn from the left. The last item is the calculated value of coefficient of determination for each regression equation.

As the estimated coefficient of "basic research" $\hat{\beta}$ proves to have a weak statistical significance, we set it zero and estimated a revised equation (Equation 10.13b):

$$\ln(TTR)_t = \ln\alpha + \gamma \ln(ASY)_{t-1} + \delta(ASZ)_{t-1} + u_t \quad (10.13b)$$
$$t = 1976, \cdots, 2004$$

The results are shown in the line of Equation 10.13b of Table 10.3. This equation makes it clear that Japan's technological strength has been fostered almost solely by the efforts of the private sector. In this situation, the effect of governmental research activities on the progress of industrial technology is regarded to be almost negligible.

We examined the effect of basic research by industry instead of public research activities, based on Equation 10.13c:

$$\ln(TTR)_t = \ln\alpha + \beta \ln(ASX)_{t-1} + \delta(ASZ)_{t-1} + u_t \quad (10.13c)$$
$$t = 1976, \cdots, 2004$$

The results are shown in the line of Equation 10.13c of Table 10.3.

They show a strong role of the industrial development activities more clearly. The effect of industrial basic research on the technological strength becomes weaker in terms of its statistical significance than that of public activities.

In the case of Japan it is important to remember that the first boom of central research institutes took place in the 1960's (METI). But, before the 1980's, Japanese firms were not yet competent to carry out innovations by their own effort and thus, relied heavily on foreign technologies. Imports of overseas innovations and government financed research schemes were the main sources of technological "seeds" for Japanese industry in those days. This is recognized from the figures on technological trade by Japan's industry (ratios of overseas earnings from royalties and technical services to payments overseas for them) as shown in Table 10.2. Another index from other sources showing similar results is given in Table 10.4.

Table 10.4 Japan' Technological Trade

Year	Export/Import	Year	Export/Import
1970	0.136	1991 – 1995	0.540
1971 – 1975	0.152	1996 – 2000	0.805
1976 – 1980	0.237	2001	0.902
1981 – 1985	0.300	2002	1.015
1986 – 1990	0.347	2003	1.116

Source: MEST.
Note: Figures are based on Bank of Japan's statistics on balance of payments.

However, in the second boom period (i.e. from 1982 to 1995) companies no longer relied on the government to the same extent for R&D support. As a matter of fact, the V-th Generation Computer project, for instance, which was carried out under the initiative of AIST from 1982 to 1995, could not get a very active cooperation from industry that past consortia had received. As a result, the project has not been rated very successful in accomplishing targeted objectives (Callon,(1995; Nakayama, 1995).

CONCLUSIONS

In this chapter we have examined the role of the cooperative R&D scheme led by government for the enhancement of national industrial technology. The behavior of private firms in that national strategy has also been assessed. The cooperative policy scheme which was implemented by post-war Japan has been observed sometimes cautiously by foreign competitors. Some industrialized countries such as the U.S. have even been in doubt regarding the validity of state intervention in civilian economic strategies such as industrial R&D.

The problem has been assessed using a simple model of cooperative research activities by two parties, i.e., industry (private firms) and government, each of which has its own objectives. The government has a target for the level of national R&D but executes no coercive power over the private sector to fulfill its objective. It only uses financial measures for the governmental scheme of research consortia, to induce private firms to take part in them. On the other hand, private firms, having their own research facilities, decide how much they can contribute to the cooperative activities for their own benefit. An essential point affecting their decisions is that, whereas the fruits produced by firms' in-house laboratories give them the revenues from patents and other intellectual products and services, research results by the national consortia are basically supplied to the society as a "public good" free of charge. The fruits in either work for basic research affect equally the industry's development activities as a technological prerequisite for the second phase of its research process.

This structure of the model led us to an analysis in a simple game-theory framework of a sub-game perfect Nash equilibrium. The first stage of this process is industry's decision about its contribution to the consortium and the second stage consists of industry's and government's decisions about research funds to be invested in their own labs and the consortium, respectively. We investigated the standard case where there is no difference in research productivities (specifically, in probability of success functions) between the industry's basic labs and the government-led consortia. Under these conditions we obtained the following results:

i. Industry decides the magnitude of its basic research efforts as the total value of investment in both its independent research works at the in-house labs and the possible contribution to the consortium.
ii. Corresponding to industry's action, the government concurrently decides the optimum value to be financed publicly for the consortium projects only after considering the state of industrial technology and the desirable level of research as a nation, without regards to how much industry is willing to contribute to the shared activities in the research association.
iii. As for the industry's contribution to the consortium, they (i.e. private firms) tend to invest all the R&D resources in their own in-house research activities and refrain from sacrificing their funds or resources in the cooperative research at the consortium as far as they do not recognize any other benefits in it.
iv. The total amount of the industry's investment in basic research increases as they expect greater revenue from the R&D products, i.e., revenue from patents and other intellectual products and services and it lessens as the government has a greater national target for basic research.
v. The government optimum decision for the consortium is the reverse of industry's decision concerning a relationship between research funding and above two factors, i.e. the possible industrial research revenue and the national target.
vi. Total funding for basic research optimally chosen by both industry and government is directly related to probable industrial research revenue at that time.

A firms' attitude toward the consortium may change in a situation where the probability of success at their in-house labs is less than at public institutions due to a lack of qualified research facilities and researchers at the former. In addition, when a government cannot have an aggressive target for national research standard, firms may choose to participate in the joint research activities in the government-led scheme, instead of trying basic research by themselves with the associated greater risk of failure given their own scarce and insufficient resources. A government should supply public funds so as to fill any deficiency in the essential expenses of the consortium. That is, the government may supply a larger quantity of community funds when industry cannot contribute sufficiently. However, our model gives the essential answer to the attitudes of both industry and government in such a cooperative research scheme as the consortium.

In empirical examinations where actual data were applied to the theoretical results, we have had some assurance that the structure represented in our model has been basically working in Japan's R&D policy featured by the national research consortium. Industry has certainly shown the attitude of a minimal contribution to the government-led cooperative activities in such a way that our model leads its optimal value for x_c to zero. Estimations using historical data indicate that the fruits of R&D have been produced almost only by development of research activities undertaken by industry. These statistical investigations indicate that basic research activities along with government-funded activities including those by the consortia have not rendered positive results to the advancement of Japan's industrial technology during the thirty year period of the study. This could be said to be a natural result rather than a failure of estimation since basic research has generally and intrinsically no direct relationship to economic performance as compared with development research of new products and processes.

In the national strategies for industrial technology after WWII and up to the 1970's, Japan's industry assumed a positive and cooperative attitude toward the initiatives taken by MITI since Japanese manufacturing firms had not yet sufficiently developed their international competitiveness. In that period, government-financed consortia successively produced considerable research results in cooperation with major private firms, which jointly contributed to activities by supplying, for example, their gifted researchers. The strategy of undertaking key research projects by utilizing combined public and private research funds and resources was certainly effective for reducing the risk that should otherwise be brought upon private firms. Results were diffused fast enough throughout the industry as a sort of "public good", having the effect of giving Japanese manufacturing industries an edge over other advanced industrial economies. Examples include a Super High Performance Computer project in the latter half of the 1960's and a Super LSI project in the latter half of the 70's.

Since the 1980's, however, Japanese industry has been equipped with sufficient R&D resources to accomplish breakthroughs by its own efforts in basic research, which is necessary for further developments of product and process innovation. Companies which were motivated to achieve technological breakthroughs in basic research brought about the so-called "second boom of central research institutes" in the period from 1982 to 1995, during which private firms established in-house research laboratories vigorously and competitively. Historically speaking, it is probably only after the 1980's that Japanese private firms, especially in the fields of highly sophisticated technologies such as computers, microelectronics, biotechnology and advanced materials sciences, have been equipped with sufficient research resources and acquired confidence in their own ability to carry out technological breakthroughs.

Companies are now situated in a state of basic research that was assumed in our model to have the probability of success which is on an equal or higher footing with that of governmental research institutions. As a result, their present strategies are to concentrate their efforts on their own research activities employing in-house basic laboratories and to hold their contribution to cooperative undertakings in the government-led consortia to a minimum so as to obtain information about competitor firms' strategies and government policies.

There is no way to prove definitely whether or not the advance of Japan's industrial technology can be attributed to the government intervention coupled with public funds. As far as we understand from the results obtained in our analysis, Japanese industry has basically strengthened its technological competence by relying on the private sector's own efforts and its own resources, whereas the government has only played a role of supplying industry with subsidies in the period when it was not yet technologically and financially developed. The government has played the same role for the agricultural industry. It may be said that national strategies using such research consortia, which we explored in this chapter, did not have as much of an effect on the advancement of industrial technology as the government had expected. Further investigations are needed in this area in particular with regards to the optimum decision making process. It may be more realistic to integrate the respective goals of firms and government into one cooperative goal or objective of the research consortium by regarding them as a "team". This may bring us additional knowledge about the relationship between national strategies and private firms' choices in the arena of industrial R&D activities.

REFERENCES

AIST (Japanese Agency of Industrial Technology) (1972), Ohgata Purojekuto niyoru Cho-Koseinou Dennshi-Keisannki (Super-Performance Electronic-Computer on Large-Scale Project)

Callon, S.(1995), Divided Sun: MITI and the Breakdown of Japanese High-Tech Industrial Policy, 1975-1993. Stanford, Stanford University Press

Dockner, E., Jorgensen, S., Long, N. V., and G. Sorger (2000) Differential Games in Economics and Management Science. Cambridge: Cambridge, Cambridge University Press

Fudenberg, D. and J.Tirole (1991), Game Theory. Cambridge: MIT Press

Grossman, G. M. and C.Shapiro (1987), 'Dynamic R&D Competition,' The Economic Journal, 97, 372 –387

Jaffe, A. B. and J. Lerner (2001), 'Reinvesting Public R&D: Patent policy and the commercialization of national laboratory.' Rand Journal of Economics 32, 67-198

MEST (Japanese Ministry of Education, Science, and Technology)(2003), Kagaku Gijutsu Hakusho (White Paper on Science and Technology). 1984-2003 edition

METI (Japanese Ministry of Economy, Trade, and Industry). http://www.meti.go.jp /policy / innovation_policy/index.html

Nakayama, S. (1995), Kagaku-Gijyutsu no Sengo-Shi (Post-War History of Science and Technology), Tokyo, Iwanami

Neumann, J. von and O. Morgenstern (1953), Theory of Games and Economic Behavior. Princeton: Princeton University Press

Sah, R. K. and J.E. Stiglitz (1987), 'The invariance of market innovation to the number of firms,' Rand Journal of Economics 18, 98 – 108.

Thurow, L. C. (1992), Head to Head: the Economic Battle among Japan, Europe, and America, New York, Harper Collins Publishers

EPILOGUE

Hans W. Gottinger and Mattheus F. A. Goosen

"Growth does not generate high productivity or technological change, although technological change generates high productivity and growth"
(Alice H. Amsden, Asia's Next Giant, 1989)

Renowned economist Larry Summers (2003), former US Secretary of Treasury and Chairman of the US Council of Economic Advisers is quoted as saying:"[The] rate at which countries grow is substantially determined by three things: their ability to integrate with the global economy through trade and investment; their capacity to maintain sustainable government finances and sound money; and their ability to put in place an institutional environment in which contracts can be enforced and property rights can be established. I would challenge anyone to identify a country that has done all three of these things and has not grown at a substantial rate."

While we do not pretend to challenge this dictum one can assert that those premises are much too comprehensive in that they do not fully explain the varied and substantial different rates of growth observed even for economies that may satisfy all those terms.

In this book a multilayer analytical framework was developed for modern economic growth and performance driven by continuous long-run economic rivalries between nations and larger regional economic entities. This was done on the basis of industry/ technological advancement for creating income and accumulating wealth. The persistent pursuit of economic growth is a legitimate and compelling reason for a national economic policy that aims to achieve desirable social goals such as combating poverty, inequality, regional disparities and discrimination. Achieving economic growth also involves underlying structural change and social transformations which are the most important contributing factors to a nation's future and to global well-being. Without change and transformation we would end up with social paralysis, conflicts, crisis and ultimately communal warfare.

Economic growth over the long-run can only be achieved in the course of a real, sustainable value-creating process through industrial performance and open markets in which technology and innovation are the key facilitators. Nations with their industries engage in rival contests in what we term industrial races within a given international trade regime. This reflects a micro-economic based behavioral focus on economic growth (positive or negative). It builds a deeper foundation to explanations of economic growth than conventional macro-economic texts. It also uncovers the true sources of growth as a tool for growth diagnostics (Rodrik, 2007a) allowing to embrace other observations on urban growth (Chapter 5) and non primarily economic factors reviewed in Chapter 7. In an influential paper in Foreign Affairs entitled 'Can India overtake China' Huang and Khanna (2003) first looked at macro-economic factors, which favor China. They then considered micro-economic structures and behaviors such as competent indigenous entrepreneurship, a sound capital market, an independent legal system, property rights and a grass roots approach to development. The latter all favor India in the long run, say over the next fifty years.

In a widely covered empirical investigation on global growth patterns we concur with Easterly and Levins' (2002) finding that it is not factor accumulation, per se, but total factor productivity that explains cross-country differences in the level of GDP growth rates. This total productivity in turn is derived from technology (innovation) transfer and diffusion, its' supporting institutional characteristics and cultural dependence. Of course, on a deeper level, considerations of merely formal institutions may not suffice for explanations but instead forms of economic mechanism design may be called for that effectively deal with (enforce rules on) 'moral hazard' and 'adverse selection' issues (Myerson, 2006). As a basic starting point in Chapter 3 we emphasized a neoclassical type structural model based on capital accumulation rates but extended to include the impact of technology diffusion and inefficiencies caused by institutional rigidities. In the reference model adopted technology becomes one possible mechanism through which the effective capital stock may increase. The impact of social institutions arises by allowing the potential technology gap to be modified by them. The resulting model only slightly modifies the steady state and rates of convergence predicted by a typical neoclassical model. However, it also allows for more complex growth dynamics, including non-random relative income shifts while maintaining a high degree of tractability. This approach accomplishes reconciling a neoclassical model with slow technology diffusion and institutional variations as outlined in the economic history (cliometric) approach to economic development.

In Chapter 4 we found that follower nations benefit significantly from the technology gap with the leader and that adoption rates could differ greatly between regions. Furthermore, countries vary in average efficiency levels and these differences seem consistent with common beliefs and are robust to diverse econometric estimations. Dissimilarities in average efficiency levels, for instance, are notably explained by a set of institutional variables including bureaucratic (in)competence, as well as political and civil rights. It should be sufficient to point out that specific types of institution act as the driving force behind nations' (in)efficiency. For example, taking three regions, Europe, East Asia and South America, it shows that the latter has a relatively high technology adoption rate but fails to take advantage of its potential because of poor political and social institutions that could be sourced to historical colonial origins (Landes, 1999,Chap. 20).

Aggregated data can only point toward probable explanations for the basic reasons behind cross-country growth differences. Yet, there emerge some clear policy implications from such collective results. First of all, we can conclude that technology diffusion is an important source of growth for follower nations. Next, states seem to differ in their ability to take advantage of newer and better expertise. Thus, in general, any strategy that allows follower nations to better adopt foreign technology should boost their expansion rate, at least in the short run. Since the difference in skill adoption capability appears to be related to a nation's institutional efficiency, the results suggest that governments are well-advised to pursue policies that increase the efficiency of markets.

Improved technology adoption is complementary to the pursuit of efficient institutions. For example, consider two follower nations that face identical initial technology gaps. Their growth paths will be different according to their ability to close this gap. If one nation does not incorporate foreign know-how into their production it will have to rely solely on accumulation of factor inputs as a source of growth. If, on the other hand, the other adopts better technology, then rapid growth is expected until the gap is removed, at which time the nation is left with factor accumulation or the coming up with new ideas (innovation) as the sources of growth. However, the latter nation will be richer and more productive at all points in time.

In concluding this argument, higher income can be achieved not only from increases in the savings rate (i.e. the neoclassical prediction) but also from institutional change. As indicated in Chapter 4 and more explicitly in Chapter 7, the institutional framework of states cannot be ignored in any attempt to explain cross-country growth. But little could be said in the aggregate about the quantitative impact of each specific institution on growth. Consequently, we wish to investigate if particular institutional rigidities lead to inefficiencies which cause heterogeneous rates of catch-up. For example, given the available technology, the efficient use of factor inputs depends on aspects such as tax structure, regulations, education, infrastructure, and social and legal rights. In addition, given the institutional environment, implementation of more productive technologies increases the production efficiency of nations. This diffusion of technology depends on factors such as distance from the source country, language, as well as trade barriers.

What we can obtain from neoclassical expansion models is that economies, in addition to having different accumulation rates, also differ in levels of skill. Thus flows of technology (i.e. innovations) present an additional opportunity for growth. Adoption of expertise from abroad is one possible mechanism through which the capital stock of a nation increases, as better proficiency improves the productivity of the existing capital stock.

As shown in Chapter 2 growth can be viewed as being induced through a nation's deviation from technological leaders by multiple industrial races, plus different rates of factor accumulation, not by a deviation from a hypothetical steady state, as suggested by the standard neoclassical model. Gerschenkron (1962), for instance, demonstrated the historical rationale of a rival industrial performance in the description that relative late-comers can benefit from entering the development race with the latest skill without necessarily repeating the path of technical innovation that produced them. Earlier development leaders, on the other hand, suffer from embedding their infrastructure, capital and labor in outdated technology or products. The result could establish a possible leapfrogging process whereby relative latecomers catch-up and leaders fall behind. Along those lines, in the catch-up phase, the economy needs the help of change agents, most notably the government, to push closer towards the technology frontier. Thus the more a country lies behind the leader, the more it needs a publicly induced innovation system or a strategic industrial policy.

To capture some of Abramovitz (1986) ideas on social capabilities, we suggest that in addition to economies' varied abilities to adopt the technology gap they may also differ in their ability to recognize or to use the available know-how. To incorporate this into the model a term, labeled inefficiency, is included which acts to reduce the available technology gap to economies. To account for varied institutional rigidities the given level of labor productivity is some fraction of the leader's productivity, and that fraction is determined by the nation's level of inefficiency. Consider, for example, the possibility that countries adopt technology only slowly over time. Specifically, assume that technological innovations introduced at the beginning of time t are only partially adopted and the adoption speed, ρ_i, may differ across countries:

$$\alpha_{it} = (1 - \rho_i)\alpha_{it-1} + \rho_i \alpha_{it}^*$$

with α_{it}^* as the country i's optimal productivity level, for $0 \leq \rho_i \leq 1$. When a firm adjusts its production technology in this fashion, the inefficiency level must be correlated with its lagged levels. Let the productivity level be given by:

$$\alpha_{it} = \alpha_{it}^* - u_{it}$$

where u_{it} (≥ 0) is country's i technical inefficiency level at time t. Then one can show from observations in Chapter 4 that the long-run average technical inefficiency level of nation i is given by:

$$u_i^{LR} \equiv \lambda_i / \rho_i = \kappa_i + (1 - \rho_i)\gamma / \rho_i$$

where κ_i measures the long-run inefficiency due to country i's inability to comprehend and to fully utilize newly introduced production technologies while the second component $(1 - \rho_i)\gamma / \rho_i$ captures the long-run efficiency loss due to the country's sluggish adoption of technical innovations which are negatively related to adjustment speed ρ_i

Let us have a look at the inefficiency of follower nations, i.e., the negative effect on the potential technology gap stemming from inefficient social and institutional factors. The relative efficiency of nations within some sample regions appears to conform to common beliefs. For example, in Europe, the Netherlands, Germany, Switzerland and Sweden are the most efficient while Italy, Portugal and Greece are the least efficient. In East Asia, Hong Kong, Singapore, Taiwan and South Korea are the most efficient while Indonesia, Thailand and the Philippines are the least. In Latin America, Mexico and Chile are at the top while Nicaragua, Bolivia and Ecuador are at the bottom. Thus, even for countries who are benchmarked close to others in technology gap they may differ significantly in relative efficiency and therefore may stay under their technologically induced growth potential.

From the viewpoint of relative ranking consider the time required to catch-up, that is, to calculate the required time period until nations reach their frontier when only the catch-up term and inefficiency are allowed to vary across regions and countries. Two frontiers need to be considered: nations' inefficiency frontier and the leader nation's frontier. For catch-up the latter requires that the inefficiency levels reduce themselves in time occurring at the rate of ρ. Most of the EU countries seem to have reached their inefficiency reduced frontier. The same is true for most of the NIEs in East Asia. Thus, these nations will not catch-up with the current benchmark industry leader (say, the US) without higher accumulation rates or improved efficiency. Other developing economies are still catching-up with their inefficiency frontier so that if accumulation rates were the same, catch-up would still take place through diffusion of disembodied technology. Of course, if inefficiency levels remain constant over time then a follower could never wholly catch-up with the leader. This begs the question of what determines these inefficiencies. A substantial amount of literature has used several variables to capture this aspect of a nation's institutional framework as previously reviewed in Chapter 7. One major group belongs to the realm of government policy.

With technology as the driving factor, in response to catch-up, our model also allows for the potential of leapfrogging which would likely result for a company or even an industry in case of radical innovations. Observations show that leapfrogging only occurs for countries or regions incrementally and in the long run.

In general, the effect of government policies can be of two kinds: either the government provides growth promoting public goods and designs taxes which close the gap between private and social costs, or alternatively, the government wastes funds and imposes taxes and regulations that distort private decisions. As an example for identifying proxies of broad institutional variables we refer to the work of Mauro (1995) who restricts his attention to nine different indictors of institutional efficiency which are all independent of macro-economic variables and apply to both domestic and foreign firms. These nine indicators are grouped into two categories: political stability and bureaucratic efficiency. The political stability index contains the following six indicators: political change – institutional, political stability, social change – probability of takeover by opposition group, stability of labor, relationship with neighboring countries, and terrorism. The bureaucratic efficiency index consists of three variables: judiciary system, red tape bureaucracy and corruption. Openness to international trade as another contributing factor is included for two reasons: its relation to the diversion of resources from their free market allocation, and because international trade is a leading source of technology diffusion (Trindade, 2005).

Trade serves as a scale multiplier and acts like an increasing returns mechanism (IRM) as developed in Chapter 6. The significance of the level of education in particular when intrinsically related to technology skill acquisitions is likely to play a role through its impact on efficiency levels. Whenever sources of growth are identified then they can be qualitatively ranked. As contributors it does not mean that they are equally important, even more so when they contribute equally at every phase of the growth process. If the past fifty years of modern economic growth show statistically something for a wide range of countries in major regions of the world it is that some factors that worked for some countries at a given time did not work for others at the same or at a similar stage, as Rodrik (2007b) reviewed the evidence for growth clubs.

The statistical inconsistency of weighing possible factors of economic expansion is also reflected in retrospective growth regressions as reported by Easterly (2000). Calculating the prior probability of a nation attaining a growth miracle equivalent to at least five percent annual per capita growth we have among the most probable for the period 1960 to 1985: Japan, Singapore, Malta, which also realized miracles, as there were Greece, Portugal, France as highly probable (twenty percent) but not realized, while there was Korea with only eight percent probability but clearly realized. Performing growth diagnostics with only the common factors of production is not sufficient to explain the growth process. This may not apply in the long-run, if we define the long-run to be when technology has diffused uniformly to all nations, and countries' rates of growth are functions of input accumulation. However, this steady state story does not hold presently as countries are different in levels of technology.

Our models in Chapters 4 and 8 contain three growth effects in addition to varying accumulation rates. Each nation is faced with a technology gap approximated by the difference to the leader in per worker output which can increase the productivity of capital. This is interpreted as the catching-up potential described by Abramovitz(1986). Also we included heterogeneous absorption capacities and adoption rates in the growth term. Thus a nation might not take advantage of the catch-up potential if it either fails to adopt foreign technology or knowledge adoption is seriously compromised due to the nation's level of inefficiency. Such a model provides a mechanism for explaining why some countries forge ahead while others fall behind, while maintaining all the steady state predictions in the long run. The policy implications on running a successful industrial policy in a catch-up phase has been shown for the case of Japan in Chaps. 9 and 10 A paper by William Baumol (1986), showing that a group of sixteen industrial countries has caught up to the leader over the past century, was repeatedly criticized because of statistical selection bias using them as a group as pointed out by Easterly (2002, p. 64). But this criticism does not explain the substantive issue related to convergence on economic growth. It is more convincing to argue that those countries selected had adopted a set of similar sources (i.e. capital accumulation, industrial technology pursuit, and institutional forms) that promote economic growth and catch-up leading to convergence while others did not.

REFERENCES

Abramovitz, M. (1986) ,'Catching Up, Forging Ahead, and Falling Behind,' *Journal of Economic History* 46(2), 385-406.

Baumol,W. (1986), 'Productivity Growth, Convergence, and Welfare: What the Long Run Data Show', American Economic Review 76(5), 1072-1085

Easterly,W.(2000),'Explaining Miracles: Growth Regression Meet the Gang of Four', in Ho,T. and A.O. Krueger eds., East Asian Economic Growth, Cambridge,Ma., Harvard Univ. Press, 267-299

Easterly,W (2002) ,The Elusive Quest for Growth, Cambridge, Ma, MIT Press

Easterly,W. and R. Levins (2002), 'It's not Factor Acumulation: Stylized Facts and Growth Models', Central Bank of Chile, Working Papers No. 164, June

Gerschenkron, A. (1962), Economic Backwardness in Historical Perspective, Cambridge,Ma., Harvard Univ. Press

Huang, Y. and T. Khanna (2003), 'Can India Overtake China', Foreign Affairs, July-Aug.

Landes, D.S.(1999), The Wealth and Poverty of Nations, New York, Norton

Mauro, P. (1995) ,'Corruption and Growth,' *Quarterly Journal of Economics, August*, 681-712.

Myerson,R.B. (2006), 'Fundamental Theory of Institutions: A Lecture in Honor of Leo Hurwicz, http://home.uchicago.edu/~rmyerson/hurwicz.pdf

Rodrik, D.(2007a), 'Growth Diagnostics', Chap.2 in Rodrik,D., One Economics, Many Recipes, Princeton, Princeton Univ. Press, 56-84

Rodrik, D.(2007b), 'Fifty Years of Growth (and Lack Thereof):An Interpretation', Chap.13 in Rodrik,D., One Economics, Many Recipes, Princeton: Princeton Univ. Press, 56-84

Summers, L.H.(2003), Godkin Lectures, JFK School of Government,, Harvard University, April

Trindade,V. (2005), 'The Big Push, Industrialization and International Trade: The Role of Exports', *Journal of Development Economics* 78, 22-48

ABOUT THE EDITORS

Hans Gottinger studied mathematics and economics at the University of Goettingen and the University of Munich, Germany. He received a diploma and Ph.D. in economics from the University of Munich, and habilitation in statistics and econometrics from the Technical University of Munich. Dr. Gottinger has held the following positions:

- Ford Foundation Fellow, University of California, Berkeley
- Professor of Economics, IME, University of Bielefeld, Germany
- Professor, Dept. of Systems Engineering and Operations Research, University of Virginia, Charlottesville, Virginia
- Senior Research Director, Oxford Institute for Strategic Economics and Energy Analysis (OIES)
- International Institute of Management Science, Maastricht, NL
- Visiting Professor, IIR, Hitotsubashi University, Tokyo
- Executive Research Director, STRATEC Consulting, Germany, since 2007 (http://stratec-con.com)

Major consulting assignments include IBM, San Jose, California; Stanford Research Institute International, Menlo Park, California; Battelle Memorial Institute, Columbus, Ohio; Nomura Research Institute, Tokyo, Japan; and National Economic Research Associates, Inc. (NERA), London, England.

Mattheus (Theo) F. A. Goosen, Ph.D.
Associate Vice President for Research and Graduate Studies

Dr. Goosen joined Alfaisal University in Riyadh, Saudi Arabia, in March 2008 and currently serves as Associate Vice President for Research and Graduate Studies. Previously he held the position of Campus Dean (CAO) at the New York Institute of Technology in Amman, Jordan. Dr. Goosen has also held the position of Dean of the School of Science and Technology at the Universidad del Turabo in Puerto Rico, USA, and Dean of Engineering as well as Dean of Agricultural & Marine Sciences at the Sultan Qaboos University in Muscat, Oman. He has been on the Board of Directors of two companies.

He obtained his doctoral degree in Chemical/Biomedical Engineering from the University of Toronto, Canada, in 1981. After graduation he spent three years as a post doc at Connaught Laboratories in Toronto and then ten years at Queen's University in Kingston Canada in the Department of Chemical Engineering.

Dr. Goosen has published extensively with over 160 refereed papers, book chapters, books, and patents to his credit. His research interests are in the areas of environmental management and sustainable economic development, water purification and treatment, as well as bioengineering and membrane technology.

INDEX

A

Age
    chronological 5
    technological 5
aggregate racing behavior 44, 61-87
    leapfrogging 44, 50-53
aggregate technological racing, modeling 61-87
    endogenized growth model 65
    industrial racing between nations 63-65
    technology adoption, modeling 65
anarchies, autocracies and democracies 130-132
Asian countries 134-136, 155, 158-178, 179-200, 201-222
    GDP statistical evidence 173
        see also Gross Domestic Product
    historical change in GDP 134
Asian economies 157-178, 179-200, 201-222
    Asian miracle, the 124, 161
    dynamic cooperative industrial policy 179-200
    fundamental structure 176
    GDP data, actual 134, 158, 173, 174
        see also Gross Domestic Product
    historical change in country GDP 136, 158, 174
    industrialization 158-160
    innovative systems and Japanese R&D policies 201-222
        see also Japanese economic growth
    Japan's catching-up with US 170
    take off 158
    theoretical model and growth paths 162-168
        growth trajectories 169
        initial conditions and policy efforts 169
        one-time changes 176
        sustained growth 168
        trade theories 159
        zero growth 171
Asian miracle, the 124, 134-136, 157-178, 179-200, 201-222
    and the North –South trade 160
    theoretical model and growth paths 162-168
asymmetries in firm capabilities 30-32

B

Backwardness,
    technological 44, 52
        see also modeling technology and industrial races
        see also technology and institutions
behavior
    leapfrogging 10, 50-52, 53
'big push' 64
Britain 125-154
Business International (BI), indices from 79

C

Capital
    country's social capability 62
    cultural heritage hypothesis, North's 126, 132
    human 46
        see also growth and institutions
catching-up 1-2, 9-11, 61-86, 144-146
    American leadership by Japan, to 6, 157-222
catch-up for economic growth 1-2, 6, 9-11, 61
    leapfrogging 9-11
        see also industrial and macrocompetition
        see also technology and industrial races
CCI Control of Corruption Index (CCI) 140

China 44, 174
cliometric approaches to development 41, 51
Cobb-Douglas production function 74
competition 1-2, 4, 5, 7-12, 61-86, 144-146
    see also race(s)/racing
conditional convergence 46
conditional probability 55
consensual political orders 148
consortium, research 179, 203-204
convergence 46
    conditional 45
    dynamics 70
    factor accumulation 46
    fundamentals 46
    human capital 46
    openness 546
    path 71
cooperative R and D scheme 202
    see also research and development
corrupt countries, the most 133
corruption and growth 139-142
    Control of Corruption Index (CCI) 140
    Corruption Perception Index (CPI) 140
    industrial racing and catch-up 144
    International Country Risk Guide (ICRG) 141
    International Crime Victims Survey (ICVS) 140
    most corrupt countries, the 141
    public debt and economic growth 142-144
country specific economic policy, Olson's 126, 132
CPI Corruption Perception Index (CPI) 140
    see also corruption and growth
cultural dependent learning and economic emergence 128
    adaptability 129
    debate over whether or not institutions cause economic growth, the 126
    disorder 128
    key characteristics of countries 128
    overheads 129
    Spain and Britain, example of 129
cultural heritage hypothesis, North's 126, 132

D

Debate over whether or not institutions cause economic growth, the 146-148
development traps 63
    see also industrial racing
    role of government 63-64
differential game formulation 22-24
Douglas North's cultural heritage hypothesis 126, 128-130
    see also growth and institutions
    cultural dependent learning and economic emergence 128-130
        adaptability 129
        disorder 128
        key characteristics of countries 128
        overheads 129
        Spain and Britain, example of 129
dynamic cooperative industrial policy, Japan's 179-200
    modeling R and D policy 181
        government, problem of the 184
        private sector, problem of the 182
        problem and analytical setup 181
    salvage value model 194
        government's alternative objective 194
        maximum net benefit of R and D 198
        simulation results 187
    solution of the R and D differential game 178
        government 178
        maximum net benefit 191
        optimal strategies 189
        private sector 185
        simulation results 193

E

Econometric issues 41-60, 75
    framework for urban growth 93
economics
    corporate governance, and 136
    dimensions 137
    evolution of institutions 136
    governance 126-139
    measures of institutional quality 138
    performance and evolution of institutions 136
economic growth
    catch-up and 41-55
    development, and 41-60
        aggregate leapfrogging 44
        catch-up hypothesis 43
        conditional probability 55
        convergence and conditional convergence 45
        effect of institutions 125-154
        endogenous growth models 47

factor accumulation 42
increasing returns mechanism 103-124
Japan 155, 157-178, 179-200, 201-222
leapfrogging 50-52, 53
neoclassical versus endogenous growth models 48-50
overview 41-60
probability of movement 54
R and D spillovers 47
rank mobility measures 53
    see also growth and institutions
technology and institutions 42
urban economic growth and development 87-103
education, 80, 125-154
    see also growth and institutions
efficiency, determinants of 78, 80
    education 80
    government market supporting policies 79
    impact of social institutions 83
    openness 79
    Pearson correlation coefficient 80
empirical evidence of urban growth 94
    covariance matrix 89
    exclusion of externality based variables 98
    interaction effects 99
    ordinary least squares (OSL) estimates 95
empirical relations of urban growth 90
    traditional economic factors 90
    geographic factors 90-92
endogenized growth model 48, 65
    convergence path 71
    determinants of efficiency 78
    econometric issues 75
    efficiency levels of countries 74, 78
    extension of model 73
    knowledge gap 68
    model, the 66
    prerequisites 65
    rate of growth 72
    steady state 68
    technology adoption function 68, 78
    transition dynamics 70
    versus neoclassical growth model 48-50
Europe 4
evolution, technological 3-19

F

Factor accumulation 46

firms
    capabilities, asymmetries in 30-32
    capital investment parameters 31
    innovation resource productivity 31
    lagging and leading 63
    obsolescence parameter 32
        see also modelling technology and industrial races
    spillover factor 32
frontier 4, 5, 8, 10-12
    evolution, technological 3-19
    firm level technology (FTF) 8-9
    industry technological (ITF) 8-9, 15
    sticking behavior 4
    technological 7-10
        see also race(s)/racing
FTF see frontier, firm level technology

G

GDP see Gross Domestic Product
General Electric (GE) 104
geographic production externalities 90
    localization, economies of 91
    specialization, economies of 92
    urbanization, economies of 91
governance see economic governance
government market supporting policies 79
Gross Domestic Product (GDP)
    historical change for Asian countries 134, 158, 174
    statistical evidence 165
growth and institutions 125-154
    Asian countries 134-136
        historical change in GDP 134
    corruption and growth 125, 139-142
        Control of Corruption Index (CCI) 140
        Corruption Perception Index (CPI) 140
        industrial racing and catch-up 142
        International Country Risk Guide (ICRG) 141
        International Crime Victims Survey (ICVS) 140
        most corrupt countries, the 140
        public debt and economic growth 142-144
    country specific economic policy, Olson's 126, 132
    cultural dependent learning and economic emergence 128

adaptability 129
disorder 128
key characteristics of countries 128
overheads 129
Spain and Britain, example of 129
cultural heritage hypothesis, North's 126, 132
debate over whether or not institutions cause economic growth, the 146
economic governance 136-139
dimensions 137
evolution of institutions 136
measures of institutional quality 138
incentives and economic growth 138
differences between cultural-dependent and country-specific theories 132
Olson's order maintaining political systems 130
see also Asian economies
growth effects 228
growth equations 163-169, 176
growth in cities 88-90
see also urban economic growth and development
capital and labor growth 95-100
econometric framework for urban growth 93
economies of localization 91
economies of specialization 92
economies of urbanization 91
empirical evidence 94
empirical relations 90
geographic factors 90-92
traditional economic factors 90
Herfindahl index 92
growth trajectories, phase plane of 169

H

Herfindahl index 92
historical change in per capita GDP 158
human capital 46
hypothesis, catch-up 43-45, 61-86, 144-146

I

ICRG International Country Risk Guide (ICRG) 141
ICVS International Crime Victims Survey (ICVS) 140
see also corruption and growth
incentives and economic growth 130-134
differences between cultural-dependent and country-specific theories 132
Olson's order maintaining political systems 130
see also Asian economies
income shifts 41
increasing returns in industrial competition 116
structural change and development paths 118
increasing returns mechanism 103, 109
ergodic markets 110
industrialization policies and development 118
increasing returns in industrial competition 116
network externalities 115
Schumpeterian mechanism 105
cost reducing learning 104
demand side increasing returns 108
learning-by-doing 107
learning-by-using 107
standards and increasing returns 115
structural change and development paths, an example of 118
supply-side scale economies 104
technological competition, and 120
technological competition under uncertainty and inertia 112
technological trajectories 113, 114
winner-takes-all markets 121
India 224
indicators, statistical 9
industrial and macro competition 3-19, 21, 61, 155,
patterns 4
see also catch-up for economic growth
industrial racing, indicators of 12-15
see also racing and racing behaviour
catch-up statistics 13
domination period statistics 13
frontier pushing, assessment of 13
interfrontier distance 14
leapfrogging statistics 14
race closeness measure (RCM) 14
trends across industries 15
industrial policy 3, 118, 155, 179, 201
industrial races 21-38, 61-87, 144
see also racing and racing behaviour
modeling technology and industrial races 22
aggregate technological racing 61-88
analysis of sequential differential game 27-30

asymmetries in firm capabilities 30-32
differential game formulation 22-24
sequential differential game 24-28
theorems and proofs 34-38
industrial racing between nations
see industrial racing, indicators of
see industrial races
industrialization policies and development 118-120
see also increasing returns mechanism
industry/-ies
industry technology frontier (ITF) trends 8, 12, 15
inefficiency, institutional 45
innovation resource productivity 31
innovation, modeling technological 26, 226
innovative systems and Japanese R&D policies 201-222
effect of R and D expenditures 218
empirical analysis 210
fundamental features of analytical model 203
Japan's R and D performance 215
Japan's technological trade 218
Ministry of Economy, Trade and Industry (METI) 201
model, the 203-207
analysis 207-210
functions of industry and government 204
industrial R and D structure 203
industry-government R and D structure 204
national consortium 203
probabilty of achieving success 206
R and D expenditures 211
role of cooperative R and D 218
institutional factors and economic growth, weighing 149
institutional quality, measures of 138
see also growth and institutions
institutions 125-154
inefficiency 45
soundness 45
ITF see frontier, industry technological

J

Japan 42, 124, 134-136, 158-222
catching-up with US 170
post war 157-220
Japan's R and D performance 215
Japan's technological trade 218
Japanese economic growth 158-222
and Asian economies 157-178
dynamic cooperative industrial policy 179-200
innovative systems 201-222
R&D policies 201
Japanese R and D policies 201-222
cooperative R and D scheme 202
innovation systems ,and 201
research consortium 179, 203-204

K

Knowledge gap 67-68

L

Leading edge technology 9
leapfrogging 50-52, 53
neoclassical model, and 50
new growth theory 51
liquid crystal displays (LCD) 179
and cooperative production 179

M

Macro-competition 3-19
see also industrial and macro-competition
Mancur Olson's country specific economic policy hypothesis 126, 130-134
see also growth and institutions
maximum net benefit of R and D, salvage model 198
micro racing environment 63
in comparison to macro level 63
modeling R and D policy 181
government, problem of the 184
maximum net benefit of R and D 191
optimal strategies 189
private sector, problem of the 182
problem and analytical setup 181-182
salvage value model 195
simulation results 193
solution of the R and D game 185
modeling technology adoption 22-24, 26, 28, 30-32, 34-38, 44, 52, 61-88
endogenized growth model, in an 65

convergence path 71
determinants of efficiency 78
econometric issues 75
efficiency levels of countries 74, 78
extension of model 73
knowledge gap 68
model, the 66
prerequisites 65
rate of growth 72
steady state 68
technology adoption function 68, 78
transition dynamics 70
model/modeling 22-24, 26, 28, 30-32, 34-38, 44, 52, 61-88
aggregate technological racing 61-88
asymmetries in firm capabilities 30-32
backwardness, technological 44, 52
differential game formulation 22-24
salvage value model 192-194
government's alternative objective 194
maximum net benefit of R and D 198
simulation results 195, 198
sequential differential game 24-28
sequential differential game, analysis of 25-30
spillover effects 26
Stackelberg equilibrium investment 28
theorems and proofs 34-38
movement, probability of 54
mobility matrix 54

N

National consortium 203
and industrial R and D structure 203-204
model, the 203-207
neoclassical model 41, 42, 46
empirical objections 50
objections to 49
steady state predictions 46
versus endogenous growth model 48-50
network economy 7, 18
network externalities 115
new growth theory 51

O

Obsolescence parameter 32
see also modelling technology and industrial races

OLS Ordinary Least Squares estimates and growth 95
see also urban economic growth and development
Olson's order maintaining political systems 130
openness 46
overview of economic growth and catch-up 1-2, 41-51, 223-230

P

Pearson correlation coefficient 80
performance and evolution of institutions 136
policy efforts 175
probability function of achieving success 206
analysis for Japanese R and D policies 207-210
empirical analysis 210
public debt and economic growth 142-144

R

Race(s)/ racing
between nations 4, 5, 8-9, 10-12, 63
catch-up 6, 10
dynamics of 3-20
cluster-of 5
firm-led 5
frontier 4, 5, 7-9, 10-12
frontier-sticking behavior 4, 10
hypothesis, catch-up 43-45, 61-86, 144-146
industrial 12-16, 21-38, 61-88, 144
catch-up 6, 10, 13
conditional probability 55
convergence and conditional convergence 45
domination period 13
endogenous growth models 47
frontier pushing 4, 5, 8, 10-13
industrial racing patterns 11-12
interfrontier distance 14
leapfrogging 14
neoclassical versus endogenous growth models 48-50
probability of movement 54
R and D spillovers 47
race closeness measure 14
rank mobility measures 53
statistical indicators of 12-16
labour productivity 5

lagging company 5
leapfrogging 4, 9, 10
market asymmetries 4
network economy 7
racing patterns 11-12
research and development 11
resource based 4
risk driven 4
rivalry 4
statistical profiling of technological evolution 8
    performance criteria 8
technology/technological 1, 3, 5, 8-9, 18, 21-39, 61, 155
trailing countries 5
types of 4
racing patterns 11-12
R and D see research and development
rank mobility measures 53
research and development (R and D)
    catch-up/leapfrogging 9-11
    effect of expenditures on R and D performance 217
    expenditures of industry and government, historical 211
    investment in 5
    Japan's performance 214-216
    Japan's technological trade 217-218
    profits, monopoly and duopoly 5
    spillovers 47-48
research consortia, government-led 202-204
    fundamental features 202-203
Russia 45
    per capita GDP 45

S

Salvage value model 194
    government's alternative objective 194
    maximum net benefit of R and D 198
    simulation results 195, 198
Schumpeterian mechanism 105
    cost reducing learning 106
    demand side increasing returns 108
    learning-by-doing 107
    learning-by-using 107
sequential differential game 24-28
sequential differential game, analysis of 28-30
social capabilities 225
    productivity, and 226

    technical inefficiency level 226
Solow model 42, 69
    convergence path 69
    rate of convergence 68
    transitional dynamics 70
solution of the R and D differential game 185
    government 187
    maximum net benefit 191
    optimal strategies 189
    private sector 185
    simulation results 193
spillover effects 26
    R and D 48
spillover factor 32
Stackelberg equilibrium investment 28, 35-38
standards and increasing returns 115
statistical analysis see statistical metrics
statistical profiling of technological evolution 8
    performance criteria 8
statistical metrics
    catch-up 13
    conditional probability 55
    convergence and conditional convergence 45
    domination period 13
    endogenous growth models 47
    frontier pushing 13
    industrial racing patterns 11-12
    interfrontier distance 14
    leapfrogging 14
    neoclassical versus endogenous growth models 48-50
    probability of movement 54
    R and D spillovers 47
    race closeness measure 14
    rank mobility measures 53
    statistical indicators of industrial racing 12
steady state growth 68-70
    Solow growth diagram 69
supply-side scale economies 104

T

Technological competition 1, 3, 5, 8-9, 12, 112
    and increasing returns mechanism 120-122
    under uncertainty and inertia 112-115
technological frontier 3, 5, 7-9, 12, 21-39, 61, 155
    company, of (TFC) 8, 15
    evolution and innovation 8
    firm, of (TFF) 8, 15
    industry, of (TFI) 8, 15

statistical profiling 8
   trends 15
technology 1, 3, 5, 8-9, 12, 21-39, 61, 155
   adoption function 65-73
   efficiency 78
   inefficiency, institutional 45
   knowledge gap 68
   modeling in an endogenized growth model 68
   Pearson Correlation Coefficient 80
   rates 78
   steady state 68, 69
technology and industrial races 1, 3, 5, 7-9, 12, 21-39, 61, 155
   modeling 22-30
technology and institutions 42-43
theorem(s)/theory
   new growth 51
   sequential play game 34-38
TFC technological frontier of a company (TFC) see technological frontier
TFF technological frontier of a firm (TFF) see technological frontier
TFI technological frontier of industry (TFI) see technological frontier

U

United States 4
urban economic growth and development 88-102
   econometric framework 93
   empirical evidence 94
      covariance matrix 98
      exclusion of externality based variables 98
      interaction effects 99
      ordinary least squares (OSL) estimates 95
   empirical relations 90
      geographic factors 90-92
      traditional economic factors 90
   growth in cities 88
   level of human capital 92
   political and social variables 93

W

World Bank Report
   development of East Asian economies, on 158

Z

Zero growth 171